1988 Licensing Law Handbook

The Clark Boardman
Licensing Law Library

The Law and Business of Licensing
Edited by the Licensing Executives Society

Technology Management
by Robert Goldscheider

Forms and Agreements on Intellectual Property and International Licensing
by L.W. Melville

Licensing Law and Business Report
Edited by Willian Brinks Olds Hofer Gilson & Lione, Ltd.

Eckstrom's Licensing in Foreign and Domestic Operations
by Steven Z. Szczepanski

Eckstrom's Licensing in Foreign and Domestic Operations: The Forms and Substance of Licensing
by Robert Goldscheider

Eckstrom's Licensing in Foreign and Domestic Operations: Joint Ventures
by Terrence F. MacLaren

The Law of Merchandise and Character Licensing— Merchandising Law and Practice
by Gregory J. Battersby and Charles W. Grimes

1988 Licensing Law Handbook
edited by Arnold, White & Durkee, P.C.

Licensing Law Library

1988 Licensing Law Handbook

by Arnold, White & Durkee

Clark Boardman Company, Ltd.
New York, New York   1988

ISSN: 0731-5783
ISBN: 0-87632-596-7

Preface

This book is an expansion and revised update of **1984 Licensing Law Handbook**. The addition of new chapters on pricing the technology as well as bankruptcy law's ambiguous application to licensing, with its sometimes shocking results, renders the work much more complete than its parent.

In addition there are major revisions of such existing areas as the liability of licensors for catastrophies occurring with respect to the licensee's product or plant operations—for example, the Bhopal, India, accident that killed or maimed thousands.

The authors of this book are all lawyers with Arnold, White & Durkee of Houston. While many contributed to the drafting and updating process, it is particularly appropriate to mention the following as principal contributors: Tom Arnold, Christopher R. Benson, J. Timothy Headley, Earl Horn, Christopher D. Kiers, Craig M. Lundell, Thomas A. Miller, Paula D. Morris, Michael B. Schroeder, and D.C. Toedt III.

The authors acknowledge the role of the Licensing Executives Society in inspiring this work and providing much of the background that went into it.

The views expressed are those of the individual authors and are not necessarily those of either the Licensing Executives Society or the firm of Arnold, White & Durkee.

Arnold, White & Durkee

Table of Contents

Licensing

Licensing

Licensing

Licensing

Part 1

Basic Considerations in Technology Transfer Licensing

Chapter 1

Context for Licensing

§ 1.01 Ways to Exploit a Technology

The proprietor of a technology may exploit his technology, *i.e.,* may reach markets:

(1) By one location manufacture and sale to all markets, including export sale to distant markets ("make at home and sell abroad" exploitation);

(2) By establishing a manufacturing division in the locale of each market—an inherently high capital and high risk approach ("make abroad and sell abroad" exploitation);

(3) By joint venture manufacture and sale ("joint venture" exploitation);

(4) By foreign contract manufacture with the technology proprietor's know-how and specifications with either proprietor direct sales or contract sales ("contract manufacture" exploitation);

(5) By license ("license" exploitation);

(6) By any one of those devices addressed to selected geographic or field of use[1] market segments in combination with other[s]of those devices addressed to other geographic market segments or field of use market segments;

(7) By some unique combination of these.

---

[1] Many technologies are applicable to multiple fields of use so diverse from one another as to be markets served by different sales channels and different manufacturers, *e.g.,* lithium batteries for heart pacemakers versus for automobiles. A manufacturer or seller in one such field of use may be ill equipped for the other and may make and sell in one while licensing out the other.

§ 1.02 Factors Influencing Choice of Strategy

If you have a new technology to market, it is a helpful study to develop perhaps a page or so of data on the factors that influence technology transfer licensing. Let's start by calling a number of those factors to mind:

(1) Market structure.
   (a) nature and number of competitors and potential competitors if the new technology proves profitable;
   (b) geographic area of competitive activity;
   (c) available different fields of use of the technology;
   (d) market niches or divisions in the fields of use of the technology;
   (e) types of companies (and their names) within and without the industry that could make or market the new technology, and that thereby are worth considering as a potential licensee;
   (f) place of the licensor, the potential licensee, and their product line in that market structure—
   for example, if you have a new tobacco product to develop in Europe, do you seek established tobacco companies as licensees? They will be your competitors. How about a joint venture with the Bic cigarette lighter company, a noncompetitor with excellent marketing, including good contacts with every cigarette counter in Europe?
   (g) contemplated growth or other change, either in that market structure or in the proprietor's or potential licensee's role in it—either independently occurring or caused by the entrance of the new technology into the market.
(2) Position of the technology along the time line of its life cycle.
   Technologies are born in a conception, pass through a stage of being half-developed, through a stage

where capability and economics are demonstrable (for example, after a first full-scale demonstration plant is operable), through a maturity of the product and the markets for it, and eventually into a decline.

While this handbook discusses one very early license of xerographic technology to Battelle and one license of bread-making technology that was so far past its prime as to be thought of as obsolete (*see* § 2.01), for a variety of reasons the vast majority of licenses occur after capability and economics are demonstrable and before the product's markets are fully matured.

(3) Government regulations.

    (a) regulations of the industry involved, as by the Food and Drug Administration or the Environmental Protection Agency;

    (b) regulation of the license terms and of the licensing process, as in Canada and most Latin American countries, where the license itself is a highly regulated item, or as in the Comecon countries, where the government itself is often the real party in interest and the chief negotiation protagonist.

    But don't be a slave to such regulations. When Mexico had an apparently rigid rule against royalties over 5 percent or 5 years, a licensor went to the regulators with a lot of data on Mexico's need for the technology and the regulations of the industry (ROI) to be expected. The rigid rule yielded to 20 percent for 20 years;

    (c) legal restrictions on sources of supply, on location of a perhaps dangerous installation in relation to housing, on use of expatriate employees vs. forced use of native employees whose safe-operations may be unreliable even with good training (*cf.* the catastrophe at Carbide's Bhopal, India, subsidiary/licensee, where local Indian managers apparently were not attentive to maintenance of all the safety interlock systems and training employees in their use).

(4) Tariffs.

(5) Taxes.

(6) Restrictions on international payments, which may make it necessary for consideration to be paid partly in buy-backs, or by barter in leather or some mineral ore, or by some circuitous route.

As an example, once a licensor had money in Peru that was subject to restriction on transfer. He wanted to repatriate that money into U.S. dollars. A deal was struck with Braniff Airways, which then flew to Peru. In rotation, Braniff flew each of its planes to Peru and left them there overnight for service. The first-class seats were replaced with very fine Peruvian leather seats, paid for in Peruvian money by the technology licensor, and then flown out of Peru. Braniff paid the licensor for the seats in hard currency, U.S. dollars.

This story is but one illustration of the fact that many a license succeeds or fails in direct proportion to the imagination displayed by the parties. The evaluation and manipulation of factors present in licensing can be as simple or complex as the licensor chooses—a licensor could dream up a whole series of barters, contract parts manufacture, buy-backs, or other deals by which to effect payment. "Evaluation" and "manipulation" of the many factors—a pair of words we will come back to.

(7) Shipping costs.

(8) Labor costs and their influence upon the licensee's capacity to compete with the licensor.

(9) Necessary sales techniques. For example, selling heart pacemakers through doctors is sharply different from selling auto batteries though Sears.

(10) Sales know-how.

(11) Sales muscle, including strong trademark and sales organization or lack thereof.

When Xerox had neither marketing know-how nor marketing organization in Europe, it licensed what became Rank Xerox, a joint venture with J. Arthur Rank, which had a great European marketing organization but which had no copy machine technology. The marriage turned out to be a win for Xerox and a win for Rank.

(12) Availability of manufacturing or service labor with education and skills trainable for the work. The capability of the local work force to safely build, maintain, and operate the technology.[2]

Particularly in some developing countries, the cost of training service personnel may render a given transaction economically impossible.

Some years back one of our clients was seeking to license some very sophisticated electronic gear to Hungary. The negotiations went smoothly until the cost of training the service personnel was examined. At that time Hungary had no television, no English-speaking population, and very little native language population who were experienced electronic technicians. After some discussion of the need for reliability and the related cost of training the labor force that was then available in Hungary, it was the Hungarians who first observed that, given the small market they hoped to serve, there was no way they could afford to pay the cost of training the service and operating personnel.

This phenomenon is not rare in the developing world, although sometimes the government is so interested in having its labor force trained that the government will subsidize the contract.

(13) Capital requirements, capital availability, and capital cost.

(14) Start-up time requirements.

---

[2] *See Principles and Guidelines for the Safe Transfer of Technology,* Counseil Europeen des Federations de l'Industrie Chimique, Avenue Louise 250. Btd 71, B-1060, Bruxelles, App. A *infra.*

(15) Special design problems to localize a product or service for local markets.

On one occasion I was truly shocked to see the difficulty an old-line U.S. manufacturer had in converting his 110-volt electric motor manufacturing habits over to 220-volt production for foreign markets.

(16) Patent strength or weakness and patent scope, country by country.

(17) The nature or mix of the technology.

    (a) as an embryonic idea or matured development (Very early in a technology's life cycle the technical feasibility, warranty, and market-size risks all tend to be high, while very late in the life cycle the technology may not be worth licensing.);

    (b) as patentable, or partly so;

    (c) as know-how inherently protectable by secrecy;

    (d) as know-how easily reverse-engineered by competitors;

    (e) as merely an assemblage of common knowledge to be taught to plant operators and salesmen, *i.e.,* as nonproprietary "show-how";

    (f) as dependent for value upon the life cycle of some other product or technology—and just what is the stage of that other life cycle, *e.g.,* the market for an improved mechanical timing mechanism for watches is dead; it was buried by quartz crystals.

(18) Trademarks and their value.

(19) Projected value of ongoing R&D.

(20) Availability of local contract manufacturers for possible use in lieu of a licensee; availability of a good licensee.

(21) Raw material availability.

(22) Local product liability law and the duty to have provided technology having "the highest degree of safety reasonably practicable according to the cur-

rent stage of knowledge," as recited in *Principles and Guidelines.*[3]

(23) Physical Environment: the impact of the technology on the environment,[4] and the effects of local climatic conditions on the technology (*e.g.*, certain automatic operations with fabrics are difficult in cool, dry climates where static electricity is high on the fabric).

§ 1.03 Evaluation and Manipulation

Most of those factors are so important and vary so much from case to case that a chapter on each topic, including many case examples, would be required to give a reasonable background in and feel for evaluation and manipulation of the factors as found in a given situation.

But the key thought here is in those two words:

evaluation of the factors, and

manipulation and change of the factors

in order to fit them most effectively into a make-and-sell mode of exploitation, a joint venture mode of exploitation, a license mode of exploitation, or some unique combination of those.

---

[3] N. 2, *supra.*

[4] *Id.*

Chapter 2

Why License Technology?

§ 2.01   Why to License out Your Own Technology

There are more reasons to license out your own technology than we sometimes think of. Some licensors' reasons for licensing out include:

(1)   To earn royalty income.

Royalty and fee income from U.S. licenses to foreign buyers exceeded $4 billion in 1978. Surely it must be higher today. Domestic U.S. license income I don't know, but surely it is of the same order of magnitude.

Royalty income is best made by developing the classic win-win situation, a win for the licensor and a win for the licensee, because a license is rarely very profitable to the licensor unless it is also very profitable to the licensee. And vice versa.

(2)   To buy technology.

Yes, everybody knows that licensors license to earn a royalty income. But Chester Carlsen, the patent lawyer who invented xerography, had a better idea.

When he ran out of development money, he licensed Battelle Development Corporation in exchange for Battelle's agreeing to carry on the development—a license by which the *licensor* rather than the licensee purchased ongoing technology development, and by which the licensor bought technology rather than immediate royalties.

It turned out to be a win-win deal, a win for Carlsen and a win for Battelle.

That Carlsen-to-Battelle license is notable because it occurred early in the life cycle of the technology, at a time when licenses tended to be unusual to rare. IBM, Kodak, and other manufacturers had been offered a license but turned it down as an unduly high-risk investment in the context of the technological uncertainty and the market they could then visualize. The refusal of the manufacturers to take a license, as is usual at early stages of a technology development, sets the stage for the Battelle license.

(3) To acquire marketing strength, capital and market assets, or an interest in them.

Xerox can again serve as our example. Some while after Xerox had acquired Carlsen's and Battelle's technology, Xerox had technology in an area where J. Arthur Rank had none. Rank had marketing structure and strength in European markets, where Xerox had neither. Xerox licensed its technology in exchange for a substantial ownership in what became the Rank Xerox joint venture. Xerox acquired virtually instant market success at a rate of penetration surely impossible for Xerox had it tried to go it alone in Rank's market area. A win for Xerox and a win for Rank.

So there we see a license to a joint venture by which to buy marketing strength—including the capital associated with Rank's marketing structure.

Note that this license, like many licenses, was entered into after complete early-model commercial development of the technology but before its maturity.

(4) To reduce the capital requirement for reaching a market by other means such as erection of a local plant for manufacture.

(5) To test a market later possibly to be exploited by manufacture-and-sale or joint venture exploitation.

(6) To adapt a product to a local market.

(7) To reach a geographic market not otherwise reachable. For example, Russia is simply not reachable by proprietor-owned manufacture in the subject market and often is not reachable by export sales.

(8) To reach fields of use in which the technology proprietor does not operate.

Some while back Union Carbide developed a very promising technology, but one which required a lot of technical support service that was not natural to the mass producer of bulk chemicals. After failing to do very well in the area, Carbide licensed Lord Corporation, a company long on the skills of customized customer service. Lord did more than well enough to pay Carbide royalties greater than Carbide's modest profit and earned a handsome profit for itself as well—a successful "win-win" example of matching the technology to its user.

(9) To avoid waste of by-product technology outside the proprietor's area of operations, technology that arose perchance as a by-product of other R&D. The Carbide-Lord story above is a good example also of this practice.

(10) To profit from residual value in an old technology.

My example here is the bread factory for Egypt, originally programmed to be a monument to new, fully automated technology. But what does a licensing man see instantly in that simple expression of the proposal that faults it?

In the U.S., capital is cheap and labor is very costly, so the investment of big capital in the labor-saving automated factory makes sense. But in Egypt, hard-currency capital is very dear while labor is dirt cheap, cheap enough to make bread at less cost per loaf with man labor than with machine labor. And indeed Egypt needs jobs even more than it needs bread.

A vintage bread factory design, 15 years out of date for the U.S., fit the Egyptian need much better than the latest automated design and gave the proprietor a windfall return on its "obsolete" technology.

This license is noteworthy because it came late in the life cycle of the technology. Unusual but not really rare.

Of course developing nations sometimes resist buying what they regard as secondhand wares, the technology of a decade or two ago. But often that is the product that fits the market, and what we should convince them they really want.

(11) To improve a foreign subsidiary's performance by lending it technical assistance, and in the process moving profit figures around for tax advantage.

(12) To obtain future technology, as by grant-back of:

(a) existing licensee technology, or

(b) results of future licensee R&D or experience with the licensed system—as in the UOP catalytic cracking license example, below.

The legal considerations are different in some countries for (a) and (b).

UOP has a very successful licensing program built upon the licensee's interest in future R&D. Some 50 or 60 catalytic cracking refiners of oil—I don't know how many—are too small and technically unsophisticated to do catalytic cracking R&D effectively. How do they compete with the eight or so major refiners in an area of continuously developing technology? By licenses from UOP.

UOP keeps one or more pilot plants continuously operating to try out new catalysts, new reactor temperatures, residence times, etc. And UOP collects grant-back information from its licensees. Then UOP conducts annual seminars to give its licensees the latest updated technology.

These licensees are licensees not just of past-developed technology but also of future-developed technology.

(13) To reduce risk, as for example, risk of expropriation by an erratic government.

(14) To avoid local foreign country social legislation.

(15) To fulfill local law patent working requirements.

(16) To avoid antitrust or trade regulation problems, and to profit in the process.

For example, a manufacturer with an 80 percent market share and a questionable patent may not want to risk an antitrust counterclaim in a suit to enforce the patent. So he assigns his patents, perhaps to a charitable university-based foundation for 80 percent of all royalty income, and takes a royalty-bearing license back.

The charitable assignee with no market share can sue infringers with sharply reduced or no exposure to the antitrust counterclaim from the infringer.

If the patent stands up, the assignor and the assignee both make money.

As a second example, suppose a patent on a sort of dirt that can be made out of two very voluminous industrial pollutants is owned by a company in the business of engineering and construction of plants to dispose of the pollutants by making the patented dirt-like material.

The practicalities of building plants to dispose of the pollutants are such that a patent owner cannot both seek the design, engineering, and construction contract from the producer of the pollutants and enforce his patent against them, his customer group.

His interest is to enforce his patent on the patented material against competing designers and builders of plants that dispose of the pollutants by making the material, who are inducing infringers under 35 U.S.C. § 271(b). But to sue them is to seek to restrain their trade in unpatented engineering and construction services, which some might argue to be outside the scope of the Supreme Court's 1980 opinion in *Dawson Chemical v. Rohm and Haas,* 448 U.S. 176, 206 U.S.P.Q. 385, *reh'g denied,* 448 U.S. 917 (1980), founded on 271(a).

But if the patent owner assigns to a third party and takes a license back, the third party, who is not in the engineering and construction business, can without uncertainty of patent misuse law enforce the patent against all direct and inducing infringers without biasing customers to buy unpatented engineering and construction services from himself.

(17) To avoid or settle litigation with patent infringers or those wrongfully appropriating trade secrets.

The potential licensor who refuses to license may be confronted with a host of infringers of his patents. Licensing can then become a virtually forced alternative to an excessively burdensome and risky series of litigations.

(18) To help sell products, services, raw materials, or equipment.

For example, make and sell major equipment and license replacement parts or maintenance service to support the major equipment sale. But beware of tie-ins that may violate antitrust or trade regulation laws.

(19) To sell a company.

Sometimes it is necessary to grant a license to the new owner of a company being sold.

(20) To buy an equity interest in a company.

For example, Conoco went into many, many joint ventures in which it provided the technology in exchange for half interest and the partner supplied the capital and local labor force for his half interest.

(21) For access to a low-cost labor pool.

A licensor like RCA may desire to establish a source of supply of a manufactured part or component like TV circuit boards used in its own finished TV product, wherein the manufacture is in a low-cost labor pool like Taiwan.

§ 2.02   Why Not to License Your Technology

A proprietor might be biased against licensing in order:

(1)   To avoid the risk of setting up a future competitor, for licensees tend to become future competitors.

(2)   To make the potentially bigger profit commonly resulting from direct manufacture and sales—though at higher risk and capital cost.

(3)   To make a longer term profit, *i.e.,* to retain a secure hitch to a share of long-term future markets projected to be growing as time passes. For licenses tend to expire; licensees have a tendency to become unhitched from the licensor.

And still we can observe the Standard Oil of Ohio acrylonitrile process first licensed in about 1960 and still bringing in royalties and even new licensees after 28 years—over $300 million in royalties.

Licenses, you see, are not *all* short-term arrangements.

(4)   To retain control over product liability or plant catastrophe liability exposure.

The Counseil Europeen des Federations de l'Industrie Chimique (CEFIC) produced in 1987 a document entitled *Principles and Guidelines for the Safe Transfer of Technology,* Appendix A *infra.* CEFIC issued the *Principles and Guidelines* in response to the Bhopal catastrophe, where the Indian government required Indian management for a Carbide Indian subsidiary licensee. This document contains two sections, Principles and Guidelines, and though it is flawed, it is useful as a checklist in license negotiations. Presently the International Affairs Group, U.S. Chemical Manufacturers Association, is studying this document.

Section 2 of *Principles and Guidelines* presents the principles that its authors feel should be considered and agreed upon by the various parties concerned in providing the conditions for a safe transfer of technology. The main responsibilities lie with the licensor and licensee; yet the host state must establish the necessary framework not only for a safe transfer of technology, but for safe ongoing use of it after transfer—which seems not to have occurred at Bhopal.

This document states that the licensor's duties include the responsibility for a safe process design, the initial technical training, the supervision of commissioning, start-up assistance, and information for the safe operation and handling of products, used or manufactured.

The licensee's duties are said to include the responsibility for detailed engineering, plant erection, process operation, plant maintenance and modifications, provision of information to local authorities on safety issues, training and supervision of the work force, and establishment of safety and security check systems.

Section 3 of *Principles and Guidelines* presents guidelines ensuring that the degree of safety of the licensee's plant is of an internationally accepted level and equivalent to that achieved in the country of origin. This section develops each phase in a transfer of technology, the initiation phase, the negotiation phase, the design and engineering phase, the procurement and erection phase, the emergency plan phase, the commissioning phase, and the operational phase.

The *Principles and Guidelines* document is not law anywhere, but it will have an influential role in license negotiations, in license terms, and in expert witness testimony of standards of license practice in cases of serious accidents in using the licensed technology.

The document seems to present some bias against licensing and some bias toward misplacing liability in some factual contexts. In addition this document raises some possible antitrust questions of its own.

(5) To retain control over product quality and product marketing deemed requisite for successful penetration of a market—a penetration that may be missed by a sloppy licensee.

(6) To support the proprietor's ongoing R&D effort.

With a license only and no ongoing manufacture and market experience, the practical quality of any ongoing R&D results and improvement development surely will dissipate, thereby debilitating the capacity to keep licensees hitched. With proprietor manufacture and sale and with close customer contact, the ongoing R&D is much more likely to generate fully competitive or competition-leading ongoing advances in the art.

Thus the bias long term is importantly influenced by the proprietor's confidence in his own future R&D in the area and by his need to have manufacture, sales, and associated customer contact to support his R&D effort.

(7) To avoid the burdens of technology transfer, training of support and service personnel, and guarantees—particularly if the licensee's market is not assured of being large, thereby to return large sums to the licensor.

Recall here the story of a proposed license to Hungary. Our client sought to license a sophisticated electronic technology to Hungary at a time when Hungary had no TV, had no labor force trained to handle electronic operation, maintenance, and repair of complex electronic equipment. The result was that the deal fell through because the modest market to be served would not support the cost of training the work force from a square-one starting point.

But often a developing nation is so desirous of getting its work force trained that it may subsidize such a contract if you are so bold as to ask.

Another burden of technology transfer is illustrated by the story of the French buyer of a U.S. tire making technology. The contract was a turnkey contract for a U.S. company to design and build a tire factory guaranteed to make X tires per month at Y reject rate and Z cost, etc., for a French buyer. When the plant had been completed and the contract training program completed, the buyer was able to get only 80 percent of the tires promised at twice the guaranteed reject rate and cost, or some such.

The licensee in good faith blamed the factory. The licensor in good faith blamed the stupidity of the licensee.

The court was about to get a case which it was totally incompetent to decide on the kind of evidence that can be brought to a courtroom.

If the case were litigated, the licensor could not feel confident of winning a good faith swearing match without strong evidence; the licensor needed dramatic evidence that the plant did meet specifications. So the licensor stripped its U.S. plants of 100 or so personnel, took them to France, and in 45 or so days had rejects at half the guarantee and production at 112 percent of guarantee. (Note that good license contract men never guarantee the ultimate limits of their technology because they must leave room for some licensee inefficiency, as by the licensee in this story—perhaps because the licensor did not teach well.)

Having developed the evidence for the lawsuit, the licensor did not need it. But neither did he ever get fully repaid for the cost of developing the evidence: repayment for out-of-pocket costs did not repay the lost production of the 100 or so men.

So we see that additional supervisory assistance, instruction, or supply of data occasionally burden a licensor beyond the point originally anticipated in the formulation of royalties and other income payments.

In short, demand for technical assistance, quality control, and the like often make contracts unprofitable, particularly if the contract does not provide for adequate front money or if the licensee does not realize a large market volume out of which to earn large royalties.

§ 2.03 Licensee's Reasons for Licensing in

Some licensees' reasons for licensing in include:

(1) To acquire a needed technology.

The scope of what can be purchased varies widely. Sometimes an entire operating plant and related know-how package of technology is licensed, patents being mere incidentals.

Sometimes only unpatented technology is licensed.

Often a single patent is licensed; often several dozen patents.

Or a licensee may wish to obtain pieces of compatible technology from several licensors: a chemical process from one licensor, a supplementing refinement from another licensor, a catalyst from another.

(2) To acquire a needed right to operate.

For example, the licensor may own key patents or may have appropriate licenses under other dominating patents or permits from the controlling governmental authorities that are not available to the licensee other than by taking a license.

(3) To supplement the licensee's own research and/or to obtain continuing access to technical help or ongoing R&D by others.

To restate the earlier UOP example, UOP takes grant-backs from its catalytic cracking licensees throughout the world, keeps pilot plants running studies at all times, and licenses worldwide both the licensee's and UOP's refinements in catalytic cracking know-how.

Most of the world's refiners could not afford such an R&D effort and also could not stay competitive with the big eight or big ten oil refiners without access to such as UOP's ongoing R&D.

(4) To avoid the risk that the R&D expense does not produce a return on investment, particularly in a circumstance wherein experienced and proven research people in the subject area are difficult to come by.

(5) To settle a patent or trade secret dispute.

(6) To cash in on the good reputation of the licensor, like BURGER KING, IBM, or XEROX.

Chapter 3

Nature of the Different Licensable Properties

Having assumed the possibility of a desire to license, it becomes fundamental to get a mental handle on the different natures of licensable properties. This is a prerequisite to being able to mold the various license terms, royalties, barter exchanges, buy-backs, component supplies, and obligations of confidence into patterns that are compatible with each other, with the law, and with the reality of the marketplace.

§ 3.01 Show-How

Show-how is a teaching service, a technical support service. It is the product offered by consulting engineers when they are using only the common knowledge of the art to advise, by contrast with doing engineering design work.

For example: the technology for design, construction, and operation of a conventional high-pressure polyethylene plant is now available from the published literature. The published literature includes masses of what we might call chaff information, themes only marginally operable or perhaps now totally out of date, which misleads researchers and designers, as well as a relatively few kernels of currently useful wheat information.

The wheat information, *i.e.,* the set of parameters of that technology that work effectively, with good cost efficiency, good quality control, and good safety for the workers, is thoroughly blended and mixed with quantities of chaff knowledge, and only very skilled people working at high cost can screen the wheat from the chaff information.

Some professional engineers with general experience in the area, however, without designing a plant, can teach or show the broad public-knowledge *concepts* of how to build or operate such a plant and can specify roughly the production cost and quality obtainable from their concept—in the manner and to the degree of the college engineering professor in his class.

What they are thereby selling is show-how—their *time* for teaching public knowledge. And they are paid for teaching services.

Similarly, engineers often provide technical support services in an ongoing relationship after the plant is on stream, using mostly or only nonproprietary/public information.

Every technology transfer contract (as distinguished from naked patent license or naked immunity from charge of patent infringement) includes important elements of show-how. And that show-how carries with it its own set of costs, values, and tax treatments that often differ from tax treatments of proprietary know-how and patent licenses, not infrequently warranties of performance and quality and manufacturing cost, and its own set of applicable antitrust and trade regulation laws. Each must be addressed in the study for the license contract negotiation.

Show-how of nonproprietary information blends imperceptibly from public information into confidential and patented know-how, both of which significantly distinguish public information by their capital asset nature and by their proprietary character. The contract negotiator and draftsman has tremendous freedom to bias the tenor of a given contract and its monetary consideration more toward or away from show-how services for antitrust, tax, contract, or other purposes, at his option if he but has the imagination.

For example, a patent royalty in the U.S. terminates by operation of law upon invalidity or expiration of the patent. A trade secret royalty may terminate upon competitive development and/or other publication of the secret. But a participation in the gross income from a plant for X years, contractually in exchange for having provided nonsecret start-up show-how services, may go on for an entire term of years contracted for. For the consideration agreed upon is not dependent upon the continued proprietary character of a *res,* a thing, that is conveyed, but upon the hours and quality of personal service that is put into the project.

I know of one such contract for 1 percent of the gross income of an entire company for the life of the show-how performer but not less than 25 years—a fully enforceable contract.

Another example: Income from show-how service is unavoidably taxed as ordinary income. But in a proper case during capital gains tax years in which I expect to return promptly, an income from an exclusive license or sale of proprietary know-how or a patent may be taxed as capital gains. And a careful draftsman can move a lot of the consideration from one tax treatment to the other.

One of these two recited examples evidences a strong bias in favor of show-how services, the other a strong bias against show-how treatment. The two together illustrate the difficult trade-offs that are commonly necessary in license work.

Query: Is it proper for there to be an obligation to quit using nonconfidential, nonsecret, nonpatented show-how information readily available from other consulting engineers upon the event of nonpayment of consideration? Or should the seller of show-how services involving only public knowledge be relegated to his monetary remedy on grounds that he cannot be irreparably injured by lack of the injunctive remedy while the competitive structure of the industry can be disruptively injured by injunctions enforced against the use of nonproprietary show-how information? The answer to that question teaches us that the antitrust law impacts the termination and default clauses differently with respect to show-how and proprietary know-how.

§ 3.02   Know-How, Both Nonconfidential and Secret

The subject matter shown in a show-how service or technical assistance contract, *i.e.,* the *res,* is of course know-how.

25

But know-how comes in two varieties: it may be non-secret, nonproprietary know-how or secret, proprietary know-how.

Know-how may be common knowledge of the subject art with no unique value, as is the material taught by the college professor from the freshman text book, or it may be the secret design of a plant for ethylene oxide production and the instructions on how to operate it.

In some situations, deliberate confusion of proprietary and nonproprietary know-how may be advantageous. For example, a sale of technology including nonsecret information packaged with secret information and patents may hurt or improve the tax treatment of the total consideration. Or, tying of royalties to nonsecret technical assistance services or rights to future technological developments may make them lawful for many years after patents expire and patent royalties terminate.

But that nonproprietary know-how must never be confused with proprietary know-how. For the law and practice are sharply different for each.

Commonly, however, a proprietor distills from the haystack of public knowledge a unique set of parameters of process and plant which, for example, will produce X tons of Y product of Z quality at Q cost with R personnel who can be trained in S man-hours to operate the plant—all guaranteeable by the licensor.

Every feature of the process and plant may, as separate features, be within the knowledge and ordinary skill of the art. Still, it may take $10 million and three years to develop a set of parameters that will work together at certifiable cost, safety, quality, etc. Anyone who steals the package of plans and specifications has stolen a value of perhaps $50 million—the result, the work product, of a lot of design, engineering, and testing even when the concepts are in the public domain.

Though the value of a particular plant design may dissipate as new plant designs come into competitive use, a plant

26

design need *never* become generally known public knowledge.

If a plant design and know-how package is preserved in confidence, the package, *i.e.,* the compilation or combination of the parameters, is both confidential know-how and a trade secret. It is also thereby proprietary information and a capital asset.

And it is legitimate to require licensees to keep the design confidential in perpetuity, as in Sohio's acrylonitrile licenses, which have brought in some $300 million in the past, with new know-how licenses still being issued.

Often it is the guarantee that most interests the licensee. He knows he could hire the process and plant design to be developed by those of ordinary skill in the art using only public domain technology. But he doesn't trust them to effect plant safety until one or more men have been killed or maimed in the shake-down or de-bugging process. He doesn't trust them to meet quality control specifications and cost of production specifications or to de-bug the whole undertaking—all on the time schedule of the marketing program. He often will pay a premium price for a guarantee by which he avoids all those risks, and both the licensee and the licensor should study the scope and the value of the guarantee before the license negotiation commences.

Recall that pursuant to the *Principles and Guidelines,*[1] the responsibility for the safe process design, the initial technical training, the supervision of commissioning, start-up assistance, and information for safe operation and handling of products used or manufactured may, depending upon the terms negotiated in the particular circumstance, be part of the licensor's duties.

Proprietary know-how commonly is a selected blend of individually nonsecret elements wherein the blend rather than any element is secret. But that is not all.

In the development of know-how the developer often conceives some unique relationships or mechanisms or process control steps or chemistry, which as individual parts are

---

[1] *See* App. A, *infra.*

valuable secrets not known to competitors—for example, a special lubricant for extremely high-pressure compressors that will afford an extra 2,000 hours of running time between overhauls. Such a discrete, individual trade secret may be licensed along with the package of know-how blend or may be licensed separately on its own terms.

Thus we see that the proprietary trade secret, which is the know-how package and its blend, commonly also includes some discrete technical trade secret elements—elements that may advantageously be licensed separately for their own consideration and term.

Every know-how contract has in it some element of show-how cost that must not be overlooked and commonly includes both discrete trade secret details and patented concepts as well as both proprietary, confidential know-how and nonconfidential, nonproprietary know-how.

Each proprietary and nonproprietary know-how and trade secret attracts its own set of contract treatments, its own value as support for front money payments or other sums certain, its own value as support for royalty type payments, its own law for its protection, its own export control, its own set of applicable tax law, its own set of antitrust and other trade regulation law, and its own practicalities of dissipation of confidentiality and/or value with time and in light of competitive development of similar know-how.

Query: Should licensed know-how be the subject of an injunction against its use upon nonpayment of royalties, when the know-how is available to members of the public who will but reverse engineer the products on the market and use the publicly available knowledge to design plant and process?

Should know-how license contracts provide for an injunctive remedy against use of licensed know-how upon default of royalty payment occurring five years after the license? Under what circumstances?

If a first licensee is contractually free to use and include in his licenses all he knows after five years from his license date, may the original proprietor require a subsequent know-how licensee to keep the confidence for a subsequent five years, or to pay a royalty during a subsequent five years, or not to use the know-how if he doesn't pay?

Is it ethical or fair for a know-how licensee to take the licensor's disclosure to the licensee and use it as a guide-map for a search through all the public knowledge to separate out the wheat knowledge from the chaff knowledge and as instructions whereby to piece the wheat elements together into the license package—then to argue either that he owes nothing because the information given to him is not secret or that he is not subject to an injunction against its use because such an obligation with respect to nonsecret information would be in restraint of trade?

How should your contract treat that common practice of licensees?

§ 3.03   Trade Secrets

In the United States the most commonly used definition of a trade secret is that found in the 1939 *Restatement (First) of Torts:*

> A trade secret may consist of any formula, pattern, device or compilation of information [very important phrase, that last one] which is used in one's business and which gives an opportunity to obtain an advantage over competitors who do not know or use it. It may be a formula for a chemical compound, a process of manufacturing, treating or preserving materials, a pattern for a machine or other device, or a list of customers. . . . Generally it relates to the production of goods, as for example, a machine or formula for the production of an article. It may, however, relate to the sale of goods or to other operations in the business such as a code for determining discounts, rebates or other concessions in a price list or catalogue, or a list of specialized customers or a method of bookkeeping or other office management.[2]

According to this definition, which includes "compilation of information," almost every know-how package is by its

---

[2] *Restatement (First) of Torts* § 757, comment b (1939).

29

compilation and packaging also a trade secret—subject of course to the loss of its secrecy either by the nature of its use, by the practicalities of independent discovery, or by operation of law.

Note that a compilation of engineering and process data, shall we say for a chemical refinery, can be preserved in secrecy forever and independent development of the same compilation can never occur—not until a chimpanzee types the Bible on a typewriter. The value of the compilation may dissipate as new designs come onto the competitive stream, but the life of the compilation trade secret may be perpetual.

But there are often discrete trade secrets (*e.g.*, a special lubricant for a high-pressure compressor that trebles the life between overhauls of the compressors used in high-pressure chemical processes) that are separately licensable, are capable alone of sustaining a suit for misappropriation of trade secrets or for injunction against use if not paid for, and the secrecy of which is commonly lost by independent discovery.

Commonly, many of these discrete trade secrets are covered by pending applications for a patent or patents.

And there are nuances scattered through the law applicable to trade secrets that may be materially biased by the law of patents, the antitrust and trade regulation law, tax law, and the treatment of contract language.

Query: May one obtain an injunction against use of a trade secret covered by but not disclosed in a patent? Or a trade secret that is no longer secret? Major papers and many court opinions have been written on those subjects.

§ 3.04 Patent Applications

Many items of licensable knowledge may be the subject of applications for patent.

As such they may be confidential and secret for a while, perhaps until the secrecy is lost or perhaps only diluted through issue of a patent disclosing the secret.[3] Or through

---

[3] Recall that patents generally do not disclose much engineering detail

the laying open of an application for public inspection in some country that does that. Or perhaps through marketing of products in which the secret is revealed by the product or by publication of advertisements or service manuals for it. Or through competitive development of the same knowledge.

But it is not realistic to assume that all that is revealed in any patent or publication or marketed product, anywhere, is both known to and its value appreciated by all or even any of the actual workers in a given technology. The fact of publication or patenting may itself be substantially secret, in actuality, from the competitive workers in the art.

Back at the time of the end of the life of vacuum tube amplifiers, this story occurred. The technology proprietor had designed a very sophisticated geophysical amplifier, a $10,000 unit then, before inflation. It could handle input signals that varied in amplitude by a factor of a million. It could amplify the input signals by a factor of a million. All without ringing or going into an oscillation mode. It was a stable amplifier.

One key feature that contributed to that stability was the use of a photo-sensitive variable resistor in one of the feedback circuits. The circuit diagram was a part of a service manual that went as a loaner with each unit sold. A defecting employee group offered a similar design, and the technology proprietor sued.

The defendant alleged that the unique feature was published in the service manual because hundreds of copies had been given out. But the court found that the service manual was loaned to customers for purposes of service of their equipment, in contrast with being sold or published to competitors. The audience that would read the service manual were technicians, not circuit designers. Technicians could pull out a bad resistor and plug in a new one without ever comprehending the significance of this device in rendering the amplifier stable. So that court afforded protection.

---

of value. *Christianson v. Colt Indus. Operating Corp.,* 822 F.2d 1544, 1562, 3 U.S.P.Q.2d 1241 (Fed. Cir. 1987).

Thus, the words secret and nonsecret usually *say* more about a situation than is real, because the very common quasi-secrecy often involves much commercial value. Your license contract negotiation must often address that issue in a variety of ways.

There are those in many countries, including some courts in the United States, who perceive the law of trade secrets to be governed *de jure* by such publications as may *de facto* be nonenabling to the industry.

But where the facts of ongoing quasi-secrecy can be shown, as is commonly the case, to be contrary to the *de jure* presumptions that follow a publication, the contractual license negotiation patterns and the litigation patterns should be influenced by the *de facto* continuing degree of quasi-secrecy even after some publication, *e.g.,* an ongoing contract that the licensee shall keep the confidence even after the money is fully paid and no injunction lies for ongoing use of the information.

It is of course clear law, everywhere, that a mere application for patent gives no right to preclude use of the subject matter. Only when the patent issues does that right arise.

Yet it is very common to find license agreements that, in idiomatic expression, purport to "license the pending application for patent."

But in the ultimate sense, what is a license? A license is the *withholding* of a right to preclude others from use and enjoyment. It is not a grant of anything; it is a withholding of a right to exclude others.

So how do you license a patent application that at law grants no right to exclude others?

The alleged licenses of applications for patent are thus seen to be clear errors at least of grammatical form, if not of substance and reality. The purported license of a patent application is more accurately a license either of the trade secret or of the patent when it issues, or both; and normally the accurate expressions serve best.

The purported license of a patent application is a common error with which the business and industrial community lives very well. Still, lawyers, and more importantly, courts, sometimes trip over this idiom.

§ 3.05 Patents

And now we come to patents, duly issued patents.

[1] Issue Time and Term

Patents most commonly issue in the time frame between one and four or five years after filing, sometimes much longer.

In the United States patents expire 17 years after issue, which is very roughly 20 years after filing the application. In most European countries the expiration is explicitly 20 years after filing. In some few countries of possible interest shorter terms, like 14 years, obtain.

With some rare exceptions patents may not be renewed after expiration.

[2] Subject Matter Covered by Patents

In the United States the patent law extends to the "useful arts," as distinguished from the literary and fine arts, which are protected by copyright.

While pure computer software as such, the conceptual process of which is not novel, is protectable by copyrights and trade secrecy, such software is not protected by patents. On the other hand, computer hardware programmed to perform a conceptually novel process can be protected by patents.

New, nonobvious compositions of matter including new, nonobvious chemical compounds as such, may be protected. This means that the U.S. system affords easy, practical protection of new insecticides, new herbicides, new pharmaceuticals, and new foods as fully as new mechanical and electrical contrivances, a sharp contrast to the patent law of Italy, China, Romania, and a number of other countries, where new compounds and/or pharmaceuticals per se are for some inexplicable reason excluded from patent protection.

Plants and animals other than human, insofar as they are man-made, may be protected in the U.S. The law as to patents on animals other than human is not established in most other countries and indeed is under reexamination in the United States.

[3] Standard of Innovation

Patents are granted only on innovations not obvious to those of ordinary skill in the art to which the invention pertains. Therefore, a patent may not take from the public domain anything which theretofore was within the capacity of those of ordinary skill in the art to make and use.

[4] Rights Granted

Patents do not grant the right to use the invention. Rather, subject to compulsory license regulations in some countries, patents grant the right to exclude others from

(1) making the claimed invention,
(2) using the claimed invention, or
(3) selling the claimed invention in the country that grants it.

The right to use your invention is a natural right subject to prior patents and government regulations.

With rare exception there are no true international patents. The most important partial exception is the European Patent, which is enforceable in many of the countries of Europe but by the national law of the individual country involved.

Not in every circumstance but by and large, patents are said to be exhausted with respect to any patented product once it has been sold by the patentee or under his license or authority. Thereby, the right to exclude others from use or resale of the particular item so sold terminates with the first sale of any particular item.

Within the EEC the exhaustion in one country generally applies also to the counterpart patents of other EEC countries, though the exhaustion in one country is not always a complete exhaustion in other countries.

[5] Patent Coverage Is More Vague and Indefinite Than Is Commonly Thought

The scope of the patent's right to preclude others is measured by a series of one-sentence paragraphs at the end of the patent, called claims. The claims attempt to define the invention in words.

Unfortunately, words are a poor vehicle for precise definition of technological thought that keeps evolving as you study it. And so there are often major ambiguities in the application of claims to independently designed devices not in contemplation when the claims were drafted. *I.e.,* there are major ambiguities with respect to the patented invention as compared to the accused infringement, which must be essentially the same as the invention in order for infringement to be found.

There are also major ambiguities with respect to the invention as compared to the prior art, which the claims must distinguish in order to be valid.

These and other ambiguities in the patent law beget much patent litigation at very high expense. The uncertainty and cost are perhaps greater in United States practice than in most other countries.

The risk of such litigation, its uncertain results, and its contingent cost must be factored into the evaluations of many clauses in any license. One common accommodation of that cost and uncertainty, where it is feasible: license primarily the know-how, with an immunity from any charge of infringement of any of the licensor's patents by the use of the licensed know-how thrown in as an incidental. This can be done without even identifying the patents, as in UOP's catalytic cracking licenses.

But that practice of drafting the instrument as primarily a know-how license with patents thrown in as incidental, although desirable for one purpose, precludes the licensor from enjoying the privileges of the block exemptions from notification under the January 1, 1985, EEC block exemptions—a privilege that you do have under a license that is primarily a patent license with the know-how thrown in as an incidental.

Also, an agreement drafted primarily as a know-how license with patents thrown in as incidental tends significantly to reduce the damages recoverable in a subsequent successful patent infringement suit.

Consideration of these sophisticated tactical trade-offs is a necessary part of the licensing process.

In the United States an infringer can attack a patent both in the Patent and Trademark Office and in our courts. In most foreign countries, there is only one forum for such attack.

Patents are often invalidated or held unenforceable by reason of deficient disclosure of the invention, deficient definition of the invention in the claims, inequitable conduct in the solicitation of the patent, and misuse of the patent after it issues, as in a license in violation of the antitrust laws.

[6] Patents Do Not Necessarily Preempt Trade Secret Protection

The disclosure detail of patents varies markedly from country to country. But patents generally disclose the concept of an invention and how to make it sufficiently for the person of ordinary skill in the subject art to make and use it with his own engineering. Patents do not disclose the engineering detail of any particular embodiment of a product nor the production engineering for its commercial manufacture.

The omitted engineering detail is often vital to cost and quality control with respect to a particular embodiment of the invention. But often engineering detail for a particularly good model is not developed until after the patent issues or often after the patent expires, which is one of several reasons for the law's not requiring its inclusion in the patent disclosure.

Thus, while patents often disclose trade secrets, and by the patent's publication render the secrets no longer completely secret and unlikely to enjoy further protection as trade secrets, patents often do not disclose important secrets that nevertheless are within the scope of the patent's effective control.

Consider an example. The J-59 jet engine, which now powers many of our jumbo jet aircraft, was designed merely as a larger-size engine after the expiration of the basic patents on the jet engine. Yet it cost half a billion dollars to develop—half a billion, using essentially all publicly available knowledge to reconcile the new larger gas thrust with turbine size and speed, with blade metallurgy and dimensions to stand the centrifugal forces of the jet rotor at the new higher temperatures, with low noise levels and high fuel efficiency.

The know-how produced with that development is of tremendous value, independently of the fact that conceptually the engine was more or less old hat.

The documentation of that know-how fills many dozens of volumes, linear yards of shelf space, and it is not disclosed in any patent. Patents print out usually in less than a dozen pages.

The Federal Circuit was explicit on the point in a 1987 decision, *Christianson v. Colt Indus. Operating Corp.,* 822 F.2d 1544, 3 U.S.P.Q. 2d 1241 (Fed. Cir. 1987): manufacturing and production detail is not a part of the statutorily required best mode disclosure of a patent. And it is not normally to be found there.

I focus on this because many courts and even many patent lawyers seem prone to assume that because the patent statute requires a best mode disclosure, patents necessarily disclose or preempt all the trade secrets that are useful in the practice of the invention.

That is flat wrong. But licensing practitioners need to anticipate the problem presented by the common error.

[7] Avoidance of Infringement Liability

One of the most significant considerations by the business that would enter a new market is possible unwitting infringement by itself or its licensee of intellectual property rights owned by others. To import a product into the United States or to make, use, or sell it there, is to risk a charge of infringement of property rights owned by another.

As to rights under the copyright or the semiconductor chips acts and in trade secrets, suffice here to point out that unlike patents, you do not infringe any of those rights unless there has been a derivation from the prior proprietor. But if a second comer independently invents the same thing previously patented to another, he infringes the patent even without derivation from the prior patentee.

About half of all patents litigated in the United States are held invalid or unenforceable, indicating the major ambiguity in the application of patent law in business ventures, to which I alluded earlier. It follows that a thorough search for patents that may possibly be infringed should be performed either by the licensor or by the licensee long before launch of the product in the United States.

Once patents potentially to be infringed are found, validity searching and studies must be performed against each such patent. And efforts must be made to design around or get a license under those patents found arguably to be infringed. All of which takes time and money.

In a distinct majority of instances, the threat of the patents owned by others may be avoided either by design-around, license, invalidation, or proof of unenforceability by reason of inequitable conduct in soliciting the patent or by reason of misuse of the patent after its issue. So it is gross business error to back away from a venture upon merely learning of a potentially infringed patent. However, the high cost of patent litigation, the uncertainty of the result, and the severity of the remedies make it very important that, before a product launch in the United States, a thorough infringement study should be made by competent litigation-experienced counsel.

Such studies sometimes cost only a few thousand dollars. Often they cost $30,000. And sometimes they cost $250,000, a lot of money unless it is anticipated that a relatively large market is going to be reached.

[8] The U.S. System of Litigation Importantly Influences License Clauses

The remedies for patent infringement include:

(1) Injunction against making, using, selling, or importing the invention.
(2) Damages.
    (a) As a minimum, a reasonable royalty whereby the infringer may still have made a profit;
    (b) or perhaps more likely for the future, a royalty to capture or exceed the infringer's profits;
    (c) the patent owner's lost incremental profits, on his own business, if any there be, which may run 50 to 70 percent of the retail sales price;
    (d) the patent owner's profits lost on his own sales, by reason of price competition with the infringer.
(3) In cases of willful infringement, a multiplication of those damages by any figure up to three times.
(4) In exceptional cases, attorney fees that may be $1 million or more by contrast with Europe's more common $50,000 to $250,000.

Further, in the United States the system of litigation affords an almost unlimited discovery by each party of the other. Requests for hundreds, thousands, and sometimes hundreds of thousands of documents have been made in patent cases. Deposition testimony in pretrial discovery is likely to be taken from 20 persons, perhaps from 40 or 50.

The result is that patent litigation to determine the valid scope of a patent costs a million dollars in a typical U.S. case, and not infrequently costs several million dollars—and typically takes four or more years of time, during which uncertainty hangs over the commercial operations.

The

(1) sometimes harsh remedies for patent infringement,
(2) high cost in money and time of uncertainty of patent
   litigation in the United States, coupled with
   (a) the rule by which a licensee can attack the valid-
      ity of a patent under which he is licensed, and
   (b) the rule that a patent held invalid in one lawsuit
      is invalid also not only with respect to all poten-
      tial future licensees but with respect to prior
      licensees and the ongoing royalty income from
      them as well

sharply bias against a number of superficially reasonable patent license clauses.

For example, favored nations clauses tend to force expensive and risky enforcement of the patent lest the late-coming infringer enjoy what amounts to a royalty-free license by virtue of the failure to sue him. Because patent litigation is so expensive, favored nations clauses and assumptions of an obligation to enforce the patents become monstrous traps for the unwary. Further, seemingly reasonable covenants of licensors at licensor expense to defend licensees against charges of infringement by third party patent owners become horror stories in some situations, particularly when and if the licensee has the freedom to hang in with his product design without making a minor product change that would obviate the charge of infringement.

Those clauses represent very complex license issues, which we have inadequate time to cover in this book. But it is unwise ever to commit to one of those clauses without thorough study and advice from competent counsel experienced in patent litigation.

[9] Patents Attract Their Own Law

Patents, like the other forms of intellectual property, attract their own monetary and nonmonetary considerations, their own law of tax, antitrust, export control, license, and enforcement.

Query: May a market be divided geographically by licensing the patents of one group of countries while not licensing counterpart patents in another group of countries? In some circumstances, yes.

If a patent right is exhausted in one country, as by manufacture and sale by the patentee in that country, may the patentee or his licensee enforce the counterpart patent of any other country against use or resale there of the goods made by the patentee in the first country? Perhaps, but not between EEC countries under the 1984 EEC block exemptions that became effective January 1, 1985. The EEC block exemptions provide that exhaustion of the patent right in one EEC country exhausts as to all countries.

May a market be divided by licensing a patent on improved bearings to one company in one field of use like electric motors under ten horsepower, and licensing to another company in a second field of use like electric motors of more than ten horsepower? Likely, no. Field of use licenses are legally safe where the fields of use are naturally divided markets—like aircraft engines vs. electric motors—but are not so clearly safe where the fields of use divide a naturally integrated market.

§ 3.06   The Hybrid Patent and Know-How License

In hybrid patent and know-how license contracts there is one point of contract structure which we ought not overlook.

Some courts confuse patent royalty rights and know-how/trade-secret royalty rights, and refuse to allocate royalties on them when one expires or otherwise terminates.[4] If your contracts don't allocate royalties to each, the court may not

---

[4] *Meehan v. PPG Indus., Inc.,* 802 F.2d 881, 886, 231 U.S.P.Q. 400 (7th Cir. 1986); *Boggild v. Kenner Prods.,* 776 F.2d 1315, 1319, 228 U.S.P.Q. 130 (6th Cir. 1985); *Pitney-Bowes, Inc. v. Mestre,* 517 F. Supp. 52, 61–63, 211 U.S.P.Q. 681 (S.D. Fla. 1981), *aff'd in part and dismissed in part,* 701 F.2d 1365, 218 U.S.P.Q. 987 (11th Cir.), *cert. denied,* 464 U.S. 893 (1983); *Veltman v. Norton Simon, Inc.,* 425 F. Supp. 774, 776, 194 U.S.P.Q. 168 (S.D.N.Y. 1977).

do so, and may terminate all royalties upon patent invalidation or expiration.

So you are well advised, whenever it is feasible, to break out the patent from the know-how license. In many know-how licenses, particularly involving future technology as in the UOP catalytic cracking licenses elsewhere discussed, the better judgment may be to treat royalties on the patents as a throw-away without attempting break-out. But where feasible, it is preferable to break them into different contracts with different royalty clauses.

And don't forget: the patent royalties can stop on date X (not later than the expiration of the patent), the know-how royalties can stop on date Y, and the obligation of confidence either on date Z or when certain specified events occur or not at all. Royalties need not necessarily be tied precisely to the term of confidence in properly constructed contracts relating to either bona fide trade secrets or to show-how. This is in contrast to *Brulotte v. Thys Co.,* 379 U.S. 29 (1964), where the Supreme Court held that royalties on a patent may not last longer than the life of the patent.

§ 3.07   Trademarks

A trademark is a symbol of the origin and quality of goods or services.

When you buy a Coca Cola, you know it won't taste like root beer and will not have alcohol in it—*i.e.,* you know at least generally the qualities of the drink you get under that trademark.

And when you buy a Coca Cola, you expect it to be made or sponsored by the same company which made or sponsored the last Coca Cola you bought, even though the maker's true name may be anonymous to you.

At least in the United States, the term trademark is commonly applied to products and the term service mark is commonly applied to services like airline services, dry cleaning services, and the like. But the law is generally the same as applied to both. The generic term is simply mark.

The term trade name is, in correct usage, applied only to company names.

But a lot of variant usages exist with all these terms.

An essential part of any license of a mark of either character is control of the quality of the goods or services marketed under the trademark or trade name—at least in many countries.

Patents, discrete trade secrets, and sometimes know-how tend to have relatively short lives. Trademarks may go on forever if they are continuously used. It follows that an appropriate package of technology licensed with trademarks may produce much longer-term rewards than the technology alone.

Chapter 4

The Apple and Its Wrappers

It is important in many situations to understand that what the licensee is buying is a single item, not separate patents, trade secrets, know-how, etc.

Patents, whether they be one or more, trade secrets, whether they be one or more, and know-how are each different protective wrappers for the same single value to the licensee—namely, an integrated and operable set of technical parameters that are useful with particular equipment with certain safety, cost, quality, etc.

Commonly the buyer wants to buy that single value without regard to how many protective wrappers it may be presented in and without regard to what the different protective wrappers effectively do or do not protect.

An apple may be wrapped loosely in wax paper for certain protection, which nevertheless lets air in. It may be further wrapped in a sealed polyethylene envelope to keep air out to help preserve its freshness. It may further be wrapped in aluminum foil to reflect the heat of the sun. It may be further wrapped in insulation to protect it from extremes of cold. And it may then be put into a box to protect it from being squashed.

These different protective wrappers for the apple are of interest, and depending upon the circumstances there may even be a desirability of putting separate values on some of those wrappers as a part of evaluating the several wrappers and whether you really need all of the protective wrappers or only some of them.

But the psychology of the buyer, and therefore a psychology that the seller must also recognize and focus upon, likely is: how good does the apple taste? That is, how valuable and useful is the technology? The taste of the apple is one thing; it is not a series of different things, like the technology is one thing and not a series of different things. The technology is the *res,* a singular thing conveyed like the apple; the plurality of protective wrappers is of considerable interest and value, but the wrappers are not the *res.*

In the courtroom and in licensing negotiations there often appears a lot of argument about the wrappers. But we must, particularly in technology salesmanship and license work, focus a primary attention upon the taste of the apple.

Chapter 5

The Sticks of License

As implied by the catalog of intellectual properties that I have discussed, there are many separate rights available to license:

(1) The right to *make.*
(2) The right to *use.*
(3) The right to *disclose* to others
    (a) as by *publication;*
    (b) as in a *marketed product or its service manual;* or
    (c) as in a *sublicense* to others.
(4) The right to *lease.*
(5) The right to *sell.*

Each such right is a discrete stick to be separately considered in the license package. Each has its own time dimensions, space or geographic dimensions, and field of use dimensions.

Ongoing R&D, grant-backs, reversions of title, rights to receive disclosure of either old or new information, best efforts clauses, running royalty changes or graduations, obligations to police trade secrets—these are additional sticks in a bundle of sticks, elements if you prefer, addressed in license contract studies and negotiations. And each has, at least potentially, a different time line from some other.

The "termination" of a license agreement, which includes several among patents, trademarks, discrete trade secrets, know-how, show-how, grantbacks, reversions, etc., thus is seen to embody many distinct sticks that commonly cannot be addressed properly by the single word termination or expiration of the agreement, for each right or obligation almost necessarily terminates at times, in circumstances, and in degrees different from some of the others.

Surely, it is the failure to appreciate this fact—that each right or duty almost necessarily terminates at a time different from at least some of the others—that gives rise to the most common malpractice in licensing, the use of clauses that purport to terminate *"the contract,"* or to terminate *"the agreement,"* rather than terminating specifically this or that obligation, right, or duty.

For example, does "termination of this know-how license agreement" (a very common clause) mean that the licensee who now has the information lawfully,

(1) must stop using it?
(2) may stop paying royalties for his ongoing use or disclosure of the information? or
(3) must stop disclosing it to his own lawful sublicensees?

That question is surely the source of most know-how license contract litigation.

It is not the *"agreement"* that terminates. The *agreement* or *contract* goes on forever. The agreement or contract is that in the event of default the right to use the information terminates. And agreement or contract on that point—that the right to use terminates—should be a perpetual agreement or contract.

Or: The agreement was that royalties are payable until January 1, 1988. Because that agreement is perpetual and still in force in 1988, no royalties are due in 1988. The agreement, therefore, should not be recited to terminate or expire in 1987. The duty to pay royalties is the thing that should be recited to expire.

So, in technology transfer work sophisticated draftsmanship (as well as sophisticated trade-outs of one value for another) is necessary to avoid stumbling over one of the many different sticks that make up the license package.

Chapter 6

Legitimate Needs and Greeds

Let me give you one additional phrase which I have found useful in license negotiation work: "Legitimate needs and greeds."

Each party has both legitimate needs and some understandable greeds, which the other party can often find a way to concede at minor cost. There is a special candor involved in talking about your own legitimate greeds and suggesting by implication that you will concede the other guy's reasonable greeds if this or that change can be made. And that special candor helps the negotiation get along.

Perhaps more important, that kind of candid discussion begets a better understanding of the other guy's pattern of hangups.

Too often both parties hang tight with their demand for the orange. But if you can talk about it candidly, you may find that Joe really just wants the peel to make marmalade, and Dick really just wants the juice. So you can give each person what he wants, if you can identify it precisely.

In your negotiation, look for and talk about the other guy's legitimate needs and greeds—and your own.

Chapter 7

Antitrust-Misuse Law as Applied to Licensing

Let's turn now to one quick point about the antitrust and patent misuse law.

Text writers, courts, and lawyers—including the Department of Justice prior to 1980—are prone to write with respect to various license restrictions that all examples of the particular restriction as a class are either lawful or per se unlawful. For example, the pre-1980 Department of Justice publicized what it called "the Nine No-No's" as per se violations. But the Nine No-No's were not only bad law, they evidence sloppy thinking and their per se illegality has been rejected by subsequent Justice officials.

In one degree or another, all the license restrictions are either good or bad in accordance with the traditional antitrust rule of reason analysis by the two words "purpose" and "effect." I can best make that point by an illustration.

Let's take graduated royalties as our example.

An inventor has made an invention of merit which fits a market now served equally by three companies. He thinks:

> If I can get all three of those companies to compete with each other in the offering of my product, then the product will be competitively priced, the public will promptly be brought to enjoyment of the invention, and I will make a lot of money from the wide use of my invention.

A more benign set of purposes can hardly be imagined.

So he says:

> I'll offer a license to all three companies, at 20 percent royalty for the first million dollars worth of annual sales, 10 percent

51

royalty for the second million dollars worth of annual sales, and 1 percent royalty for all further annual sales.

That will make all three companies compete like hell in order to get down that steep royalty curve and perfect an average royalty of only 3 to 5 percent.

The effect turned out to be competitive pricing, extensive advertising, prompt public enjoyment of the invention, and handsome royalties to the inventor in exchange for handsomely wide use of his invention.

The common writing on such a circumstance is an absolute phrase like "graduated royalties are lawful."

Don't you believe it.

Draw the curtain on that scenario and open the curtain on another scene: the board room of the corporation with 60 percent of the relevant market, which has just sued the company with 35 percent of the relevant market on a patent with flies all over it, questionable fraud on the Patent Office, close prior art, etc. The remaining 5 percent of the market is served by a dozen minor operators, each with miniscule market shares.

The President of the patent owner corporation speaks:

We must find a way to settle this lawsuit before anybody really examines that patent. We know that the defendant is a responsible corporation [translation: not a price cutter].

The defendant would be thrilled to death to pay an average 2 percent royalty to be rid of all those loft shop operators that are always upsetting the market [translation: that are discounters, price cutters].

Suppose we offer all comers a 20 percent royalty on the first million dollars in annual sales, 10 percent royalty on the second million dollars in annual sales, and 1 percent royalty on all annual sales thereafter.

The defendant is smart enough to figure out that it will be paying about 2 percent average royalty and that the loft shop operators can't price cut while paying 20 percent and don't have enough money at stake to justify litigation expenses and therefore must capitulate.

The deal is put into effect. A Japanese importer comes along and challenges the patent.

What are the first deposition questions put by defendant's counsel?

(1)   Who proposed the royalty scheme?
(2)   What was its purpose?
(3)   What was its effect?

Here you get an entirely different image of whether graduated royalties are inherently lawful or at least arguably unlawful.

The point is: there is nothing inherent in graduated royalties that make them inherently lawful or inherently unlawful. It is the purpose of their use and the effect of their use *in their particular market and industrial context* that determines whether a graduated royalty is good or bad.

That is my view, and that is the current Department of Justice view with respect to all the restrictions you are likely to consider for your license. Territorial restrictions, package licensing, tying clauses . . . you name it.

The economically and legally proper approach is the classic rule of reason analysis by purpose and effect instead of the historic per se rule of patent misuse.

Unfortunately, over the decades from the 40s through the 70s, the courts were induced to write a lot of per se conclusions, which we cannot disregard until the courts can be brought to adopt the current Department of Justice view. And that may take a while, particularly in misuse contexts where the Supreme Court has ruled and made law not likely to be reconsidered, in view of the new presence of the Federal Circuit hearing all patent appeals. Price fixing, tying clauses, and group boycotts are examples of restrictions likely to be viewed as per se illegalities.

Bills were introduced in the 1987 Congress that would convert patent misuses to rule of reason analysis, but it is not yet known whether they will pass and be signed by the President.

Licensing

Still, it is worthwhile for persons working in the licensing area to appreciate that, in truth, there is nothing inherent in a given license restriction as such which makes it socially benign or evil. Rather, it is the purpose and effect of that restriction in context of the industry and market wherein it is used that give it its character of benign or evil. And hopefully this will soon become the generally applicable rule of law for all license restrictions.

An in-depth discussion of the conditions under which U.S. antitrust law will be given extraterritorial effect is beyond the scope of this book. However, a few general observations will be made.

Restraints on exports from the United States to a foreign nation affect the export trade of the United States, and restraints on exports from foreign nations to the United States affect the import trade. Apparently, if either the licensee or the licensor is within the jurisdiction of the United States, United States antitrust law could be applicable to such foreign import or export commerce with the United States and those whose contracts affect it. How much must the effect be?

A revision in Section 7 of the Sherman Act became effective October 8, 1982.[1] The language of the revision restricts the prior extraterritorial reach of the antitrust law.

Sec. 7. This Act shall not apply to conduct involving trade or commerce (other than import trade or import commerce) with foreign nations unless—

(1) such conduct has a direct, substantial and reasonably foreseeable effect—

(A) on trade or commerce which is not trade or commerce with foreign nations, or on import trade or import commerce with foreign nations; or

(B) on export trade or export commerce with foreign nations, of a person engaged in such trade or commerce in the United States; and

---

[1] 15 U.S.C. § 7 (1982).

(2) such effect gives rise to a claim under the provisions of this Act, other than this section.

If this Act applies to such conduct only because of the operations of paragraph (1) (B), then this Act shall apply to such conduct only for injury to export business in the United States.[2]

Just what effect this new provision will have on the antitrust jurisdictional requirements, which were previously stated only in terms of effect on interstate or foreign commerce, has yet to be determined. Section 7 now requires a "direct, substantial and reasonably foreseeable effect" on commerce, a standard similar to that recently advocated by the Department of Justice and by some courts. *E.g., Industrial Inv. Dev. Corp. v. Mitsui & Co.,* 671 F.2d 876, 883 (5th Cir. 1982), *cert. denied,* 104 S.Ct. 393 (1983) (activities that directly or substantially affect flow of commerce into or out of the United States fall within the Sherman Act). Thus, Section 7 may in part have adopted a policy already followed by some courts of examining how the extent and nature of the commercial activity affects United States commerce before sustaining jurisdiction. *E.g., Rohm & Haas Co. v. Dawson Chem. Co.,* 557 F. Supp. 739, 217 U.S.P.Q. 515 (S.D. Tex. 1982), *rev'd on other grounds,* 722 F.2d 1556, 220 U.S.P.Q. 289 (Fed. Cir. 1983) (jurisdiction sustained based on an agreement between Rohm & Haas and Bayer which allegedly resulted in curtailment of exports to Costa Rica and Swaziland).

Extraterritorial application of the Sherman Act is subject to numerous exceptions and limitations. Three exceptions from the general propositions of jurisdiction enumerated above are the doctrine of sovereign immunity, the act of state doctrine, and sovereign compulsion. Limiting the general proposition are comity and conflicts of laws. *E.g., Mannington Mills, Inc. v. Congoleum Corp.,* 595 F.2d 1287, 1291-99, 202 U.S.P.Q. 321, 324-30 (3d Cir. 1979).

---

[2] *Id.*

Licensing

It is important to remember that United States courts, as the courts of any sovereign, have little power when the losing party to a lawsuit is not present in the United States and has no property located in the United States. Unless provided otherwise by treaty, a United States judgment will be enforced in a foreign nation only if comity is granted by that foreign nation. However, comity is not readily granted. Indeed, many provisions of U.S. antitrust law are considered by foreign nations to be detrimental to their own best interests. *See, e.g.,* "British Statute Signed by Queen Elizabeth on March 20, 1980, to Protect British Interests from Foreign Antitrust Judgment," 959 Antitrust & Trade Reg. Rep. (BNA) F-1 (April 10, 1980); "Commonwealth Nations Adopt Resolution Criticizing U.S. Treble Damage Judgments," 963 Antitrust & Trade Reg. Rep. (BNA) A-10 (May 8, 1980).

The 1982 revision of the extraterritorial reach of U.S. antitrust law is uncertain. However, if a technological licensing activity may have an effect on U.S. import or export commerce, it is advised that the licensing agreements be drafted with the U.S. Antitrust Law in mind.

Chapter 8

License Homework

The novice to license work sometimes thinks in terms of the "objects" before him, the patent and/or the know-how and/or the thing or use to be made of them.

But the license terms and values are importantly influenced, often critically influenced, by many other factors.

Accordingly, whenever a licensing negotiation will support the cost of the homework effort (as most of them will or else the license is likely not worthwhile anyway), a licensing negotiating team (yes, commonly more than one man) performs the following homework information collection and studies:

(1) General information on both parties to the negotiation, including their annual financial statements, their research and manufacturing capacities in the field, their sales capacities in the field, and the geography of their market structure.

(2) Familiarity with all the various alternative goods and processes and comparison of them and their costs with the subject matter to be licensed.

(3) The structure and likely patterns of change in the market and its participants.

(4) All patents and trademarks in the field, their owners, their value, related know-how values, and exposures to infringements of patents owned by others.

(5) Summary of additional materials, know-how, etc., required by or convenient to fulfillment of the licensee's needs.

(6) Evaluation of further technical and market development time and costs and manufacturing techniques and costs.

Licensing

(7) Statement of relevant past licenses granted and summary of their terms and conditions.

(8) An outline of what the potential licensor has to sell of interest to the licensee and what the licensee has to provide of interest to the licensor—and the values of each.

(9) Any likely barters or buy-backs or contract manufacturing that might be used in manipulating the license factors.

(10) Projected profit margins and market tolerance (and in many instances, governmental regulation tolerance) for various sums certain, royalty rates, royalty terms, and scopes of subject matter that is royalty bearing.

(11) A completed draft of the preferred license agreement, perhaps with some blanks in it for certain times, dates, and figures.

(12) Analysis of the cost of any show-how that is inherently a part of the deal.

Part 2

An Overview of U.S. Antitrust and Misuse Law for Licensors and Licensees

Chapter 9

Introduction to Statutes

Our ancestors were not sophisticated in the ways of the business world and the laws used to regulate it. But they had a sense of reason that they practiced, even to what many thought were unreasonable extremes.

In 1415 when the Black Death had made workmen scarce, depriving the public of workers necessary to the material well-being and welfare of the community, *The Dyer's Case,* Y.B. 2 Henry V, pl. 26 (1415), was heard. Judge Hall became vehemently enraged by an attempt to restrain a dyer from working in a town for just a half year and struck the deal void. "By God," he declared, "if the plaintiff were here he should go to prison until he paid a fine to the king."

Some 300 years later, in *Mitchel v. Reynolds,* Y.B. 1 P.Wms. 181, 24 Eng. Rep. 347 (1711), the court held that a promise to restrain oneself from trading in a particular place is good if made upon a reasonable consideration. Defendant had leased a bakery in a certain parish to plaintiff for five years, promising not to practice the trade of a baker in that parish during the term of the lease. Chief Judge Parker found the contract reasonable and useful and therefore valid. "What makes this the more reasonable," so said the judge, "is, that the restraint is exactly proportioned to the consideration, *viz.* the term of five years." 24 Eng. Rep. at 352.

As to division of markets, our ancestors rejected Pope Alexander VI's division of the Western Hemisphere between Spain and Portugal on the basis of Portugal's discoveries in the New World. Later they revolted when King George III authorized the East India Company to control the price of tea imported into the North American Colonies in recognition of the Company's services in expanding trade with India. Even in revolt, the American Colonies had the good sense to adopt the common law of their mother country.

In the antitrust and trade regulation areas the revolutionists' common law in the first hundred years following the American Revolution developed spasmodically, if it can be said to have developed at all. Meanwhile, business barons developed skillful methods to manipulate and restrain trade.

And so, on essentially the 100th anniversary of our Constitution, legislation known as the Sherman Act was enacted condemning monopolies, monopolists, and attempts to monopolize.

It was an inelegant act, grossly overstating its case. It was not the work of a craftsman. It recited no exceptions for patent owners. It reflected gross rebellion against restraints of trade without defining the elements that made them wrong.

Poor though it was in detail, through conscious adoption of parallel provisions in the law of other jurisdictions, it has to some significant extent become the Magna Carta of the world's trade regulation law.

The Sherman Act speaks to, among others, licensors and licensees in its first two sections, which have philosophic parallels in Sections 85(1) and 86 of the Treaty of Rome. Section 1 of the Sherman Act, 15 U.S.C. § 1, provides in part:

> Every contract . . . in restraint of trade or commerce among the several States, or with foreign nations, is declared to be illegal.

Section 2 of the Sherman Act, 15 U.S.C. § 2, provides in part:

> Every person who shall monopolize, or attempt to monopolize, or combine or conspire with any other person or persons, to monopolize any part of the trade or commerce among the several States, or with foreign nations, shall be deemed guilty of a felony.

The Clayton Act of 1914 was, in effect, a supplement and amendment to the Sherman Act. Section 3 of the Clayton Act, 15 U.S.C. § 14, provides:

> [I]t shall be unlawful . . . to lease or make a sale or contract for sale of goods . . . whether patented or unpatented . . . or fix a price charged therefor . . . on the condition, agreement or understanding that the lessee or purchaser thereof shall not use or deal in the goods . . . of a competitor . . . of the lessor or seller, where the effect . . . may be to substantially lessen competition or tend to create a monopoly in any line of commerce.

Section 7 of the Clayton Act, 15 U.S.C. § 18, provides:

> [N]o corporation engaged in commerce shall acquire . . . the whole or any part of the assets of another corporation . . . where in any line of commerce . . . the effect of such acquisition may be substantially to lessen competition, or to tend to create a monopoly.

Finally, Section 5(a)(1) of the Federal Trade Commission Act, 15 U.S.C. § 45(a)(1), recites in totally broad generalities:

> Unfair methods of competition in commerce, and unfair or deceptive acts or practices in commerce, are hereby declared unlawful.

§ 9.01 Misuse

Our courts have added to statutory antitrust law an appendage we call "misuse": He who uses his patent, trademark, trade secret, or know-how in violation of the antitrust law, or otherwise unreasonably, to restrain trade outside the scope of the particular grant or protected franchise is guilty of misuse.

He who misuses his patent, as in licenses violative of the antitrust laws, is said in the idiom of the law to have "unclean hands." With "unclean hands" he cannot come into a court of equity to enforce his patent. Hence, a misused patent is unenforceable even if otherwise valid—and this, even though the infringer did not suffer any from the misuse that may have occurred in a license to some other party.

Thus, you see that we have a mix of antitrust and misuse law. An antitrust violation is the basis for a legal suit by way of offensive action seeking a remedy for injury and damage suffered; a parallel patent misuse violation is a defense that an infringer can urge when sued for infringement, irrespective of the infringer's injury or damage by the misuse.

§ 9.02 Rule of Reason

You will recall that the proscriptions of the statutes quoted above condemn all monopolies and monopolists, and all acquisitions which "*may* . . . tend to create a monopoly."

The statutes made no accommodation for reasonable restraints, for patents, or for many other business dealings; for example, duly franchised utilities in metropolitan areas, in which monopoly is the standard and accepted practice of the day.

The statutes were in the nature of emotional overstatements and over-corrections of perceived abuses.

When issues came to court, the courts frequently found those proscriptions to be born of generic overstatement and therefore excessive. The courts and the Department of Justice soon began a process of refinement of the law by which only unreasonable restraints were prohibited while reasonable ones were not. *Standard Oil Co. v. United States,* 221 U.S. 1 (1911); *United States v. Addyston Pipe & Steel Co.,* 85 F. 271 (6th Cir. 1898), *aff'd,* 175 U.S. 211 (1899).

The Department of Justice participates in new law making, both by way of issuing position papers and policy statements for the Congress and the Administration[1] and also by

---

[1] On January 23, 1985, the Department of Justice issued guidelines stating the Department's views on antitrust implications of vertical distribution restraints. The guidelines set forth a two-step rule of reason analysis that the Department will apply when evaluating allegedly anticompetitive restraints.

being selective in cases that it prosecutes and cases in which

---

Under the first step of this new approach, the Department will employ a "market structure screen" to weed out businesses the Department views as too small to have an anticompetitive effect on the marketplace. This "market structure screen" is essentially a threshold, below which the Department will not concern itself. The use of vertical restraints by a particular business will not be challenged if:

(1) the business employing the restraint has 10 percent or less of the relevant market; or

(2) the vertical restraints index (VRI), calculated by squaring the market share of each firm that is a party to the agreement containing the restraint and summing the squares, is under 1,200 and the coverage ratio, the percent of each market involved in the restraint, is below 60 percent in the same relevant market; or

(3) the VRI is under 1,200 in both relevant markets; or

(4) the coverage ratio is below 60 percent in both relevant markets.

If the particular business fails to meet one of the above qualifications, the Department will apply the second step of the analysis, a structured rule of reason. Under this second step, the Department first will ask whether it is easy to enter into the market supplying or distributing the product under restraint. If entry into both the supplier and dealer markets is easy, the Department presumes an anticompetitive effect is not possible and the restraint will be presumed legal. If, however, entry into either of these markets is difficult, the Department states that it will analyze other factors in order to determine if the restraint will be presumed to be anticompetitive or procompetitive. These other factors include: (1) the degree of concentration in the markets under study; (2) whether conditions in these markets are conducive to collusion; (3) the extent to which the particular restraint is exclusionary; (4) whether there is evidence of an intent to exclude or collude; (5) whether businesses engaging in the restraint can identify credible procompetitive effects of the restraint.

If, on balance, these factors suggest that a vertical practice is not anticompetitive, it will not be challenged by the Justice Department.

Department of Justice Guidelines—Vertical Distribution Restraints, [1985 Transfer Binder] Trade Reg. Rep. (CCH) § 50,473 at 56,200 (April 15, 1985).

See also National Bancard Corp. (NaBanco) v. VISA U.S.A., 596 F. Supp. 1231 (S.D. Fla. 1984), *aff'd,* 779 F.2d 592, *reh'g denied,* 785 F.2d 1037 (11th Cir. 1986) (no antitrust violation under the Rule of Reason where defendant's share of the market was "probably less than five percent").

it appears amicus curiae, advocating its perception of the public interest.

Unfortunately, the determination of "reason" has left much uncertainty as to what acts are and are not judicially reasonable and under what circumstance. For example, the Department of Justice itself did a 180 degree flip-flop about 1980 with respect to what it had theretofore called "The Nine No-no's" of licensing practice, concluding in the 1980s that all of those nine practices should be examined under the rule of reason instead of being per se violations as it had theretofore advocated.

The rule of reason of United States antitrust law, as developed by the courts, seemed to have a will of its own. It tried and tried again to find some certainty and definiteness with occasional successes of which we shall speak in a moment. But these efforts of the rule to acquire definiteness seem mostly to have been frustrated.

As recited by Richard McLaren, Assistant Attorney General in charge of Antitrust, in a speech in London, July 1971,

> The rule of reason . . . embraces three principal elements. First the restriction or limitation must be ancillary to the lawful main purpose of a contract. Second, the scope and duration of the limitation must not be substantially greater than necessary to achieve that purpose.

Those two elements seem to be inching up upon something definite, and then you get to the third element:

> Third, the limitation must be otherwise reasonable in the circumstances.

We find that different lawyers and courts have different views of what is "reasonable in the circumstances."

While an expression of the rule in a clear and universally applicable form has defied the best legal minds of our nation, the tools of analysis of the situations have not. The principal tools of analysis may be expressed as five basic elements: (1) a primary lawful purpose; (2) restraints ancillary to lawful purpose; (3) purpose and effect of the restraint in question; (4) leverage; and (5) relevant market.

Let's start with relevant market.

What is it that a monopolist monopolizes? If he monopolizes, he must monopolize something. That something is the relevant market.

Is the market digital watches, self-winding spring watches, or is it all watches?

If there is a complete cross-elasticity of market as between watches, the relevant market will be watches. But for some antitrust purposes, the relevant market sought to be monopolized might be merely digital watches, or might be all watches as distinguished from clocks and other timepieces.

Next a word about the primary lawful purpose, ancillary, and purpose and effect elements. The *primary lawful purpose* of a license may be to transfer technology and afford its use for the benefit of those who need it in applications or places not served by its owner. If the *purpose and effect* of the royalty and other license terms is to seek profits derived from licensed use of the technology, they are reasonably *ancillary* to the primary lawful purpose and are lawful; but if the *purpose or effect* of some given royalty pattern or restraint written into the license is to obtain profits from elimination of competition or to obtain profits from unpatented products not covered by the patents or outside the licensed know-how package, they are not *reasonably ancillary* and may be unlawful.

Finally, if the *leverage* of one's strength in one market area or item has been used to extract a restraint in a different market area so that a buyer is not free to choose, the restraint is likely to be held unlawful.

These, then, are the analytical looking glasses or tools of analysis that are used to measure the rule of reason. In any given situation, to fail to use every one of these looking glasses is to risk a fatal flaw in your analysis.

Both the courts and the lawyers tend to write opinions as though there were something intrinsically lawful or unlawful in some given license provision. But this is false logic and misleading. We can see this by applying the tools of analysis to, let's say, graduated royalties.

Suppose that a private inventor has made a very worthwhile invention useful in a market completely occupied by three companies having substantially equal market shares. In order to induce them to put an effort into promoting his invention in the market, he puts into a license he offers to all three companies a royalty provision calling for a 20 percent royalty on the first million dollars worth of annual sales, a 10 percent royalty on the second million dollars worth of annual sales, and a 1 percent royalty on all sales over the second million dollars worth of annual sales.

His purpose is to induce the licensees to bring the invention promptly to public enjoyment—nothing could be more noble or benign than that. The effect in this instance is consistent with the purpose. The result is to bring to the licensor a larger and more prompt return on his invention, and mere return of money to the patent owner is reasonably ancillary. So in our first example we find that graduated royalties appear to be inherently lawful.

But suppose the patent owner occupies 50 percent of the total market, a competitor charged with infringement occupies 30 percent of the total market, and the remaining 20 percent of the market is divided about equally among 15 competitors.

While sitting around the corporate conference room discussing a possible formula for settlement of a pending infringement suit against the 30 percent company, the president of the patent owning company says that the 30 percent defendant in the infringement suit is "a responsible company," which translates into being "not a price cutter." The president goes on to opine that the rest of those companies are always "upsetting the market" with their special discounts and other price cutting maneuvers. And then he proceeds to say,

> If we offer all comers a 20 percent royalty on the first million, 10 percent on the second million, and 1 percent thereafter on annual sales, the 30 percent defendant will be paying an average royalty of about 2 percent, which it will likely agree to in settlement of the lawsuit. None of the rest of those fly-

by-night operators could afford either to defend the lawsuit or pay their near 20 percent royalty rate—we will drive the price cutters out of business.

When depositions are taken the first question will be, "Who thought up the graduated royalty formula?" The next question, "What was the purpose?"

We see instantly under the purpose and effect analysis that in this different industrial marketplace context, the same graduated royalty that we found to be lawful in the first instance is clearly and affirmatively unlawful.

The point here is to illustrate that there is nothing intrinsically lawful or unlawful in graduated royalties, discriminatory royalties, tying of one product to another, or any other one of the antitrust violations and misuses that will be discussed. Rather, they take on legality or illegality depending upon their *purpose* and *effect—in the context of the particular market structure and circumstance.*

One of the problems that is often overlooked is this: The market structure and the circumstance often change during the life of the license. Thus the tying—in the computer industry they called it "bundling"—of the software and hardware was clearly legal in the early days of the computer industry. There was no independent software source that a customer could use as an alternative. But as the software industry matured the application of reason to the new circumstance changed the conclusion, and unbundling of software from hardware became necessary. *See Digidyne Corp. v. Data Gen. Corp.,* 734 F.2d 1336 (9th Cir. 1984), *cert. denied,* 473 U.S. 908, *reh'g denied,* 473 U.S. 926 (1985).

The grandfather case for the rule of reason, as applied to patent licenses, is *United States v. General Electric Co.,* 272 U.S. 476 (1926), which recites:

> The patentee may make and grant a license to another to make and use the patented articles but withhold his right to sell them.... If the patentee goes further and licenses the selling of the articles, may he limit the selling by limiting the method of sale and the price? We think he may do so *provided the conditions of sale are normally and reasonably*

adapted to secure pecuniary reward for the patentee's monopoly. Id. at 490 (emphasis added).

Since 1926, limitations on the application of that rule have dominated the evolving law, as we shall soon see.

For example, the Seventh Circuit Court of Appeals has held that in order to state a cause of action under the rule of reason, a plaintiff must allege and prove that the defendant's conduct has caused injury to competition and not just to a competitor. Absent such a showing, the court held that the plaintiff failed to state a claim upon which relief may be granted. *Hennessy Indus., Inc. v. FMC Corp.,* 779 F.2d 402, 404 (7th Cir. 1985).

The Seventh Circuit also rejected the plaintiff's claim under 15 U.S.C. § 2, holding that the plaintiff's claim "is also defective because it makes no allegations as to defendant's market power." *Id.* at 404. "[T]he first step in any rule of reason case is an assessment of market power." *Id.* at 405. *See also Brunswick Corp. v. Riegel Textile Corp.,* 752 F.2d 261, 265 (7th Cir. 1984), *cert. denied,* 105 S. Ct. 3480 (1985).

Over 60 percent suggests possible monopoly power and hence whets interest in the possibility of an antitrust violation; 5 percent or less is deemed de minimis for purposes of market power analysis. *A.I. Root Co. v. Computer/Dynamics, Inc.,* 806 F.2d 673, 675 (6th Cir. 1986) (2–4 percent of the small computer market is insufficient as a matter of law to infer market dominance).

§ 9.03 Per Se Violations

Reference has been made to an occasional "success" of the antitrust law in finding definiteness. These "successes," if they may be called that, take the form of rules applied to specific fact patterns in which the courts find illegality without consideration of reason—so-called "per se" illegality. Said the Supreme Court in *Northern Pac. R.R. v. United States,* 356 U.S. 1 (1958):

However, there are certain agreements or practices which because of their [presumed] pernicious effect on competition and lack of any redeeming virtue are conclusively presumed to be unreasonable and therefore illegal without elaborate inquiry as to the precise harm they have caused or the business excuse for their use. This principle of *per se* unreasonableness not only makes the type of restraints which are proscribed by the Sherman Act more certain to the benefit of everyone concerned, but it also avoids the necessity for an incredibly complicated and prolonged economic investigation into the entire history of the industry involved, as well as related industries, in an effort to determine at large whether a particular restraint has been unreasonable—an inquiry so often wholly fruitless when undertaken. Among the practices which the courts have heretofore deemed to be unlawful in and of themselves are price fixing, *United States v. Socony-Vacuum Oil,* 310 U.S. 150 (1940); division of markets; *United States v. Addyston Pipe & Steel Co.,* 85 F. 271 (6th Cir. 1898), *aff'd,* 175 U.S. 211 (1899); group boycotts, *Fashion Originators' Guild v. Federal Trade Commission,* 312 U.S. 457 (1941); and tying arrangements, *International Salt Co. v. United States,* 331 U.S. 392 (1947).

Id. at 5.

Note that the per se rule finds a wrong in the absence of evidence of a socially bad purpose or effect. The very reason for having the per se rule is to cut off the evidence—to eliminate the burdens of marshalling the evidence, presenting the evidence, and analyzing the evidence.

In *United States v. Arnold, Schwinn & Co.,* 388 U.S. 365 (1967), the Supreme Court found vertical territorial restrictions to be per se illegal. Before the ink was well dried on the *Arnold, Schwinn* per se rule, a trial court in California perceived that more justice can be done with evidence than without it. The court elected to hear evidence on the reasonableness of vertical territorial restrictions. The case went up to the United States Supreme Court. Continental T.V., Inc. v. GTE Sylvania, Inc., 433 U.S. 36 (1977). Under the per se rule that the Supreme Court had announced in *Arnold, Schwinn,* the Court never should have had before it any evidence on which to base a reversal of its per se rule. But in *Sylvania,* the Supreme Court reversed its *Arnold, Schwinn* per se rule. The Court urged an analysis of the purpose and effect of the restraint under the rule of reason.

Thus, while fearsomely rigid, it is worth noting that even the per se rules are *not always per se* in every context. An example is *National Collegiate Athletic Ass'n v. Board of Regents of the University of Oklahoma,* 468 U.S. 85 (1984). Horizontal price fixing and output limitation were at issue, restraints which would ordinarily be held illegal per se. The Supreme Court held that it would be inappropriate to apply a per se rule in cases involving industries in which horizontal restraints on competition are essential if products are to be available at all. Though using the rule of reason analysis, the Court found an anticompetitive effect in the broadcasting plan proposed by the N.C.A.A., a common result in cases involving horizontally imposed restraints. See also *Regents of Univ. of Cal. v. ABC, Inc.,* 747 F.2d 511 (9th Cir. 1984); *Car Carriers, Inc. v. Ford Motor Co.,* 745 F.2d 1101 (7th Cir. 1984), *cert. denied,* 470 U.S. 1054 (1985); *Rothery Storage & Van Co. v. Atlas Van Lines,* 597 F. Supp. 217 (D.D.C. 1984), *aff'd,* 792 F.2d 210 (D.D.C. 1986), *cert. denied,* 107 S. Ct. 880 (1987). Another example—and there are many—is *Broadcast Music, Inc. v. CBS,* 441 U.S. 1, 201 U.S.P.Q. 497 (1979). Two classical per se illegalities were indicated, price fixing and conditional package licensing, but the Court adopted a *purpose and effect* analysis of the activity in the context of the particular market to reach the conclusion that the rule of reason standard had to be applied.

At least one court has voiced its reluctance to apply the *per se* rule to conduct that falls anywhere outside the strictly proscribed classifications of judicially defined anticompetitive conduct.

> Although *Hennessy* characterizes the alleged concerted restraint of trade as a *per se* violation of Section 1, attachment of the *per se* label is inadequate in itself to sustain a Section 1 violation without a showing of injury to competition. In *Car Carriers, Inc. v. Ford Motor Co.,* 745 F.2d 1101 (7th Cir. 1984), this court adopted a stringent test to determine whether a violation is illegal *per se.* We held that the *per se* label must be applied with caution and we will expand that

class of violations "only after the courts have had considerable experience with the type of conduct challenged and application of the Rule of Reason has inevitably resulted in a finding of anticompetitive effects."

Hennessy Indus., Inc. v. FMC Corp., 779 F.2d 402, 403–04 (7th Cir. 1985).

As we proceed further, it will become apparent that the per se label is in fact only a tough rule of reason with which courts play verbal games. Additionally, legislation was introduced in Congress during 1987 (H.R. 557) that would require courts to apply the rule of reason standard rather than per se rules in evaluating patent licensing arrangements.

§ 9.04 Remedies

The remedies for antitrust violations are many and varied. For the purposes of two books, we abbreviate them as follows:

(1) Criminal remedies, including fines and felony jail sentences, usually reserved for cases of quite deliberate and willful conspiracy to fix prices.

(2) Civil liability for treble damages actually suffered by any plaintiff as a result of the violations. And our courts are pretty liberal in responding to projections of lost profits as damages.

(3) Where a patent license is directly involved in the unlawful restraint, a "misuse" is said to occur; the remedy is loss of enforceability of the subject patent. The extent of the misuse doctrine as applied to trademarks, trade secrets, and know-how is not well defined in our law; but neither is their immunity from misuse concepts.

To licensors and licensees, the "misuse" remedy is the one most commonly of interest, but the others are also of great interest.

§ 9.04 / Licensing

Premises and general conclusions stated, let's consider briefly a few of the many areas where antitrust/misuse is at least awash over the patent owner's historic rights in patent exploitation.

Chapter 10

Specific Patent Antitrust Areas Considered

§ 10.01 Fraudulent Procurement of Patents and Enforcement of Patents so Procured

[1] Historical Perspective

Over the years prior to 1965, the solicitation of patents was generally considered an adversarial proceeding in which the patent applicant appeared before the Patent and Trademark Office (PTO), presenting his case in the best light possible but not bound by law to volunteer any admissions against interest. Since 1965 we have witnessed an acute judicial interest in insuring that the applicant and applicant's counsel have submitted all "material" information to the Patent and Trademark Office.

In 1944 and 1945 the Supreme Court defined some rules of conduct that governed behavior before the Patent Office in prosecuting applications for patent. There was to be "an uncompromising duty to report to . . . [the Patent Office] all facts concerning possible fraud or inequitableness underlying the applications in issue." Little guidance was given, however, on how this was to be done. *Precision Instrument Manufacturing Co. v. Automotive Maintenance Machinery Co.,* 324 U.S. 806, 818, 65 U.S.P.Q. 133, 139 (1945); *Hazel-Atlas Glass Co. v. Hartford-Empire Co.,* 322 U.S. 238, 61 U.S.P.Q. 241 (1944). The cases involved overt acts of willful deception far beyond mere failure to volunteer prior art or test data or admissions against interest. The words of those opinions had little influence upon the common practice of the bar not to volunteer evidence against patentability.

This held true until *Walker Process Equip. Co. v. Food Mach. & Chem. Corp.*, 382 U.S. 172, 147 U.S.P.Q. 404 (1965). There it was recognized that the adversarial nature of the proceedings in the PTO, ex parte as they are, was severely limited. Patent unenforceability, attorney fees, and antitrust liability were remedies wedded to a duty of uncompromising candor in dealing with the Patent Office. The Court held that failure to disclose known, relevant evidence could be fraud on the PTO. Enforcement of a fraudulently obtained patent is an attempt to unlawfully monopolize and could form the basis of an antitrust cause of action under Section 2 of the Sherman Act[1] if the other elements necessary to prove such a violation were present. By showing that Food Machinery knowingly and willfully misrepresented facts to the Patent Office in prosecuting its patent and then by proving the exclusionary power of the fraudulently acquired patent in terms of the relevant market for the product involved, monopolization or an attempt to monopolize a part of a trade or commerce under Section 2 could be shown. 382 U.S. at 177, 147 U.S.P.Q. at 407.

Thus, a knowing and willful misrepresentation or nondisclosure of relevant evidence to the Patent Office could now expose the enforcer of a patent to a threat of the punitive remedies of antitrust liability.

[2] Current Standards of Advocacy Before the PTO

[a] Rule 1.56

The current standard of candor in practice before the PTO is codified by 37 C.F.R. 1.56[2] and has been adopted by

---

[1] 15 U.S.C. § 2.

[2] 37 C.F.R. 1.56(a):

A duty of candor and good faith toward the Patent and Trademark Office rests on the inventor, on each attorney or agent who prepares or prosecutes the application and on every other individual who is substantively involved in the preparation or prosecution of the application and who is associated with the inventor, with the assignee or with anyone to whom there is an obligation to assign the application. All such individuals have a duty to disclose to the

the Court of Appeals for the Federal Circuit.

The court has summarized the Rule as follows.

> A breach of duty of candor owed to the PTO, that prevents the grant of a patent or causes it to be held invalid or unenforceable, occurs when material information is misrepresented or withheld, and such misrepresentation or withholding is intentional or accompanied by gross negligence or bad faith.

Hycor Corp. v. Schlueter Co., 740 F.2d 1529, 1538, 222 U.S.P.Q. 553 (Fed. Cir. 1984). Thus, the Court will first focus its attention on (1) the intent of the patentee and (2) the materiality of the misrepresentation or failure to disclose, in determining whether or not fraud or inequitable conduct was practiced in the procurement of a patent. As we shall see later (§ 10.01[2][c], *infra*), the two criteria are interrelated. Sanctions for violation of Rule 1.56 include (1) unenforceability of the patent, (2) attorney fees in litigation, (3) restitution of license fees and royalties, and, likely in a proper case, (4) treble damages.

[b]   Fraud vs. Inequitable Conduct

Enforcement of a patent procured by willful and deliberate acts constituting fraud may violate the antitrust laws through monopolization of, or an attempt to monopolize, a relevant market. *United States v. Westinghouse Elec. Corp.,* 471 F. Supp. 532, 200 U.S.P.Q. 514 (N.D. Cal. 1978).

The Federal Circuit, however, has held "inequitable conduct in the PTO to be a more appropriate label than fraud" for common patent-invalidating behaviors. *Atlas Powder Co. v. E.I. duPont de Nemours,* 750 F.2d 1569, 1577 (Fed. Cir. 1984), *citing J.P. Stevens & Co. v. Lex-Tex, Ltd.,* 747 F.2d

---

Office information they are aware of which is material to the examination of the application. Such information is material when there is a substantial likelihood that a reasonable examiner would consider it important in deciding whether to allow the application to issue as a patent. The duty is commensurate with the degree of involvement in the preparation or prosecution of the application.

1553 (Fed. Cir. 1984), *cert. denied,* 474 U.S. 822 (1985). This was a deliberate and meaningful change by the court, not a mere accident of grammar.

[c] Materiality

A party seeking to establish fraud on or inequitable conduct in the Patent Office as the basis for either an infringement defense or an antitrust claim must show that the nondisclosed or misrepresented information was "material," but that word has had many definitions.

Four tests for the "threshold degree of materiality" have been used. First, there was the "objective but for" test, wherein a misrepresentation is material if the patent would not have issued "but for" the fraud. *Brand Plastics Co. v. Dow Chem. Co.,* 267 F. Supp. 1010, 168 U.S.P.Q. 133 (C.D. Cal. 1967), *aff'd in part and rev'd in part,* 475 F.2d 124, 177 U.S.P.Q. 33 (9th Cir.), *cert. denied,* 414 U.S. 1039 (1973).

Second was the "subjective but for" test, where the court examines whether the examiner who handled the application would have rejected claims had he known all the facts, not whether the patent is objectively valid given the withheld or misstated information. *Schnadig Corp. v. Gaines Mfg. Co.,* 494 F.2d 383, 181 U.S.P.Q. 417 (6th Cir. 1974); *Norton v. Curtiss,* 433 F.2d 779, 167 U.S.P.Q. 532 (C.C.P.A. 1970); *Charles Pfizer & Co. v. FTC,* 401 F.2d 574, 159 U.S.P.Q. 193 (6th Cir. 1968).

Third was the "but it may have been" test for materiality, which is the least stringent in that a misrepresentation or omission is deemed material if it may have had an effect upon the examiner's decision to allow the application to issue as a patent. If it could not be determined why the patent examiner allowed the patent to issue, doubt was resolved against the culpable patent applicant and the patent found unenforceable. *Timely Prods. Corp. v. Arron,* 523 F.2d 288, 187 U.S.P.Q. 257 (2d Cir. 1975); *Hercules, Inc. v. Exxon Corp.,* 497 F. Supp. 661 (D. Del 1980); *SCM Corp. v. RCA Inc.,* 318 F. Supp. 433 (S.D.N.Y. 1970).

For many years it was a generally accepted practice for an applicant to disclose only prior art that he knew would invalidate the sought-after patent. Prior art that may be pertinent to a consideration of obviousness but which the applicant in good faith did not believe would invalidate was often not disclosed. Arguably, this idea was put to rest so that now any relevant material must be disclosed. *Argus Chem. Corp. v. Fibre-Glass-Evercoat (Argus I),* 759 F.2d 10 (Fed. Cir.), *cert. denied,* 474 U.S. 903 (1985). It has now been held that an applicant's nondisclosure of prior art references on which the examiner, after independently discovering the references, rejected claims previously allowed, most of which were then allowed after amendment, rendered the patent unenforceable. *A.B. Dick Co. v. Burroughs Corp.,* 798 F.2d 1392 (Fed. Cir. 1986).

Inequitable conduct requires proof by "clear and convincing evidence of a threshold degree of materiality of the nondisclosed or false information." *Atlas Powder,* 750 F.2d at 1576. *See also Hycor Corp.,* 740 F.2d at 1538; *Orthopedic Equip. Co. v. All Orthopedic Appliances,* 707 F.2d 1376, 217 U.S.P.Q. 1281 (Fed. Cir. 1983).

The fourth test seems now to have become the applicable law. 37 C.F.R. § 1.56(a) phrases it as whether "there is a substantial likelihood that a reasonable examiner would have considered the omitted reference or false information important in deciding whether to allow the application to issue as a patent." *J. P. Stevens Co. v. Lex-Tex, Ltd.,* 747 F.2d at 1559, *citing American Hoist & Derrick Co. v. Sowa & Sons, Inc.,* 725 F.2d 1350, 220 U.S.P.Q. 763 (Fed. Cir. 1984). Said the court, "The PTO 'standard' is an appropriate starting point for any discussion of materiality, for it appears to be the broadest, thus encompassing the others, and because that materiality boundary most closely aligns with how one ought to conduct business with the PTO." *American Hoist* at 1363.

Accordingly, while the first three tests may still be used to cast light upon PTO Rule 56(a)'s substantial likelihood of importance to a reasonable examiner, those tests are now subordinate to Rule 56(a) itself.

[d] Intent

An element of intent is generally required to sustain a finding of inequitable conduct in dealing with the Patent and Trademark Office. Proof of intent "may be lacking entirely or may be shown by any relevant degree of proof—from inference to direct evidence, *i.e.,* from gross negligence or recklessness to a deliberate scheming." *American Hoist,* 725 F.2d at 1363. Some element of wrongful conduct, intentional misrepresentation, or inequitable, reckless, or grossly negligent conduct is a necessary predicate in rendering a patent unenforceable in the courts under Rule 56. *International Tel. & Tel. v. Raychem Corp.,* 538 F.2d 453, 461 (1st Cir.), *cert. denied,* 429 U.S. 886 (1976); *Carter-Wallace, Inc. v. Davis-Edwards Pharmacal Corp.,* 443 867, 882 (2d Cir. 1971).

The intent necessary to sustain a finding of inequitable conduct need not be proven with direct evidence. *Hycor Corp. v. Schlueter Co.,* 740 F.2d 1529, 1540 (Fed. Cir. 1984). "The intent element . . . may be proven by a showing of acts the natural consequences of which are presumably intended by the actor." *Rohm & Haas v. Crystal Chem. Co.,* 722 F.2d 1556, 1571 (Fed. Cir. 1983), *citing Kansas Jack Inc. v. Kuhn,* 719 F.2d 1144, 1151, 219 U.S.P.Q. 857 (Fed. Cir. 1983). The lower threshold of intent may be satisfied by a showing of gross negligence, which is present when the actor, judged as a reasonable person in his position, should have known of the materiality of a withheld reference. *Driscoll v. Cebalo,* 731 F.2d 878, 885 (Fed. Cir. 1984). It has been said that the risk is on the patentee to figure out what must be disclosed. *Precision Instrument Mfg. Co. v. Automotive Maintenance Mach. Co.,* 324 U.S. 806, 815, 65 U.S.P.Q. 133, 140 (1945). The necessary element of wrongfulness will exist whenever patent counsel knew or should have known of the relevance of the prior art. *J. P. Stevens & Co. v. Lex-Tex, Ltd.,* 747 F.2d at 1559; *USM Corp. v. SPS Technologies Inc.,* 514 F.

Supp. 213, 234, 211 U.S.P.Q. 112 (N.D. Ill. 1981), *aff'd,* 694 F.2d 505, 216 U.S.P.Q. 959 (7th Cir. 1982), *cert. denied,* 462 U.S. 1107 (1983). Counsel's subjective good faith will not necessarily negate inequitable conduct. *Argus I,* 759 F.2d at 14.

On the other hand, "simple negligence, oversight or an erroneous judgment made in good faith is insufficient" to sustain a finding of inequitable conduct. *Atlas Powder,* 750 F.2d at 1577–78, 224 U.S.P.Q. at 415; *Hycor Corp. v. Schlueter Co.,* 740 F.2d at 1520, 222 U.S.P.Q. at 561.

Whereas gross negligence has been perhaps erroneously equated with neglect of duty or failure to disclose that which one should have known, *Driscoll v. Cebalo, supra,* simple negligence may be equated with misstatements of fact or nondisclosure due to honest disagreements as to what constitutes prior art. *Arbrook v. American Hospital Supply Corp.,* 645 F.2d 273, 279, 210 U.S.P.Q. 84 (5th Cir. 1981); *Lam Inc. v. Johns-Manville Corp.,* 668 F.2d 462, 213 U.S.P.Q. 1061 (10th Cir. 1982).

> [T]o deny enforcement [of an otherwise valid patent] as a matter of law merely because of an innocent or good faith nondisclosure would go beyond what is necessary to protect the public against the improvident granting of a monopoly. Such a standard could also have the harmful effect of forcing a patent solicitor to flood the Patent Office in each case with a mass of data of doubtful materiality.

Xerox Corp. v. Dennison Mfg. Corp., 322 F. Supp. 963, 968, 168 U.S.P.Q. 700 (S.D.N.Y. 1971).

However, at least twice the Federal Circuit has defined gross negligence in reasonably prudent man terms:

> Gross negligence is present when the actor, judged as a reasonable person in his position, should have known of the materiality of a withheld reference.

Reactive Metals & Alloys Corp. v. ESM, Inc., 769 F.2d 1578, 1584, 226 U.S.P.Q. 821, 825 (Fed. Cir. 1985), *quoting J. P. Stevens & Co. v. Lex-Tex, Ltd.,* 747 F.2d at 1560.

That seems to be a classic definition of simple negligence, rather than of gross negligence, which is tantamount to intentional disregard of the law or facts. In *Reactive Metals* itself the court recited the above-quoted definition as a statement of law, but went on to find a lack of culpable intent or gross negligence in falsely answering an interrogatory with a "no on-sale" answer—even though sales brochures had been distributed, and so-called "trial sales" had been made and invoiced at regular market prices.

In a recent case, the Federal Circuit has held that a patent must have been procured by "intentional fraud" on the Patent Office in order to establish a *Walker Process* claim (*see* § 10.01[1]). *Argus Chem. Corp. v. Fibre Glass-Evercoat Co.,* (Argus II), 812 F.2d 1381 (Fed. Cir. 1987). In a concurring opinion, Judge Nies set up three lack-of-candor standards, each with its own remedy, as follows:

(1) misconduct which makes a patent unenforceable (which we have termed "inequitable conduct");
(2) misconduct which is sufficient to make a case "exceptional" under 35 U.S.C. § 285 so as to warrant, in the discretion of the trial judges, an award of attorney fees; and
(3) misconduct which rises to the level of common law fraud and which will support an antitrust claim.

Argus II, 812 F.2d at 1387.

[e] The Balancing Act

Once the thresholds of materiality and intent have been established, the court must balance them to determine whether, as a matter of law, inequitable conduct has occurred.

Questions of "materiality" and "culpability" are often interrelated and intertwined so that a lesser showing of the materiality of the withheld information may suffice when an intentional scheme to defraud is established, whereas a greater showing of the materiality of withheld information would necessarily create an inference that its nondisclosure was wrongful.

American Hoist & Derrick, 725 F.2d at 1363, *citing Digital Equip. Corp. v. Diamond,* 653 F.2d 701, 716, 210 U.S.P.Q. 521 (1st Cir. 1981).

Therefore, where an objective 'but for' inquiry is satisfied (but for the omission the patent would not have issued), even though one is not grossly negligent in failing to anticipate a judicial resolution of validity, a lesser showing of facts from which intent can be inferred may be sufficient to justify holding a patent invalid or unenforceable either in whole or in part. On the other hand, if a reasonable examiner would merely consider particular information highly interesting but not crucial to his decision not to reject, a showing of facts that show something more than gross negligence or recklessness may be required and simple negligence or mistake should suffice as a defense. *American Hoist & Derrick,* 725 F.2d at 1363.

The Federal Circuit has established an inverse relationship between the materiality and intent factors needed to find inequitable conduct. In other words, if materiality of the misrepresented or nondisclosed information is great, then wrongful intent can be inferred from the circumstances. On the other hand, if the materiality of the information is not readily apparent, the court may require a showing of actual intent to deceive. Where the nondisclosed prior art, although patent defeating, is less clearly material to the claimed invention and less clearly suppressed, no fraud will be found. "Although appellant's actions may raise a suspicion of misrepresentation, we cannot base a holding of fraud on suspicion." *Vandenberg v. Dairy Equip. Co.,* 740 F.2d 1560, 1569, 224 U.S.P.Q. 195, 200 (Fed. Cir. 1984).

Once the thresholds of materiality and culpability are established and the court concludes that inequitable conduct has been found, the patent claims themselves must be held unenforceable, even though with proper conduct the patent would have been enforceable. *J. P. Stevens,* 747 F.2d at 1560; *Norton v. Curtiss, supra.* The Supreme Court has discussed inequitable conduct as a defense to a claim of patent infringement in terms of unenforceability as well. *See Precision Instrument Mfg. Co. v. Automotive Maintenance Mach. Co.,* 324 U.S. 806, 818, 65 U.S.P.Q. 133 (1945); and *Walker Process Equip. Co. v. Food Mach. & Chem. Corp.,* 382 U.S. 172, 147 U.S.P.Q. 404 (1965). Some courts have interpreted *Walker Process* as defining two defenses: (1) "fraud," which renders the patent invalid, and (2) "other inequitable conduct," which renders the patent unenforceable. *See Timely Products Corp. v. Arron, supra; In re Frost,* 398 F. Supp. 1353, 185 U.S.P.Q. 729 (D. Del. 1975).

[3]   Inapplicability of the Per Se Rule

Once a party seeking to recover under the antitrust laws has established the defense of fraud on or inequitable conduct in the Patent Office (*i.e.,* carried its burden of proof of the defense of patent unenforceability by showing the requisite intent and materiality), it is well settled that the claimant must establish the other elements of an antitrust claim before recovering the affirmative remedy of damages.

Although the Court specifically refused to address this issue in *Walker Process,* subsequent decisions have indicated that an attempt to enforce a fraudulently obtained patent is not a per se antitrust violation, and a violation of the antitrust laws will not be found absent the necessary finding of the other elements of the violation. *See, e.g., American Hoist & Derrick Co. v. Sowa & Sons, Inc.,* 725 F.2d 1350, 220 U.S.P.Q. 763 (Fed. Cir. 1984); *Rohm & Haas Co. v. Dawson Chem. Co.,* 635 F. Supp. 1211 (S.D. Tex. 1986); *Foster Wheeler Corp. v. Babcock & Wilcox Co.,* 440 F. Supp. 897, 902, 195 U.S.P.Q. 649, 652 (S.D.N.Y. 1977) (attempted enforcement of patents obtained by fraud does not constitute a per se violation of the antitrust laws).

Thus, a patent is not presumed to effect monopoly power over a relevant market, and indeed the vast majority of patents do not do so, with a few possible exceptions. The courts have stated that an antitrust plaintiff must prove the elements of a Section 2 Sherman Act violation[3] (*i.e.,* exclusionary power, relevant market, cross-elasticity, injury, etc.) in addition to proving the existence of intentional and material misrepresentations before the Patent Office. *American Hoist & Derrick, supra; Oetiker v. Jurid Werke GMBH,* 671 F.2d 596, 215 U.S.P.Q. 21 (D.C. Cir. 1982); *Mannington Mills, Inc. v. Congoleum Corp,* 595 F.2d 1287, 1295, 202 U.S.P.Q. 321, 326–27 (3d Cir. 1979); *Rohm & Haas, supra; United Ventures, Inc. v. Fountain Indus., Inc.,* 211 U.S.P.Q. 693, 697 (D. Minn. 1981); *Reinke Mfg. Co. v. Sidney Mfg. Corp.,* 446 F. Supp. 1056, 1067, 199 U.S.P.Q. 401, 410 (D. Neb. 1978), *aff'd,* 594 F.2d 644, 201 U.S.P.Q. 344 (8th Cir. 1979); *Reynolds Metals Co. v. Aluminum Co. of Am.,* 457 F. Supp. 482, 511–12, 198 U.S.P.Q. 529, 556 (N.D. Ind. 1978), *rev'd,* 609 F.2d 1218, 204 U.S.P.Q. 7 (7th Cir. 1979), *cert. denied,* 446 U.S. 989 (1980).

Acme Precision Prods., Inc. v. American Alloys Corp., 484 F.2d 1237, 179 U.S.P.Q. 453 (8th Cir. 1973), is exemplary. In that case, the Eighth Circuit Court of Appeals reversed a lower court holding that a violation of Section 2 of the Sherman Act had occurred in connection with the enforcement of a fraudulently procured patent. In doing so, the court indicated that sufficient facts to establish monopolization or an attempt to monopolize a relevant market had not been shown. *See also Forbro Design Corp. v. Raytheon Co.,* 532 F.2d 758, 190 U.S.P.Q. 49 (1st Cir. 1976) (proof of market dominance "went to patent-related issues which involved different considerations than antitrust claims . . . there was no showing that in this case the questions were the same"); *Erie Technological Prods., Inc. v. JFD Elecs. Components Corp.,* 198 U.S.P.Q. 179, 186 (E.D.N.Y. 1978) (court specifically required a showing of the market size and plaintiff's share of that market); *Tapeswitch Corp. of Am. v. Recora Corp.,* 196 U.S.P.Q. 348 (N.D. Ill. 1977).

The Ninth Circuit has followed suit in *Handgards, Inc. v. Ethicon, Inc.,* 743 F.2d 1282 (9th Cir. 1984), *cert. denied,* 469 U.S. 1190 (1985). There, the defendant was found liable

---

[3] 15 U.S.C. § 2.

under Section 2 of the Sherman Act because he had prosecuted patent infringement suits in bad faith, knowing the patent to be invalid. The court also found that there was a dangerous probability of defendant success in monopolizing the market, since the evidence showed that no competition emerged until after the district court declared the patent invalid.

[4] Elements of Antitrust Violation

As to the various antitrust elements, one must generally show: (1) the exclusionary power of the illegal patent; (2) proof defining the relevant market that was attempted to be monopolized, that is, a market somewhat isolated in terms of buyer interest, a market with little if any cross-elasticity with markets for similar products (as watches are not cross-elastic with clocks, though both tell time); and (3) damages resulting from the patentee's anticompetitive acts.

The exclusionary power of an illegal patent must be proved in terms of the relevant market. *See, e.g., American Hoist & Derrick Co. v. Sowa & Sons, Inc.,* 725 F.2d 1350, 220 U.S.P.Q. 763 (Fed. Cir. 1984); *Kistler Instrumente, A.G. v. PCB Piezotronics, Inc.,* 220 U.S.P.Q. 631 (W.D.N.Y. 1983); *Christen, Inc. v. BNS Indus., Inc.,* 517 F. Supp. 521, 216 U.S.P.Q. 928 (S.D.N.Y. 1981); *Foster Wheeler Corp. v. Babcock & Wilcox Co.,* 440 F. Supp. 897, 902, 195 U.S.P.Q. 649, 652 (S.D.N.Y. 1977).

The presence of this exclusionary power has been shown in some cases. *See, e.g., Kearney & Trecker Corp. v. Cincinnati Milacron, Inc.,* 562 F.2d 365, 373, 195 U.S.P.Q. 402, 408 (6th Cir. 1977). But parties have often failed to make the required showing. *Forbro Design Corp. v. Raytheon Co.,* 532 F.2d at 765, 190 U.S.P.Q. at 55; *United Ventures, Inc. v. Fountain Indus., Inc.,* 211 U.S.P.Q. 693, 698 (D. Minn. 1981) (motion for summary judgment on issue of relevant market denied since neither side provided the court with sufficient information concerning the cross-elasticity of demand to allow determination of relevant market); *Reinke Mfg. Co. v. Sidney Manufacturing Corp.,* 446 F. Supp. 1056,

1067, 199 U.S.P.Q. 401, (D. Neb. 1978), *aff'd,* 594 F. Supp. 644, 201 U.S.P.Q. 344 (8th Cir. 1979) (where patent related to circular irrigation system, the court found that the record "suggested . . . thriving competition in the center pivot irrigation system industry among a variety of manufacturers a number of whom employed under truss pipe support structures" so that the Section 2 counterclaim must fail even if defendant had successfully proved fraudulent patent procurement); *Reynolds Metals Co. v. Aluminum Co. of America,* 457 F. Supp. at 511–12, 198 U.S.P.Q. at 556 ("National has provided no evidence by which it is possible to appraise or define the relevant market, its size nor the shares and shareholders therein").

A *Walker Process* antitrust claimant must also prove injury, *i.e.,* damages resulting from the patentee's anticompetitive acts. *E.g., Reinke Mfg. Co., supra; Reynolds Metals Co., supra. Cf. Indium Corp. of Am. v. Semi-Alloys, Inc.,* 566 F. Supp. 1344, 219 U.S.P.Q. 793 (N.D.N.Y. 1983), *motion denied,* 591 F. Supp. 608 (N.D.N.Y. 1984) (claimant must allege facts that patentee has sought or threatened to enforce its fraudulently obtained patent against claimant itself). Damages may include costs and expenses of defending an infringement action. *See, e.g., Kearney & Trecker,* 562 F.2d at 374, 195 U.S.P.Q. at 409. The damages, when proved, will be trebled and may be recovered from any party enforcing the patent, provided the party enforcing the patent did so with the knowledge that it was fraudulently obtained. *See, e.g., Lewis Mfg. Co. v. Chisholm-Ryder Co.,* 82 F.R.D. 745, 751, 210 U.S.P.Q. 514, 518 (W.D. Pa. 1979).

Finally, it has been held that since the fraud allegations necessary to invalidate a patent are identical to the fraud allegations that provide the basis for the antitrust claim, even though grounded in different legal theories they are logically related. As such, the defenses are compulsory counterclaims and must be so pleaded. *USM Corp. v. SPS Technologies, Inc.,* 102 F.R.D. 167, 225 U.S.P.Q. 715 (N.D. Ill. 1984), *motion granted,* 770 F.2d 1035 (Fed. Cir. 1985).

[5] Liability for Prior Royalty Income and for Fraud of Others

Another interesting aspect of a fraud violation is its potential time-bomb nature. Suppose a patent is procured in the name of an inventor who conceals the real source of his idea, which is clearly the most relevant prior art. The patent is licensed to bring in $500,000 yearly. One infringer then decides to litigate rather than take a license and proves fraud in the procurement of the patent.

Is the patentee-licensor liable for repayment of treble the royalties received under the patent for perchance 10 years? If so, a delayed action bomb has gone off.

Assume now that the inventor was an employee of the patent owner, acting under its control and direction, and assume that the employer never asked him where he got his idea. Would the employer-licensor be liable with him if the best prior art was known to him and not cited to the PTO?

We do not yet have a good fabric of case law directly on point. However, the answers to the questions appear to be that the employee and the employer may both be liable for at least restitution. In *Ampex Corp. v. Memorex Corp.*, 205 U.S.P.Q. 794, 797 (N.D. Cal. 1980), the court stated that a patent assignee had a duty to disclose prior work to both the Patent Office *and to a licensee* who had paid the assignee $100,000 for a worldwide license. The court then found that the evidence disclosed an actual fraud on the licensee, entitling the licensee to rescind the license agreement and to recover $100,000 by way of restitution. However, because there was an inadequate showing to justify relief under Section 2 of the Sherman Act, no reference to treble damages was made. *See also Transitron Elec. Corp. v. Hughes Aircraft Co.*, 649 F.2d 871, 210 U.S.P.Q. 161 (1st Cir. 1981) (restitution of royalties); *USM Corp. v. SPS Technologies, Inc.*, 514 F. Supp. 213, 211 U.S.P.Q. 112 (N.D. Ill. 1981), *aff'd*, 694 F.2d 505, 216 U.S.P.Q. 959 (7th Cir. 1982), *cert. denied*, 462 U.S. 1107 (1983).

It is therefore always good practice, as a licensing attorney, to thoroughly interview both the inventor and the attorney who prosecuted the patent prior to proceeding with any licensing of the patent. This will insure that the true inventor is of record and enables the attorney to be sure all relevant prior art was disclosed during prosecution of the patent.

[6] Effect of Inequitable Conduct on Other Patents

Generally, fraud or inequitable conduct practiced in obtaining one patent will not render other patents unenforceable even when the patents are closely related. *DeLong Corp. v. Raymond Int'l Inc.,* 622 F.2d 1135, 206 U.S.P.Q. 97 (3d Cir. 1980); *Beckman Instruments Inc. v. Technical Dev. Corp.,* 433 F.2d 55, 167 U.S.P.Q. 10 (7th Cir. 1970). However, a fraud in connection with one of several patents in suit procured years apart has been held to bar enforcement of all patents, provided the inequitable conduct was perpetrated in the Patent and Trademark Office. *SSIH Equip. S.A. v. United States Int'l Trade Commission,* 718 F.2d 365, 218 U.S.P.Q. 678 (Fed. Cir. 1983).

Nor has it appeared that fraud or inequitable conduct before a foreign patent office will render a related U.S. patent unenforceable. *Plantronics Inc. v. Roanwell Corp.,* 185 U.S.P.Q. 505 (S.D.N.Y. 1975); *Slimfold Mfg. Co. v. Kinkead Indus. Inc.,* 600 F. Supp. 1015 (N.D. Ga. 1984), *summary judgment denied in part,* 626 F. Supp. 493 (N.D. Ga. 1985), *aff'd,* 810 F.2d 1113 (Fed. Cir. 1987). By contrast, some would argue that the U.S. antitrust laws may be violated if it is shown that a fraudulently secured foreign patent is being used in a manner to restrain or restrict United States foreign trade.

In *Mannington Mills, Inc. v. Congoleum Corp.,* 595 F.2d 1287, 202 U.S.P.Q. 321 (3d Cir. 1979), plaintiff Mannington alleged that defendant's foreign patents were secured by fraud and that bringing and threatening to bring infringement suits in foreign countries on the basis of those patents resulted in a restraint of U.S. export trade by restricting plaintiff's foreign business and, hence, such activity was an antitrust violation under the *Walker Process* doctrine. Determining that the Act of State doctrine did not apply in the circumstances of this case, the court remanded the case to the district court for evaluation of concerns such as international comity, foreign policy, and the like before deciding whether jurisdiction should be exercised to enforce U.S. antitrust laws. At the very least, U.S. entities should hereafter give consideration to the *Walker Process* doctrine before seeking to enforce foreign patents against other United States entities.

[7] Partial Invalidity

Once a court concludes that inequitable conduct has occurred, all the claims, not just the particular claim or claims to which the inequitable conduct is directly connected, are unenforceable. *J.P. Stevens & Co. v. Lex-Tex, Ltd.,* 747 F.2d 1553, 1561 (Fed. Cir. 1984). "Inequitable conduct goes to the patent right as a whole, independently of particular claims." *In re Clark,* 522 F.2d 623, 187 U.S.P.Q. 209 (C.C.P.A. 1975). Where a patentee has failed to discharge his duty in dealing with the Patent Office in an equitable manner, the fact that the lack of candor did not directly affect all the claims in the patent has never been a governing rule. *Gemveto Jewelry Co. v. Lambert Bros., Inc.,* 592 F. Supp. 933, 943, 216 U.S.P.Q. 976 (S.D.N.Y. 1982).

Moreover, if the affected claims were considered invalid as opposed to unenforceable, the entire patent would still be affected. "Whenever, without deceptive intention, a claim of a patent is invalid, an action may be maintained for the infringement of a claim of the patent which may be valid." 35 U.S.C. § 288.

"Section 288 by its express terms rules out infringement actions to enforce a patent in which any one of its claims is invalid by reason of fraud or deception." *Kearney & Trecker Corp. v. Giddings & Lewis Inc.,* 452 F.2d 579, 596, 171 U.S.P.Q. 650 (7th Cir. 1971).

§ 10.02   Acquisition of Technology and Patent Rights

[1]   Internally Generated Superior Technology and Patents Resulting Therefrom

To date, acquisition of a patent and accumulation of patents through internal research has presented no antitrust problem. *Automatic Radio Mfg. Co. v. Hazeltine Research, Inc.,* 339 U.S. 827, 85 U.S.P.Q. 378 (1950); *United States v. Aluminum Co. of Am.,* 148 F.2d 416, 365 U.S.P.Q. 6 (2d Cir. 1945); *Chisholm-Ryder Co. v. Mecca Bros.,* 217 U.S.P.Q. 1322, 1338 (W.D.N.Y. 1983); *United States v. United Shoe Mach. Corp.,* 110 F. Supp. 295 (D. Mass. 1953), *aff'd,* 347 U.S. 521 (1954).

However, the district court in *SCM Corp. v. Xerox Corp.,* 463 F. Supp. 983, 201 U.S.P.Q. 258, 284 (D. Conn. 1978), *remanded,* 599 F.2d 32 (2d Cir.), *on remand,* 474 F. Supp. 589 (D. Conn. 1979), *aff'd* 645 F.2d 1195, 209 U.S.P.Q. 889 (2d Cir. 1981), *cert. denied,* 455 U.S. 1016 (1982), suggested *in dictum* that an antitrust violation arguably may exist when a company with monopoly power attempts to obtain new patents on its own inventions *primarily for the purpose of blocking the development and marketing of competitive products* rather than primarily to protect its own products from being imitated or blocked by others. There seems to be no statutory justification for such a rule. *But see* Klitzke, "Patents and Section 7 of the Clayton Act: The Significance of Patents in Corporate Acquisitions," 12 Loy. U. Chi. L.J. 401 (1981).

Here, note the tool of analysis—purpose or effect of acquiring the new patents. Think a moment on the likely available proofs of that purpose or effect. Normally, a proof of purpose to acquire patents primarily for blocking will not be obtainable; in truth, however, by the nature of real-world technology and market development economics, the primary purpose is commonly going to be the lawful purpose.

But in almost every antitrust case some "smoking gun" letter has been found in somebody's file that ends up being the key to argument of possible wrongful intent. We can easily perceive some intra-company memorandum to the effect:

> We don't yet know whether the market will evolve from our present approach X to approach Y, so let's get all the patents we can on approach Y to block out all competition and thereby preserve our options.

There is no experienced patent lawyer in the country who has not received, authored, or otherwise observed such a letter without thought of its being improper or unlawful. But given the construction that such letters can sometimes be given in court, particularly against a big company in at least pseudo-monopoly position, and given the fact that these cases are decided as much by attitudinal instincts and biases of judges as by logical following of evidence and burden-of-proof law, this type of recitation by any company with near-monopoly position or power must be viewed as a serious issue under our system of jurisprudence.

United States v. Grinnell Corp., 384 U.S. 563, 570–71 (1966), is repeatedly cited for the tenet that a dominant firm that acquires or maintains its dominant position as a consequence of growth or development resulting from a superior product, business acumen, or historic accident will not, for those factors, be in violation of Section 2 of the Sherman Act.[4] While some writers suggest that this premise gives dominant firms too much latitude to maintain their position, the courts have not yet retreated from that position. The Supreme Court has overruled a long line of cases and has held that the coordinated activity of a parent and its wholly owned subsidiary must be viewed as that of a single entity. *Copperweld Corp. v. Independence Tube Corp.,* 467 U.S. 752 (1984).

Several cases, including *Berkey Photo, Inc. v. Eastman Kodak Co.,* 603 F.2d 263 (2d Cir. 1979), *cert. denied,* 444 U.S. 1093 (1980), *California Computer Prods. Inc. v. IBM Corp.,* 613 F.2d 727 (9th Cir. 1979), and *SCM, supra,* have affirmed the proposition that Section 2 of the Sherman Act

---

[4] 15 U.S.C. § 2.

was not intended to prevent dominant firms from participating in aggressive competition or innovation.

For purposes of the decision in *California Computer, supra,* the court assumed that IBM had monopoly power in the relevant market. The plaintiff asserted three Section 2 violations, the most relevant to this discussion being that IBM had made design changes on certain of its central processing units, disc drives, and controllers that were for no technological advantage, but done solely for the purpose of frustrating competition. The court concluded that even a monopolist had the right to redesign its products to make them more attractive to buyers, whether this end was accomplished by reason of lower manufacturing costs and prices or by improved performance. The court stated that IBM was under no duty to help the plaintiff or other peripheral equipment manufacturers to survive or expand. It was also noted that when an opportunity existed to increase or protect market share profitability by offering equivalent or superior performance at a lower price, even a virtual monopolist might do so.

Nor should the integrated nature of a large business having monopoly power in one or more markets, in and of itself, stand as a barrier to that firm's taking advantage of its technological innovation. *Berkey, supra.* This case involved the following five distinct markets: amateur conventional still cameras, conventional photographic film, color print paper, photofinishing services, and photofinishing equipment, with Kodak having a monopolistic or dominant position in the first three of those markets.

A primary objection by Berkey was Kodak's simultaneous introduction of a new camera and film format, which were designed to work only with each other and which were introduced without predisclosure to other camera manufacturers. The court ruled that Kodak's ability to introduce this new format without predisclosure was solely a benefit of integration and not, on the record established, the misuse of its power in the film market to gain a competitive advantage in the camera market.

It was the position of the court that so long as we allow a firm to compete in several fields, we must expect that it will seek the competitive advantages of its broad-based activities, such as more efficient production, greater ability to develop complementary products, reduced transaction costs, and so forth. These activities, according to the court, are not considered uses of monopoly power. *See also Foremost Pro Color, Inc. v. Eastman Kodak Co.,* 703 F.2d 534 (9th Cir. 1983), *cert. denied,* 465 U.S. 1038 (1984).

While the courts may be seeking to avoid uncertainties that would have a chilling effect on innovation, a line of demarcation between those activities that are merely "the benefits of integration" and those that are directed at "smothering competition" remains unclear.

As yet, there does not appear to be any direct limitation on a firm's right to innovate and to capitalize on that innovation, regardless of what the firm's position is in the relevant market prior to the technological development. John H. Schenefield, while Chief of the Antitrust Division of the Department of Justice, stated in an October 17, 1978, Department of Justice memorandum on the Domestic Policy Review of Industrial Innovation that "a firm has the green light to advance its position by the employment of innovation whose purpose is not simply to create entry barriers."

But consider the appeal of this scenario: A company advances parallel technology paths, elects to market one while using patents covering the other development as protection against competition from that parallel quarter. Surely the company has offered on the market what it perceived at the time to be the best of the two alternatives, so the public is unlikely to be injured; and unilateral refusal to license others is generally accepted as a lawful right.

But to enforce patents on the parallel approach without licensing them (*i.e.,* to block others from development of the competitive technology) somehow simply feels anticompetitive to some personality types found in the bar and on the bench, notwithstanding the statutory unrestricted patent right to exclude others. One day a case may come along in the context of other factors (like a high percentage of the relevant market already controlled and/or evidence of mischief of some kind) when the dictum, "may," of *SCM, supra,* is expressed as a Section 2 liability if the unused parallel technology patents are enforced to block, rather than to license, the competition.

[2] Acquisition of Patent Rights by Purchase or Merger

There is no basic quality of the purchase of sale of patents that renders the transaction lawful or unlawful. Given the analytical tools in the rule of reason discussion *supra (see* § 9.02), the industry context of the purchase or sale decides the issues. *See United States v. United States Gypsum Co.,* 333 U.S. 364, 76 U.S.P.Q. 430 (1948); *Hartford-Empire Co. v. United States,* 323 U.S. 386, 64 U.S.P.Q. 18 (1945); *United States v. Vehicular Parking, Ltd.,* 54 F. Supp. 828, 61 U.S.P.Q. 102 (D. Del. 1944); 35 U.S.C. § 261.

In *Kobe, Inc. v. Dempsey Pump Co.,* 97 F. Supp. 342, 89 U.S.P.Q. 54 (N.D. Okla. 1951), *aff'd on other grounds,* 198 F.2d 416, 94 U.S.P.Q. 43 (10th Cir.), *cert. denied,* 334 U.S. 837 (1952), the court awarded treble damages under the Sherman and Clayton Acts[5] to an accused infringer. The plaintiff had acquired ownership or received licenses under more than 90 patents, most of which related to hydraulically actuated pumps for installation in oil wells (*i.e.,* the plaintiff had cornered the market on one class of pumps). The patent rights had been acquired from a number of parties and were deemed to give the plaintiff a complete monopoly of all hydraulically actuated oil well pumps—a monopoly of a relevant market, a broad relevant market, not protected by any single patent.

The court found that the patents were acquired "pursuant to a plan and purpose to monopolize commerce in such hydraulic pumps" and granted treble damages. In doing so, the court also noted that many of the patents were not used

---

[5] 15 U.S.C. § 1 *et seq.*

commercially. *Id.,* 97 F. Supp. at 348, 89 U.S.P.Q. at 59; *see also United States v. Besser Mfg. Co.,* 96 F. Supp. 304, 88 U.S.P.Q. 421 (E.D. Mich. 1951), *aff'd on other grounds,* 343 U.S. 444, 93 U.S.P.Q. 321 (1952); *United States v. Parker Rust-Proof Co.,* 61 F. Supp. 805, 65 U.S.P.Q. 563 (E.D. Mich. 1945), in which the courts placed emphasis on the contractual arrangements involved.

Compare the situation in *Chisholm-Ryder Co. v. Mecca Bros.,* 217 U.S.P.Q. 1322 (W.D.N.Y. 1983). Chisholm-Ryder had acquired the rights to several patents in the area of harvesting grapes by machine. The court found that the progressive acquisition of patents occurred during development of a practical harvesting machine and followed *SCM Corp. v. Xerox Corp.,* 463 F. Supp. 983, 201 U.S.P.Q. 258, 284 (D. Conn. 1978), *remanded,* 599 F.2d 32 (2d Cir.), *on remand,* 474 F. Supp. 589 (D. Conn. 1979), aff'd, 645 F.2d 1195, 209 U.S.P.Q. 889 (2d Cir. 1981), *cert. denied,* 455 U.S. 1016 (1982), holding that no Sherman Sections 1 or 2 or Clayton Section 7 violation had occurred.

The risk of a Clayton Section 7 violation in some circumstances has been suggested. *E.g., Honeywell, Inc. v. Sperry-Rand Corp.,* 180 U.S.P.Q. 673 (D. Minn. 1973); *Dairy Food, Inc. v. Farmers Co-op Creamery,* 298 F. Supp. 774 (D. Minn. 1969). In *Dairy Foods,* the court stated:

> Section 7 prohibits acquisition of assets . . . where " . . . such acquisition may . . . substantially . . . lessen competition. . . ." Patents are assets and where two large business concerns own patents which may be similar in scope and decide not to compete but to put both into a common corporation or pool of which each owns 50% of the stock, such may tend to lessen competition.

Id. at 777. *But cf. Dole Valve Co. v. Perfection Bar Equip., Inc.,* 311 F. Supp. 459, 462–63, 165 U.S.P.Q. 337, 338–40 (N.D. Ill. 1970) (a patent may be an asset under Section 7 of the Clayton Act, but a suit for infringement of a patent acquired by an acquisition unlawful under Section 7 is not necessarily an injury "by reason" of that acquisition; rather, injury stems from misuse of the patent); *Smith-Corona*

Marchant, Inc. v. American Photocopy Equip. Co., 217 F. Supp. 39, 137 U.S.P.Q. 308 (S.D.N.Y. 1963).

In particular, if one of the two largest companies in a given market acquires a substantial package of technology from the first, second, or third largest company in the market, and between them they control over 60 percent of the relevant market, you may derive from some cases such as *Honeywell, supra,* the strong suggestion that for antitrust safety you should not only offer the subject technology to others on reasonable license terms, but should advertise the availability of the license to competitors and potential competitors as well. Without such an offer the acquisition runs a risk of being held to be anticompetitive as to small competitors suffering technological impediments to market entry or development.

The acquisition of patent rights often involves a technological merger—that is, an agreement or cross-licensing arrangement covering patents, proprietary information, and unpatented design and manufacturing technology. This kind of arrangement was one focal point in *Honeywell, supra.* Plaintiff Honeywell claimed that a technological merger between Sperry-Rand and IBM violated Sections 1 and 2 of the Sherman Act and Section 7 of the Clayton Act, resulting in damages to Honeywell. The Sperry-Rand/IBM technological merger grew out of the settlement of several interference proceedings between applications for patents by Sperry-Rand and IBM.

The Minnesota District Court found that the merger injured competition in the electronic data processing (EDP) industry in two ways. First the industry was injured by a conspiracy to perpetuate the dominance of the EDP market by the two companies who were party to the merger (95 percent of the EDP market at the time of the merger). Second, the court held that the EDP market was injured by the merger because the merger tended to protect the market share of each conspirator. While the agreement purported to be a nonexclusive cross-licensing agreement, the court found it to be *de facto* exclusive in view of the secrecy and confidentiality with which the parties cloaked the agreement, especially when coupled with the absence of any licenses.

The court found the cross-license and exchange of technical information agreement to be an unreasonable restraint of trade and an attempt by IBM and Sperry-Rand to strengthen or solidify their monopoly in the EDP industry. The court held, however, that Honeywell had failed to prove that Sperry-Rand's participation in the technological merger violated Section 2 of the Sherman Act. While Honeywell's standing to sue under Section 7 (the anti-merger section) of the Clayton Act was barred by the statute of limitations, it seems clear that this claim would have been sustained had the cause of action been timely raised. In view of the market positions held by IBM and Sperry-Rand in the EDP market, the court concluded that each of the parties to the agreement had a duty to the remaining members of the industry to make a full disclosure of the agreement and to affirmatively seek out parties such as Honeywell and offer them access to technological information equal to that offered in the technological merger.

One district court case and dicta in other cases is not necessarily controlling law. But let us not be oblivious to the handwriting on the wall—like *Honeywell.*

Existing market power and intent were key factors in the decision in *McDonald v. Johnson & Johnson,* 537 F. Supp. 1282 (D. Minn. 1982), *aff'd in part and vacated in part,* 722 F.2d 1370 (8th Cir. 1983). Johnson & Johnson (J&J) had acquired the stock of a small corporation engaged in the manufacture of electric nerve stimulators for controlling pain. After the acquisition, J&J suppressed the manufacture of the stimulator invention (at least arguably because it was not uniformly effective). Combined with the fact that J&J wanted to protect its own over-the-counter pain drug product and its dominant market position, the reason for the suppression was disregarded and J&J was found guilty of violations of both Sections 1 and 2 of the Sherman Act.

A further note with regard to a potential Section 7 Clayton Act violation on the purchase of a patent or patents arose in

SCM Corp. v. Xerox Corp., supra. The relevant product market and submarket did not exist until eight years following the acquisition by Xerox of still uncommercialized patents, and Xerox then possessed no market power whatsoever in even the inchoate market and submarket until some four years following the acquisition.

The appellate court held that the probable economic effects are to be viewed at the time of acquisition, and that if the relevant product market did not exist at the time of acquisition, Section 7 cannot be violated as a matter of law. *SCM,* 645 F.2d at 1211, 209 U.S.P.Q. at 905. Moreover, when the acquisition of patents does not violate Section 7, subsequent conduct permissible under the patent laws cannot trigger any liability under the antitrust laws because to hold otherwise would violate the policies that underlie the patent law system. *Id.,* 645 F.2d at 1212, 209 U.S.P.Q. at 906.

But what if Xerox possessed power in the inchoate market and submarket at the time of the acquisition? The court indicated in dictum that a Section 2 Sherman Act violation will occur when the dominant competitor in a market acquires a patent covering a substantial share of the same market that, when added to his existing share, will afford him monopoly power. *Id.,* 645 F.2d at 1205, 209 U.S.P.Q. at 900.

The Department of Justice and the Federal Trade Commission recently issued new Merger Guidelines to "improve the predictability of the [Justice] Department's merger enforcement policy." Merger Guidelines of Department of Justice—1982, Trade Reg. Rep. (CCH) ¶ 4500 (1982). No special provisions relating to technological mergers are included. The unifying theme of the new Guidelines is that mergers—technological or otherwise—should not be permitted to create or enhance "market power" or to facilitate its exercise.

[3] Grant-Backs

Historically, the acquisition of almost any form of patent license or title by grant-back from a patent licensee to his licensor was viewed as legal. *Transparent-Wrap Mach. Corp. v. Stokes & Smith Co.,* 329 U.S. 637, 72 U.S.P.Q. 148 (1947). *But see Chandler v. Stern Dental Laboratory Co.,* 335 F. Supp. 580, 171 U.S.P.Q. 100 (S.D. Tex. 1971).

But it is always dangerous to follow precedents of this type without going through the rule of reason analysis—including the industry context of the transaction. Acquisition of exclusive licenses or patent title by grant-backs from the licensee or by exclusive cross license is now in antitrust hot water at least up to the ankles. The Department of Justice (of a 1970s administration) announced its intent to challenge grant-backs (1) of exclusive rights and (2) when the result is an expansion or extension of the original licensor's patent licensing power.

Limited term nonexclusive grant-backs, at least if without the right to sublicense and if the rights granted back cannot be practiced without practicing the original licensor's patented invention, are on solid dry ground. *Santa Fe-Polmeroy, Inc. v. P & Z Co.,* 569 F.2d 1084, 197 U.S.P.Q. 449 (9th Cir. 1978). But long term and exclusive grants-back merit close study before putting them into any new license you may be drafting. *See* Chapter 12, "Current Thinking and Likely Enforcement Policy of the Antitrust Division Regarding Patent Licensing Practices."

[4] Patent Pools, Cross-Licensing

Patent pools and cross-licenses are generally not per se violations of Section 1 of the Sherman Act. *See Standard Oil Co. v. United States,* 283 U.S. 163 (1931); *Platt Saco Lowell Ltd. v. Spindelfabrik Suessen-Schurr,* 199 U.S.P.Q. 636 (N.D. Ill. 1978); *Honeywell, Inc. v. Sperry-Rand Corp.,* 180 U.S.P.Q. 673 (D. Minn. 1973). The antitrust inquiry is generally directed to the purpose and the effects of the particular arrangement, as always, in context of the particular industry structure. For example, one court has held that a finding that competitors' patents were blocking supported an inference that the existence of a pooling arrangement was for a legitimate, rather than an anticompetitive, purpose. *Carpet Seaming Tape Licensing Corp. v. Best Seam Inc.*, 694 F.2d 570, 216 U.S.P.Q. 873 (9th Cir. 1982), *cert. denied*, 464 U.S. 818 (1983).

Arrangements of this nature can have positive effects in extending technology to new products and geographic markets, and increasing the return available on the pooled technology, thereby increasing the incentive to innovate. The countervailing aspects include the possibility that the arrangement in some contexts may dampen the incentive for individual firms to engage in competitive technical research and development. Consider, for example, an industry-wide cross-license pool of patents on new inventions. If you are assured of access to all your competitors' new things at a reasonable royalty—"reasonable" in this context means you can pay it and still make a profit—why assume the high risks inherent in R&D? The arrangement, in some contexts, operates as a form of security blanket, reducing investments in innovation by all members of the pool.

This concern led the government to challenge the pooling arrangements in the cases of *United States v. Automobile Manufacturers Ass'n*, 1969 Trade Cas. (CCH) ¶ 72,907 (C.D. Cal. 1969), and *United States v. Manufacturers Aircraft Ass'n, Inc.*, 1976-1 Trade Cas. (CCH) ¶ 60,810 (S.D.N.Y. 1975). Both cases involved industry-wide agreements to pool patents and technology, in the first case a requirement that all members grant royalty-free licenses to other members, and in the second case, licenses at a fairly low rate set by an arbitration board. In one case it was also provided that no member would take licenses from outside parties unless similar rights and terms were available to all other members.

It was the government position in both cases that the pace of innovation among members of the pools was reduced, as was the competition for patents developed by others. The government obtained consent decrees in both cases, which provided all of the relief that had been requested.

In a decision by the federal district court in Los Angeles, the government's request for an extension of the consent decree against the automobile manufacturers was denied. *United States v. Motor Vehicle Manufacturers Ass'n of U.S., Inc.*, 1979–2 Trade Cas. (CCH) ¶ 62,759 (C.D. Cal. 1979). In reaching its conclusion, the court cited changing circumstances, specifically noting a shift in national concern to energy efficiency.

In its report "Domestic Policy Review of Industrial Innovation," dated October 17, 1978, the Department of Justice set forth the following guidelines for pooling arrangements:

(1) industry-wide pooling arrangements should be avoided;
(2) the exchanges should relate only to interfering patents;
(3) the arrangement should cover only present patents rather than future patents; and
(4) the arrangement should be of limited duration.

It is clear that the broader the scope of the particular arrangement, the more likely it is that antitrust problems will arise. Roger B. Andewelt, Chief of the Intellectual Property Section Antitrust Division of the United States Department of Justice, made it clear in 1985 that the Department of Justice favors an evaluation of pooling arrangements using a rule of reason approach rather than a rigid per se condemnation.[6]

It is interesting to note that in May, 1985, the Justice Department petitioned the U.S. District Courts of the Southern District of New York and Delaware to modify or

---

[6] Remarks of Roger B. Andewelt, Chief, Intellectual Property Section Antitrust Division, United States Department of Justice, before the National Institute On Industrial & Intellectual Property, Philadelphia, Pennsylvania, October 11–12, 1984, 53 Antitrust L.J., Issue 3, p. 620 (1985).

terminate three consent decrees that had been entered against the RCA Corporation.

The original consent decrees ended litigation the Department had brought against RCA under Sections 1 and 2 of the Sherman Act. The Department had alleged that certain patent pooling agreements, market division agreements, and restrictive patent licensing practices were in restraint of trade.

In explaining the Department's change of attitude with respect to these decrees, acting Assistant Attorney General, Charles F. Rule, noted that under certain circumstances the practices prohibited under the earlier decrees can promote, rather than harm, competition. The Department cited changing market conditions as the reason for its change of attitude and concluded that the decrees were no longer in the public interest. "Justice Dept. Seeks Termination of Decrees Relating to Patent Licensing," [Jan.–June] Patents, Trademark & Copyright J. (BNA) Vol. 30, No. 735 (June 20, 1985).

The Department of Justice has also sought to terminate a 35-year-old consent decree prohibiting two drug companies from conspiring to fix prices for hard gelatin capsules. According to the Department, many of the provisions of the decree are now obsolete since the patents involved have expired and the decree restricts competitively neutral or procompetitive conduct that the companies' competitors are free to undertake. *Parke, Davis & Co.,* Case No. 1014, Trade Reg. Rep. (CCH) No. 823, p. 4 (Aug. 25, 1987).

But consider this situation: Eight major companies in a chemical processing industry, each with big R&D budgets and two continuously running pilot plans from which to learn new efficiencies; 50 minors in the industry, each without finances to keep up in the R&D race, who pool a joint R&D effort of about the same size as most of the majors and exchange cross-licenses. Hm-m-m.

[5] Technical Interchange Contract

The tremendous costs associated with R&D efforts are a significant factor in the turn to technical interchange contracts such as joint venture arrangements.

Many projects are simply beyond the financial means of any one entity. Moreover, the time lapse between the R&D investment and any return from the marketing of the resulting technology is increasing. The financial risks are reaching such proportions that many individual companies, which may have money available, cannot, from a reasonable business standpoint, invest in R&D activity.

Another important consideration is that individual companies, which may have sufficient funds for R&D, often lack other essentials, such as a particular expertise, or the appropriate pilot plant facilities.

Finally, a joint effort may often be more efficient because needless and costly duplication of efforts may be avoided.

Joint ventures for R&D are not per se violations of Section 1 of the Sherman Act. Not even a joint venture between a monopolist and another firm in a complementary market is considered a per se violation of Section 1. *Berkey Photo, Inc. v. Eastman Kodak Co.,* 603 F.2d 263, 302–03 (2d Cir. 1979), *cert. denied,* 444 U.S. 1093 (1980).

Joint ventures are reviewed by the Justice Department under the rule of reason analysis. Ewing, Ky P., "Antitrust Enforcement: A Positive Force for Innovation," remarks made before the Institute of Electrical and Electronics Engineers, September 20, 1978.

President Reagan signed the National Cooperative Research Act of 1984, 15 U.S.C. § 4301 *et seq.* This act specifically clarifies the application of the rule of reason to joint R&D ventures. The Act also limits damages recoverable in actions brought under antitrust laws to the actual, as opposed to treble, damages suffered if the joint ventures register their venture with the United States Attorney General and the Federal Trade Commission within 90 days after entering into a written agreement to form the venture. A notice of the venture is then published in the Federal Register. See, for example, 51 Fed. Reg. 11489, April 3, 1986 (a joint research venture to explore electronic and other industrial applications of advanced ceramics); 51 Fed. Register 35706 (1986) (a joint research venture to sponsor and conduct toxological research on a pesticide ingredient).

Therefore, the legality of a joint venture will generally be determined on the basis of the circumstances and purposes leading to the particular arrangement, and on the manner in which it is implemented.

For example, in the *Berkey* case, the court found that Kodak had actually obtained agreements from Sylvania and GE that delayed new flash cube technology from hitting the market until Kodak was ready to incorporate the new technology into its cameras. This, the court felt, the jury could have found to be a clear loss to consumers with no justification other than Kodak's convenience. The court, however, held that the agreement was not a per se violation of Section 1.

The court cited the following factors as relevant variables: the size of the joint ventures; their share of the respective markets; the contributions of each party to the venture and the benefits derived; the likelihood that in the absence of the joint effort, one or both parties would undertake a similar project, either alone or with a smaller firm in the other market; and the nature of the ancillary restraints imposed and the reasonableness of their relationship to the purposes of the venture. 603 F.2d at 302.

Other factors to be considered, as set out in *United States v. Penn-Olin Chem. Co.,* 378 U.S. 158, 177 (1964), include: the number and power of the competitors in the relevant market; the background of their growth; the power of the joint venturers; the relationship of their lines of commerce; the competition existing between them and the power of each dealing with competitors of the other; the setting in which the joint venture was created; the reasons and necessities for its existence; the adaptability of its line of commerce to noncompetitive practices; the potential power of the joint venture in the relevant market; and an appraisal of what the competition in the relevant market would have been if one of the joint venturers had entered it alone instead of through the joint venture.

Also to be considered are the size of the research project proposed in relation to prior independent R&D efforts by the participants and the ability or inability of each to undertake the project on its own.

Finally, consideration must also be given to whether the joint venture is an "essential facility" that must be open to all on reasonable and nondiscriminatory terms.

One of the dangers of various forms of joint venture R&D programs is the likelihood that parties who start such a program with strict and pure guidelines soon forget to think about antitrust violations and then may inadvertently slip into an illegal pattern.

In my personal experience, for example, we once represented a major company that supplied probably 15 percent of a certain broad class of manufacturing raw material. There was one particular user of that material that consumed about 20 percent of all of that class of raw material.

These two parties put together a joint venture R&D project by which they could improve the material for use in the end product and make it perform much better in that particular application. As their success grew, the manufacturer of the end product increased its market share tremendously, in part by the quality of the raw material put in. And the manufacturer of the raw material tended increasingly to sell its output only to its joint venture customer, whose orders were growing.

When the time came to sue on the patents produced by this venture, we found a pattern that gave us considerable pause. We elected not to expose that pattern to discovery in cross-examination until we could purge it.

With respect to industry joint action, comments made in 1979 by then Deputy Assistant Attorney General Ky P. Ewing regarding U.S. industry's conversion to the metric system is of interest. It has been stated that industry conversion plans that make every effort to accommodate all members will not be attacked under Section 1 of the Sherman Act, providing that the restraints inevitably flowing from them are reasonable. However, caution must be exercised to avoid anticompetitive exploitation of the conversion process and of coordinated anticompetitive conduct such as excessively broad information exchanges and adoption of standardization proposals designed to facilitate price coordination.

[6] Justice Department Business Review Procedure

While the Department of Justice does not issue advisory opinions, it does provide a business review procedure whereby the Antitrust Division may indicate its present antitrust enforcement intentions with respect to a proposed course of action by a business, industry group, or other enterprise. This business review procedure is set out at 28 C.F.R. ch. 1, pt. 50.

Under the procedure, a requesting party or parties must submit a written request with respect to proposed business conduct and must make a full and true disclosure with respect to that proposed conduct. This means that the party or parties must submit all relevant data and materials and any additional information or documents later requested by the Antitrust Division.

The Antitrust Division may respond with its present intentions, or may decline to pass on the request altogether. Furthermore, the "business review" letter issued by the Antitrust Division only represents the Division's enforcement intention as of that date, and does not restrict the Division from later bringing whatever action or proceeding it comes to believe is required by the public interest.

Records of the Antitrust Division indicate that about thirty-four specific requests for business reviews involving research and development, joint ventures, or both, were filed between 1968 and 1982. The Antitrust Division has responded affirmatively (*i.e.,* stated a present intention not to bring an enforcement action) in about 90 percent of these instances.

Typically, favorable responses to proposed research and development joint ventures are made on the basis of certain "understandings" of the Antitrust Division, such as:

(1) the inability of one joint venturer to interest companies other than the second venturer in the project or to obtain alternative funding—recited in a June 1972 letter to Petroleum Technology Corporation and Hercules Inc.;

(2) the experimental nature of a proposed project and the limitations on its scope and duration—recited in an October 1973 response to Westinghouse Electric Corp. and Tenneco Power Systems, Inc., concerning the design and manufacture of platform-mounted nuclear power plants;

(3) the inability of the patent owner to generate the required interest among potential licensees for the testing and commercial development of patented drugs through the use of less restrictive licensing arrangements—in a December 1975 response to Salk Institute for Biological Studies;

(4) the scope of the project being limited to basic industry knowledge (as opposed to particular manufacturing practices) and the results being available on a nondiscriminatory basis to all industry members—in an April 1976 response to the Metal Treating Institute;

(5) all patentable discoveries being placed in the public domain by publication or made available on a royalty-free license to any requesting party—in a May 1978 response to the Proprietary Association;

(6) the foreign party to the joint venture to sell and manufacture energy saving systems would not remain in the U.S. market without a joint venture agreement—in an August 1981 response to RTE Corporation; and

(7) the joint venture would account for less than 10 percent the market in a designated geographical area—in a February 1981 response to Shoake Packing Co.,

Van de Graaf Ranches, Inc., and Monson & Sons Cattle Co.

In a letter dated May 16, 1979, the Antitrust Division gave a favorable response to a technical assistance agreement between two of the major automotive companies on the understanding that one was facing financial difficulties that would severely hamper its ability to compete in several submarkets without technical assistance to meet government standards and deadlines regarding emission control and passive restraint devices.

An example of a negative response is found in an opinion letter dated November 27, 1978, from the Antitrust Division concerning a proposed joint venture combining the United States television business of General Electric Co. and Hitachi, Ltd. of Japan. Elimination of significant existing and potential competition between G.E. and Hitachi in the manufacture and sale of television sets and an increased concentration in television markets were cited as reasons for the Justice Department position.

While an affirmative response from the Antitrust Division is no guarantee that future action will not be initiated, utilization of this procedure may have value in those situations in which a proposed joint venture R&D effort has some appeal to reason as well as some characteristics that would appear unfavorable if subjected later to rigid antitrust scrutinization.

Item 9 of the business review procedure indicates that the Antitrust Division has never exercised its right to bring a criminal action when there has been a full and true disclosure at the time of presenting the request for review. While this is not a binding commitment, it may be an additional incentive for using the procedure—with a full and candid disclosure.

§ 10.03 Refusal to License

[1] Unilateral Refusal to License

Historically, the unilateral refusal to license has always been thought of as lawful. *United States v. Colgate & Co.,* 250 U.S. 300 (1919); *United States v. Westinghouse Elec. Corp.,* 648 F.2d 642 (9th Cir. 1981); *Gates Learjet Corp. v. Magnasync Craig Corp.,* 339 F. Supp. 587, 173 U.S.P.Q. 203 (D. Colo. 1972). Contrast the much-criticized *Allied Research Prods. Inc. v. Heatbath Corp.,* 300 F. Supp. 656, 161 U.S.P.Q. 527 (N.D. Ill. 1969).

The law seems to remain that a patent owner, and even one that has monopoly power, may unilaterally refuse to license its lawfully acquired patent(s) covering its marketed line without incurring treble damage liability under the antitrust laws. In *SCM Corp. v. Xerox Corp.,* 645 F.2d 1195, 209 U.S.P.Q. 889 (2d Cir. 1981), *cert. denied,* 455 U.S. 1016 (1982), the court held:

> Where a patent holder ... merely exercises his "right to exclude others from making, using or selling the invention," by refusing unilaterally to license his patent for its seventeen-year term, such conduct is expressly permitted by the patent laws.

Id., 645 F.2d at 1204, 209 U.S.P.Q. at 899; *accord, GAF Corp. v. Eastman Kodak Co.,* 519 F. Supp. 1203, 213 U.S.P.Q. 356 (S.D.N.Y. 1981). The *SCM* holding must be read in light of the fact that the court found that the patents were acquired prior to the appearance of the relevant product market and that "the patents themselves afforded Xerox the power to achieve eventual market dominance." 645 F.2d at 1205, 209 U.S.P.Q. at 900.

Further, a patent owner may refrain from using its patent while at the same time refusing to license others. *Special Equip. Co. v. Coe,* 324 U.S. 370, 64 U.S.P.Q. 525 (1945); *Continental Paper Bag Co. v. Eastern Paper Bag Co.,* 210 U.S. 405 (1908); *Monsanto Co. v. Spray-Rite Serv. Corp.,* 465 U.S. 752, *reh'g denied,* 466 U.S. 994 (1984) ("A manufacturer of course generally has the right to deal, or refuse to deal, with whomever it likes, as long as it does so independently."); *contrast, Standard Sanitary Mfg. Co. v. United States,* 226 U.S. 20 (1912) (nonuse or refusal to license as part of a scheme to foreclose competition may violate antitrust laws).

Circumstances will occasionally exist that will persuade at least some courts to award relief in the form of a mandatory license. A court's refusal to award an injunction after a finding of infringement is equivalent to requiring a license. Special circumstances such as public health may prompt a court to refuse injunctive relief. *See City of Milwaukee v. Activated Sludge,* 69 F.2d 577 (7th Cir.), *cert. denied,* 293 U.S. 576 (1934). Furthermore, damage liability might arise if the refusal to license is combined with any other "injurious conduct." *See, e.g., Vitamin Technologists, Inc. v. Wisconsin Alumni Research Found.,* 146 F.2d 941, 63 U.S.P.Q. 262 (9th Cir.), *cert. denied,* 325 U.S. 876, *reh'g denied,* 326 U.S. 804 (1945); *Allied Research, supra.*

The court in *Mannington Mills, Inc. v. Congoleum Indus., Inc.,* 610 F.2d 1059, 203 U.S.P.Q. 81 (3d Cir. 1979), said, "We seriously doubt that an arbitrary or discriminatory unilateral refusal to deal by a lawful monopolist is actionable under Section 2 of the Sherman Act." *Id.* 610 F.2d at 1069, 203 U.S.P.Q. at 89. It held that Congoleum's refusal to license know-how to Mannington was not "arbitrary" because Mannington had prior manufacturing experience that other licensees lacked. However, on the separate charge that Congoleum terminated Mannington's foreign sales licenses, the court held that cancellation of a nonexclusive license *at the behest of competing licensees (i.e.,* not unilaterally) is not entitled to a patent law exemption from normal antitrust coverage. A summary judgment for defendant was reversed.

Exclusive licenses have been universally accepted, even though they carry the inherent obligation of the licensor not to grant other licenses he could have granted but for the contract with the exclusive licensee. Section 261 of the Patent Statute expressly authorizes exclusive licenses.

The most recent announcement that unilateral refusal to license is lawful comes from the Ninth Circuit in *United States v. Westinghouse Elec. Corp., supra.* The Justice Department took the position that a patent owner who grants one license should be obligated to grant licenses to all qualified applicants. The court stated:

> The antitrust laws do not grant the government a roving commission to reform the economy at will. . . . [N]o court has held that a patentee must grant further licenses to potential competitors merely because he has granted them some licenses. . . . [S]o too would the patent system be undermined if a licensing agreement, perfectly legal when signed, might later form the basis of an antitrust violation because the licensee had flourished under the agreement.

Id. at 648.

Similarly, in *United States v. Ciba Geigy Corp.,* 508 F. Supp. 1118 (D.N.J. 1976), the Justice Department was unable to convince the court that once a license has been granted to certain competitors, the law required a compulsory license to other competitors where there was no proof of an unlawful combination or conspiracy.

Together, these two cases seem to completely negate *Allied Research, supra,* insofar as it might be construed as requiring a compulsory license in the absence of some injurious illegal conduct beyond a mere unilateral refusal to license.

Even so, sophisticated licensors and licensees should be aware of the existence of some few special circumstances in which the reality of the law in action is that the burden may be upon the patent owner to justify a refusal to license after having granted earlier licenses. *See, e.g., Foster v. American Mach. & Foundry Co.,* 492 F.2d 1317, 182 U.S.P.Q. 1 (2d Cir.), *cert. denied,* 419 U.S. 833 (1974); *Vitamin Technologists, Inc. v. Wisconsin Alumni Research Found., supra; City of Milwaukee v. Activated Sludge, supra.* It should be noted that at least one court has held that unilateral *termination* of a sublicense is not exempt from scrutiny under the antitrust laws. *International Wood Processors v. Power Dry, Inc.,* 593 F. Supp. 710, 224 U.S.P.Q. 52 (D.S.C. 1984). In this case the

Court applied the rule of reason to a unilateral termination of a sublicense and found that it ran afoul of the antitrust laws.

[2] Bilateral Refusal to License

Quite a number of cases discuss, often critically, bilateral refusals to license, that is, contracts by which the licensee and licensor have veto power over the other's granting further licenses, as in an exclusive license with no right to sublicense.

The critical rulings have usually involved cases in which the right of veto over further licenses was in context of other evidence of intent to monopolize. *Noll v. O.M. Scott & Sons Co.*, 467 F.2d 295, 175 U.S.P.Q. 392 (6th Cir. 1972), *cert. denied*, 411 U.S. 965 (1973); *Mason City Tent & Awning Co. v. Clapper*, 144 F. Supp. 754, 111 U.S.P.Q. 330 (W.D. Mo. 1956); *United States v. Krasnov*, 143 F. Supp. 184, 110 U.S.P.Q. 411 (E.D. Pa. 1956), *aff'd mem.*, 355 U.S. 5, 115 U.S.P.Q. 70 (1957); *United States v. Besser Mfg. Co.*, 96 F. Supp. 304, 88 U.S.P.Q. 421 (E.D. Mich. 1951), *aff'd on other grounds*, 343 U.S. 444, 93 U.S.P.Q. 321 (1952). In *AB Iro v. Otex, Inc.*, 566 F. Supp. 419, 220 U.S.P.Q. 239 (D.S.C. 1983), the court held that the alleged conspiracy between the patentee and the exclusive licensee fell within the realm of conscious parallelism. To make out a conspiracy under Section 1 of the Sherman Act requires evidence that cannot be reconciled with a contrary innocent explanation. The court concluded no violation was proven because plaintiffs appeared to be acting in their own best interest.

In one modern case the court declined to hold a bilateral arrangement to be a per se violation. The court said the pattern presented an issue triable to the jury as to whether the restraint was unreasonable. *Moraine Prods. v. ICI Am., Inc.*, 538 F.2d 134, 191 U.S.P.Q. 65 (7th Cir.), *cert. denied*, 429 U.S. 941 (1976).

In another case, the court found no patent misuse when a "settlement license" containing an agreement between the licensor and nonexclusive licensee not to grant licenses to any other party had been approved by another district court. *Speed Shore Corp. v. Denda,* 197 U.S.P.Q. 526 (C.D. Cal. 1977), *aff'd,* 605 F.2d 469, 203 U.S.P.Q. 807 (9th Cir. 1979). *But see Duplan Corp. v. Deering Milliken, Inc.,* 444 F. Supp. 648, 197 U.S.P.Q. 342 (D.S.C. 1977), *aff'd in part, rev'd on other grounds,* 594 F.2d 979, 201 U.S.P.Q. 641 (4th Cir. 1979), *cert. denied,* 444 U.S. 1015 (1980).

[3] Refusal to Take a License

A related topic that has recently been the subject of several cases involves a patent owner's inability to get a "buyer" for his invention. In *Shapiro v. General Motors Corp.,* 472 F. Supp. 636, 204 U.S.P.Q. 461 (D. Md. 1979), *aff'd,* 636 F.2d 1214 (4th Cir. 1980), *cert. denied,* 451 U.S. 909 (1981), the inventors of a seat belt were confronted with independent refusals by both Ford and General Motors to deal directly with outside inventors and, at the same time, an arrangement between Ford and General Motors and their suppliers whereby only royalty-free second source licenses were taken. Consequently, when the inventors were directed to deal with the suppliers they found that these entities were unwilling to pay much of anything for the inventions because of the arrangements with Ford and G.M. The court found no evidence of conspiracy, a failure to show any direct injury to plaintiff caused by the defendant's practices, and thus no standing to sue. The court stated that the manufacturers "had no obligation to serve as licensees."

In *Laurie Visual Etudes, Inc. v. Chesebrough-Pond's, Inc.,* 473 F. Supp. 951, 204 U.S.P.Q. 855 (S.D.N.Y. 1979), the patent owner alleged that the defendant had violated Section 2 of the Sherman Act by using its monopoly power to delay and prevent plaintiff from entering the market (by prolonging their negotiations until defendant's own devices had reached the market). Plaintiff was found to have no standing because it had no "business or property" that was subject to injury and that its failure to enter the market was the result of its own incapacity.

Finally, in *Gould v. Control Laser Corp.,* 462 F. Supp. 685, 200 U.S.P.Q. 693 (M.D. Fla. 1978), *appeal dismissed in part, aff'd in part,* 650 F.2d 617, 213 U.S.P.Q. 1120 (5th Cir. 1981), the court held that the alleged concerted refusal of a group of industry members to deal with the patent owner was subject to a rule of reason analysis and that to the extent that *Jones Knitting Corp. v. Morgan,* 361 F.2d 451, 149 U.S.P.Q. 659 (3d Cir. 1966), held otherwise, it was no longer authoritative. The court also suggested that an agreement to share costs of litigating the validity of a particular patent could only violate the antitrust laws when there was evidence of abuse of the adjudicatory process or coercive conduct designed to use the courts for improper purposes.

[4] Bilateral Termination of License

If a licensor, not in competition with his licensees, unilaterally terminates one of the licenses there generally will not be a problem of anticompetitive overtones.

If, however, a licensor is in competition with a licensee and deals with another party in like competition before terminating a license, the spectre of anticompetitive practices will be raised.

Even the appearance of an intent to eliminate competition is of critical importance when such a licensor terminates a license. In *International Wood Processors v. Power Dry, Inc.,* 593 F. Supp. 710, 224 U.S.P.Q. 52 (D.S.C. 1984), the District Court for South Carolina applied the Rule of Reason to a termination of a sublicense and found that the termination ran afoul of the antitrust laws. The court was presented with a situation in which a licensor claimed it terminated a sublicense in order to compete "head on" with manufacturers of like products. The Court looked to the fact that the licensor had been engaged in negotiations with a prospective purchaser of the licensor's business. There was evidence to show that the prospective purchaser was only interested in purchasing the licensor's business if the business's principal asset, the licensed patent, was free of all licenses. The Court concluded that under these circumstances a jury could have concluded that the licensor and purchaser had a "unity of purpose" or "common understanding" that the licensee was to be excluded as a competitor. *International Wood Processors, supra. See also Mannington Mills v. Congoleum Indus., Inc.,* 610 F. 2d 1059, 1073 (3d Cir. 1979) ("Applying these principles, we think that a patentee's termination of a licensee, in concert with competing licensees, is not entitled to an antitrust exemption. . . . Where the patentee's anticompetitive conduct is undertaken after a number of non-exclusive licenses have been granted and in concert with competing licensees, however, there is a greater risk that the restriction is designed not to reward patent monopoly, but to increase the licensee's [sic] reward.").

Finally, the Court of Appeals for the Fourth Circuit has held that a bankrupt licensor may terminate an "executory" licensing contract to obtain better licensing terms in order to improve its situation in bankruptcy. The Court found that the licensor's unperformed, continuing obligations to notify licensee of further licensing under the patent, to notify licensee of infringement suits, and to forbear entrance into further licensing agreements with terms more favorable to a licensee meant that the contract was executory and could be rejected in bankruptcy. The Court also considered the fact that the licensee was under an obligation to undergo an independent quarterly audit to determine royalty payments in its determination that the contract was executory. *Lubrizol Enters. v. Richmond Metal Finishers,* 756 F.2d 1043 (4th Cir. 1985).

Therefore, although the Court observed that the terminated licensee was not without rights in that a suit for breach of contract could still be brought, it appears as though the financial position of the prospective licensor must now be considered before taking a license to use patented technology.

§ 10.04 Tied Restraints; Control of Unpatented Goods

Tying the sale of one unwanted, "tied" product or service to the sale of another wanted, "tying" product or service is a well-known Sherman Act Section 2 and Clayton Act Section 3 violation. From time to time there appears to be a judicial bias toward per se condemnation, rather than a rule of reason approach. The Department of Justice, however, has hinted that it will apply a rule of reason approach when it evaluates allegedly illegal tying arrangements:

> The use of tying will not be challenged if the party imposing the tie has a market share of *thirty percent* or less in the market for the tying product. This presumption can be overcome only by a showing that the tying agreement unreasonably restrained competition in the market for the tied product (emphasis added).

Department of Justice Guidelines—Vertical Distribution Restraints, [1985 Transfer Binder] Trade Reg. Rep. (CCH) ¶ 50,473 at 56,200 (April 15, 1985).

One description of the synthesis of the cases might be as follows: Tying is per se illegal if the court finds separate products tied, and legal if the court is persuaded that the two items are a single integrated whole to such a degree that it is unreasonable to treat the transaction as an illegal tie. After all, it would be legal to sell "breakfast," even if it were illegal to tie ham and eggs. *See United States v. Loew's, Inc.,* 371 U.S. 38, 135 U.S.P.Q. 201 (1962); *Brown Shoe Co. v. United States,* 370 U.S. 294 (1962); *Northern Pac. R.R. v. United States,* 356 U.S. 1 (1958); *International Salt Co. v. United States,* 332 U.S. 392, 75 U.S.P.Q. 184 (1947); *B.B. Chem. Co. v. Ellis,* 314 U.S. 495, 52 U.S.P.Q. 33 (1942); *Leitch Mfg. Co. v. Barber Co.,* 302 U.S. 458 (1938); *Carbice Corp. of Am. v. American Patents Dev. Corp.,* 283 U.S. 27 (1931); *Susser v. Carvel Corp.,* 332 F.2d 505, 141 U.S.P.Q. 609 (2d Cir.), *cert. granted,* 379 U.S. 885 (1964), *cert. dismissed,* 381 U.S. 125 (1965); *Dehydrating Process Co. v. A.O. Smith Corp.,* 292 F.2d 653 (1st Cir.), *cert. denied,* 368 U.S. 931 (1961); *Cummer-Graham Co. v. Straight Side Basket Corp.,*

142 F.2d 646 (5th Cir.), *cert. denied,* 323 U.S. 726 (1944); *Barber-Colman Co. v. National Tool Co.,* 136 F.2d 339, 58 U.S.P.Q. 2 (6th Cir. 1943) (tying sale price of unpatented article to grant of license to perform the patented method of producing the unpatented article); *Mid-America ICEE, Inc. v. John E. Mitchell Co.,* 1973–2 Trade Cas. (CCH) ¶ 74,681 (D. Or. 1973); *United States v. Jerrold Elecs. Corp.,* 187 F. Supp. 545 (E.D. Pa. 1960), *aff'd per curiam,* 365 U.S. 567 (1961); U.S. Attorney General's Report, Supplement, p. 106 (1968); Turner, *The Validity of Tying Arrangements under the Antitrust Laws,* 72 Harv. L. Rev. 50 (1958).

The Supreme Court has qualified the per se rule. In *Jefferson Parish Hospital Dist. No. 2 v. Hyde,* the Court held that tying arrangements are illegal per se when (1) the seller has market power in the tying market, (2) the tying and tied products are distinct and are not separately available in the marketplace, and (3) there is a substantial adverse effect in the tied product market due to the tying. *Jefferson Parish Hospital Dist. No. 2 v. Hyde,* 466 U.S. 2, 13–14 (1984).

The Supreme Court defined this special "market power" as the ability to control a particular market to such an extent so as to force a consumer into the purchase of the tied product.

> Per se condemnation—condemnation without inquiry into actual market conditions—is only appropriate if the existence of forcing is probable. Thus, application of the per se rule focuses on the probability of anticompetitive consequences.

Id. at 1560.

See also Will v. Comprehensive Accounting Corp., 776 F.2d 665 (7th Cir. 1985), *cert. denied,* 106 S. Ct. 1659 (1986) (Alleged tying of data processing to franchise. Court held that defendant did not have market power, and it was not established that there was a substantial danger that it would acquire market power in the tied product market.); *Ralph C. Wilson Indus., Inc. v. American Broadcasting Cos., Inc.,* 598 F. Supp. 694 (N.D. Cal. 1984), *aff'd,* 794 F.2d 1359 (9th Cir. 1986) (Court looked to fact that defendant did not have dominant market power as one reason to hold that exclusive licensing program was not a per se violation.); *Spartan Grain & Mill Co. v. Ayers,* 735 F.2d 1289 (11th Cir. 1984) (Seller of chicken feed did not have sufficient market power to support an antitrust claim). *But see Digidyne Corp. v. Data Gen. Corp.,* 734 F.2d 1336 (9th Cir. 1984), *cert. denied,* 473 U.S. 908, *reh'g denied,* 473 U.S. 926 (1985) (Court of Appeals held it is not necessary to show a market power over entire market for tying product, only that "an appreciable number of buyers" yielded to the tying arrangement. Further, the court held that the requisite economic power is presumed when the tying product is patented or copyrighted.).

The showing of "integrated whole" may sometimes be founded upon the need for assurance of associated equipment being compatible with the patented equipment. *Malsbary Mfg. Co. v. Ald, Inc.,* 310 F. Supp. 1112, 165 U.S.P.Q. 241 (N.D. Ill. 1970), *aff'd,* 447 F.2d 807, 171 U.S.P.Q. 7 (7th Cir. 1971); *Dehydrating Process Co. v. A.O. Smith Corp.,* 292 F.2d 653 (1st Cir.), *cert. denied,* 368 U.S. 931 (1961). Designing information or data processing systems that are only compatible with your own line of printers has been held not to be illegal tying. Technologically interrelated products do not constitute a per se unlawful tying arrangement. *Technicon Data Sys. Corp. v. Curtis 1000 Inc.,* 1984–2 Trade Cas. (CCH) § 66,260 (Del. Ch. 1984). *But see IBM Corp. v. United States,* 298 U.S. 131 (1936) (Lease rates for data processing machines conditioned upon purchase of punch cards manufactured by lessor held to be unlawful tying arrangement). *See also Berkey Photo, Inc. v. Eastman Kodak Co.,* 603 F.2d 263 (2d Cir. 1979), *cert. denied,* 444 U.S. 1093 (1980) (An integrated business does not offend the Sherman Act whenever one of its departments benefits from association with a division possessing a monopoly in its own market).

The Supreme Court has held that any inquiry into the validity of a tying arrangement must focus on the particular market in which the "tied" and "tying" products are sold. "Tying arrangements need only be condemned if they restrain competition on the merits by forcing purchases that would not otherwise be made. A lack of price or quality competition does not create this type of forcing." *Jefferson Parish Hospital Dist. No. 2 v. Hyde,* 466 U.S. 2 (1984).

Subject to the important qualification treated *infra* at § 10.05, tying is equally illegal when the "tying product" is a license under a patent that is granted only on condition of some staple commodity "tied product" being purchased from the patent owner—hornbook law rendered very sophisticated by the inducing/contributory infringement law of 35 U.S.C. § 271(b), (c), and (d). *International Salt Co. v. United States,* 332 U.S. 392, 75 U.S.P.Q. 184 (1947); *Mercoid Corp. v. Mid-Continent Investment Co.,* 320 U.S. 661, 60 U.S.P.Q. 21 (1944); *Mercoid Corp. v. Minneapolis-Honeywell Regulator Co.,* 320 U.S. 680, 60 U.S.P.Q. 30 (1944); *Morton Salt Co. v. G.S. Suppiger Co.,* 314 U.S. 488, 52 U.S.P.Q. 30 (1942); *IBM v. United States,* 298 U.S. 131 (1936); *Motion Picture Patents Co. v. Universal Film Mfg. Co.,* 243 U.S. 502 (1917); *United States v. Westinghouse Elec. Corp.,* 471 F. Supp. 532, 200 U.S.P.Q. 514 (N.D. Cal. 1978), *aff'd,* 648 F.2d 642 (9th Cir. 1981); *Sonobond Corp. v. Uthe Technology, Inc.,* 314 F. Supp. 878, 165 U.S.P.Q. 731 (N.D. Cal. 1970).

The District Court for the Northern District of New York confronted an interesting situation in which a patentee had licensed various manufacturers to use his patented mixture subject to a royalty based on the value of an end product. The patentee gave his licensees the option of purchasing other unpatented raw materials from him in return for a waiver of royalty payments. The patentee did not require that his licensees purchase the unpatented materials in order to obtain a license, he merely offered to not charge a royalty if they did. The Court held that such an arrangement did not run afoul of the antitrust laws. *U.S. Indus., Inc. v. Norton Co.,* 1985–1 Trade Cases (CCH) ¶ 66,341 (N.D.N.Y. 1985).

The conditioning of a trademark license on the licensee's use of a patented component from a designated supplier, when the licensor had a financial interest in the sales of the designated supplier, has been found to be a violation of the Sherman Act. *Ohio-Sealy Mattress Mfg. Co. v. Sealy, Inc.,* 585 F.2d 821, 200 U.S.P.Q. 337 (7th Cir. 1978), *cert. denied,* 440 U.S. 930 (1979).

But, illegal tying will not be found where a consumer would not perceive a product and a trademark as two separate items. *Power Test Petroleum Distribs., Inc. v. Calcu Gas, Inc.,* 754 F.2d 91 (2d Cir. 1985). *See also Bogosian v. Gulf Oil Corp.,* 561 F.2d 434 (3d Cir. 1977).

Unlawful "conditioning" by a patentee who offers only an implied or "label license"[7] to purchasers of an unpatented staple was found, pre-*Rohm & Haas,* even where no one asked for a patent license separate from the label license, which went with the unpatented staple made and sold by the patent owner. The Ninth Circuit held that a patentee who does not affirmatively offer a license program separate from the label license "runs the risk" of the court's finding an "implicit" tie-in. *Rex Chainbelt Inc. v. Harco Prods. Inc.,* 512 F.2d 993, 185 U.S.P.Q. 10 (9th Cir.), *cert. denied,* 423 U.S. 831 (1975). But it seems that this result would be different now, since the Supreme Court's opinion in *Dawson Chem. Co. v. Rohm & Haas Co.,* 448 U.S. 176, 206 U.S.P.Q. 385, *reh'g denied,* 448 U.S. 917 (1980) and the district court's opinion in *Rohm & Haas Co. v. Dawson Chem. Co.,* 557 F. Supp. 739, 217 U.S.P.Q. 515 (S.D. Tex. 1982), *rev'd on other grounds,* 722 F.2d 1556, 220 U.S.P.Q. 289 (Fed. Cir. 1983), discussed in Chapter 13, *infra.*

In *Fortner Enters. v. United States Steel Corp.,* 394 U.S. 495 (1969), the tying item was credit extended to buyers of prefabricated houses, and the Court found that summary judgment was improper because there was a question of whether U.S. Steel had the monopoly power in the credit market required for a Sherman Act violation. In a subse-

---

[7] "Label license" is a term used to identify a license, most commonly of a method-of-use patent, expressly granted on the label of the patentee's product (which is not covered by the patent), so that if the product is used in accordance with the label instructions the user infringes the patentee's method-of-use patent.

quent decision, *United States Steel Corp. v. Fortner Enters., Inc.,* 429 U.S. 610 (1977), the Court found that plaintiff had failed to establish the required economic power. Because the credit terms were not significantly different from other lenders, the conclusion that the defendant had appreciable economic power in the credit market was not supported.

A number of special justifications for ties have been identified, but they seem to be fickle theories to rely upon. In one case in which a manufacturer was able to show extreme customer dissatisfaction where his silo unloader had been matched up with silos by other manufacturers and customer satisfaction when they were sold together as a package, the justification was allowed. *Dehydrating Process Co. v. A.O. Smith Corp.,* 292 F.2d 653 (1st Cir.), *cert. denied,* 368 U.S. 931 (1961).

In *United States v. Jerrold Elecs. Corp.,* 187 F. Supp. 545 (E.D. Pa. 1960), *aff'd per curiam,* 365 U.S. 567 (1961), the court indicated that when a new product line is offered, service to that product line might justifiably be tied, but that justification expires as a separate service industry develops and becomes capable of rendering the service satisfactorily.

In *Electric Pipe Line, Inc. v. Fluid Sys., Inc.,* 231 F.2d 370, 109 U.S.P.Q. 24 (2d Cir. 1956), a warranty of performance of the package of components in an assembled whole was held in the particular context to be a justification for selling the entire group of parts. *Cf. Advance Business Sys. & Supply Co. v. SCM Corp.,* 415 F.2d 55 (4th Cir. 1969), *cert. denied,* 397 U.S. 920 (1970).

In *Ways & Means, Inc. v. IVAC Corp.,* 506 F. Supp. 697 (N.D. Cal. 1979), *aff'd per curiam,* 638 F.2d 143 (9th Cir.), *cert. denied,* 454 U.S. 895 (1981), the court held that a manufacturer's plan of renting an entire temperature taking system (including a thermometer, probe covers, other accessories, in-service training, and maintenance) wherein the user agreed to purchase 15,000 probe covers for the thermometer, did not constitute an illegal tying arrangement. The plan was held not to be illegal because both thermometers and probe covers were separately available to the customer, a substantial percentage of defendant's sales of thermometers were outside the plan, and the annual cost of a thermometer with 15,000 probe covers under the plan was more than the purchase of a thermometer from defendant and probe covers from plaintiff. Under these circumstances in which the tied and the tying product were each available separately at reasonable prices, the court stated that "no trier of fact could correctly conclude that an implicit tying arrangement existed by virtue of price manipulation." 506 F. Supp. at 703. In other words, there was no leverage exercised in effecting the alleged tie; hence, no violation.

Two cases, which do not technically come under the heading of examples of tying arrangements, demonstrate that "linking" or "leveraging" of the patent to unpatented products may result in antitrust liability.

In *SmithKline Corp. v. Eli Lilly & Co.,* 575 F.2d 1056 (3d Cir.), *cert. denied,* 439 U.S. 838 (1978), a violation of Section 2 of the Sherman Act was found on the basis of a marketing scheme that linked an unpatented drug with a group of patented drugs. Under the plan, Lilly offered a rebate when its customers purchased any three of its cephalosporins in specified quantities. No tie-in was established because there was no "conditioning" that the unpatented product be taken. However, because of the market circumstances, the unpatented product was usually taken in conjunction with Lilly's other two leading products.

The effect was that SmithKline, a competitor in the market for the unpatented drug, was forced to pay rebates on its one product equivalent to the rebates paid by Lilly based on volume sales of three products. The rebate program, in which patented products were linked to a "competitive product," was held to constitute an act of willful acquisition and maintenance of monopoly power.

In *United States v. Studiengesellschaft Kohle m.b.H.,* 200 U.S.P.Q. 389 (D.D.C. 1978), *rev'd,* 670 F.2d 1122, 212 U.S.P.Q. 889 (D.C. Cir. 1981), the trial court held the grant of an exclusive license to sell an unpatented product (produced by licensor's patented process), when the licensor had monopoly power and the arrangement was not reasonably necessary to any legitimate primary business purpose of the licensor or licensee, to be a violation of Section 1 of the Sherman Act. The lower court found a per se violation of Section 1 of the Sherman Act as a result of the use of the economic leverage of the patents covering the manufacturing processes by the licensor and licensee to restrain and prevent trade in the United States as to the unpatented goods.

On appeal, the court reversed, relying on the Supreme Court's rationale in *Continental T.V., Inc. v. GTE Sylvania, Inc.,* 433 U.S. 36 (1977), and characterized the decision below as "overly formalistic and insufficiently attentive to the real economic effects of the particular challenged restraint." 670 F.2d at 1129, 212 U.S.P.Q. at 897. Rejecting the proposition "that any restraint on products produced by a process patent is outside the protection of the patent laws and is illegal per se regardless of the effects of the restraint on the theory that licensing of the process exhausts the patentee's rights in that process," *id.,* the court held that the patentee has the "right to impose restrictions in a license that affect products that *were* made by its process." *Id.,* 433 U.S. at 1134, 212 U.S.P.Q. at 900.

By contrast, territorial restraints on the use of unpatented products of a patented process were held to be misuse in *Robintech, Inc. v. Chemidus Wavin, Ltd.,* 450 F. Supp. 823, 198 U.S.P.Q. 466 (D.D.C. 1978), *aff'd,* 628 F.2d 142, 205 U.S.P.Q. 873 (D.C. Cir. 1980).

The courts have also recognized that tying arrangements can constitute patent misuse, which renders a patent unenforceable, as well as an antitrust violation, which results in damages. *Senza-Gel Corp. v. Seiffhart,* 803 F.2d 661, 231 U.S.P.Q. 363, 368 (Fed. Cir. 1986).

In *Senza-Gel,* the court sustained a summary judgment holding of misuse where the patentee only licensed its process patent to companies that leased its machine, which was used in carrying out a step of the patented process.

The court held that a proper mode for analysis of a claim of patent misuse in a tying context included the following three step analysis:

(1) Determine whether there are two things tied, *i.e.,* whether there are separable or inseparable items; if so,

(2) Determine whether the "thing" that is assertedly tied to the patented item is a staple or nonstaple item in commerce; if staple,

(3) Determine whether in fact they are tied.

Senza-Gel, 231 U.S.P.Q. at 365.

Of course, a tie-out can be just as effective a control over unpatented goods as a tie-in. Thus, a patent licensor in many situations may not require a licensee to refrain from dealing in unpatented goods or goods patented to another. *F.C. Russell Co. v. Consumers Insulation Co.,* 226 F.2d 373, 107 U.S.P.Q. 131 (3d Cir. 1955); *McCullough v. Kammerer Corp.,* 166 F.2d 759, 76 U.S.P.Q. 503 (9th Cir.), *cert. denied,* 335 U.S. 813 (1948); *National Lockwasher Co. v. George K. Garrett Co.,* 137 F.2d 255, 58 U.S.P.Q. 460 (3d Cir. 1943); *Webstone Co. v. Daljack Indus., Inc.,* 220 U.S.P.Q. 513 (D. Mass 1982); *Robintech, Inc. v. Chemidus Wavin, Ltd.,* 450 F. Supp. 823, 198 U.S.P.Q. 466 (D.D.C. 1978); *Krampe v. Ideal Indus., Inc.,* 347 F. Supp. 1384, 175 U.S.P.Q. 688 (N.D. Ill. 1972). *But see Windsurfing Int'l Inc. v. AMF, Inc.,* 782 F.2d 995 (Fed. Cir.), *cert. denied,* 106 S. Ct. 3275 (1986) (court held that clause in a patent license agreement recognizing trademarks and agreeing not to use them is not a patent misuse).

However, the situation is often addressed by a clause requiring diligent development of a particular market by the licensee as a lawful primary business purpose. And such a clause often gives the licensor what he is entitled to—and often what he wants as well—even in the absence of a covenant of the licensee not to handle goods competing with those licensed.

§ 10.05 / Licensing

In the special circumstances of *General Fin. Corp. v. Dillion,* 172 F.2d 924, 80 U.S.P.Q. 341 (10th Cir. 1949), the court found an implied duty to diligently develop the market in patented items. But a contract clause is much more reliable than an implied duty, which often will not attach.

Be well advised, however, that side oral agreements to treat the diligent market development clause as the definition of areas in which there is to be no competition are going to make the writing as illegal as though the side oral agreement had been written. Additionally, a long-term lack of handling competing goods after the market has been diligently developed may, in some circumstances, be construed adversely unless some justification can be shown.

§ 10.05 Inducing and Contributory Infringement

There is a unique area of tying involving unpatented parts and supplies for patented inventions. The applicable law qualifies much of what is said in Chapter 12.

The early case law of inducing and contributory infringement evolved to its pinnacle of permissive tying in *Henry v. A.B. Dick Co.,* 224 U.S. 1 (1912), where a patentee was permitted to require as a condition of license that his licensee buy from the patentee unpatented consumable "staple commodity" supplies (paper and ink for a mimeograph machine) and/or component parts for the practice of the invention.

The theory: Since the patentee could lawfully preclude all infringement, there was no mischief in letting the patentee take his income from direct infringers via his profit on supplies and parts for the direct infringement rather than in royalties. These profits are in essence merely convenient alternative measurements of the licensee's use and society's enjoyment of the invention. Further, the knowing suppliers of the supplies or parts were deemed to be inducing infringers and/or contributory infringers, profiting from their inducement/contribution to tortious infringement. When they were consciously aware of or intended the direct infringement with their products, they were independently liable as co-tortfeasor infringers.

But the net effect of these licenses (whether expressed or implied by virtue of the manufacturer's failure to sue its customers) was restraint of trade in the unpatented supply or part. To antitrust purists who think in terms of what they have learned, rather than in terms of the substance of what is really going on, these restraints constituted an "extension of the patent monopoly."

Thus, there arose a line of cases evidencing the swing of the pendulum:

—From *A.B. Dick's* total permissiveness,

—swinging through *Motion Picture Patents Co. v. Universal Film Mfg. Co.,* 243 U.S. 502 (1917); *Carbice Corp. of Am. v. American Patents Dev. Corp.,* 283 U.S. 27 (1931); *Leitch Mfg. Co. v. Barber Co.,* 302 U.S. 458 (1938); and *B.B. Chem. Co. v. Ellis,* 314 U.S. 495, 52 U.S.P.Q. 33 (1942), and

—to the extreme of *Mercoid Corp. v. Mid-Continent Investment Co.,* 320 U.S. 661, 60 U.S.P.Q. 21 (1944); and *Mercoid Corp. v. Minneapolis-Honeywell Regulator Co.,* 320 U.S. 680, 60 U.S.P.Q. 30 (1944) (*Mercoid*).

In *Mercoid,* the Court used language that appeared to establish misuse as follows: even when the defendant has knowledge of his tortfeasing contribution to the direct infringement, if a patentee files suit for inducing or contributory infringement by the manufacturer of an unpatented supply or part for a patented invention, this suit is itself a patent misuse by virtue of its inherent effect of restraining trade in the unpatented supply or part. If anything remained of the venerable doctrines of inducing/contributory infringement and liabilities of such profiteering infringers as co-tortfeasors with the direct infringer, few if any could find it.

All the pendulum swings of this law in both directions were in the nature of legislation by the Supreme Court, which did not have in the records before it any evidence on the factual issues it was deciding—industry motivation and economic service to society. In 1952, Congress enacted 35 U.S.C. § 271 after extensive public hearings and drafts followed by hearings followed by redrafts, in which both supporters and critics of Section 271 construed it as reestablishing inducing/contributory infringement. Section 271 reads in part as follows:

(a) Except as otherwise provided in this title, whoever without authority makes, uses or sells any patented invention, within the United States during the term of the patent therefor, infringes the patent.

(b) Whoever actively induces infringement of a patent shall be liable as an infringer.

(c) Whoever sells a component of a patented machine, manufacture, combination or composition, or a material or apparatus for use in practicing a patented process, constituting a material part of the invention, knowing the same to be especially made or especially adapted for use in an infringement of such patent, and not a staple article or commodity of commerce suitable for substantial noninfringing use, shall be liable as a contributory infringer.

(d) No patent owner otherwise entitled to relief for infringement or contributory infringement of a patent shall be denied relief or deemed guilty of misuse or illegal extension of the patent right by reason of his having done one or more of the following:

(1) derived revenue from acts which if performed by another without his consent would constitute contributory infringement of the patent; (2) licensed or authorized another to perform acts which if performed without his consent would constitute contributory infringement of the patent; (3) sought to enforce his patent rights against infringement or contributory infringement.

But law, like mass, has inertia. Courts were reluctant to accept congressional change of Supreme Court law, and all the myriad variations upon the factual themes of inducing/contributory infringements and licenses relative thereto were not expressly covered in specific detail in the statute.

Various appellate courts wrote to the general effect that Section 271 did more to codify *Mercoid's* extreme than reverse it. *E.g., Rex Chainbelt Inc. v. Harco Prods., Inc.,* 512 F.2d 993, 185 U.S.P.Q. 10 (9th Cir.), *cert. denied,* 423 U.S. 831 (1975); *Rohm & Haas Co. v. Dawson Chem. Co.,* 191 U.S.P.Q. 691 (S.D. Tex. 1976), *rev'd,* 599 F.2d 685, 203 U.S.P.Q. 691 (5th Cir. 1979), *aff'd,* 448 U.S. 176, *reh'g denied,* 448 U.S. 917 (1980).

A Fifth Circuit reversal of the trial court decision was affirmed by a 5-to-4 divided Supreme Court, in *Dawson Chem. Co. v. Rohm & Haas Co.,* 448 U.S. 176, *reh'g denied,* 448 U.S. 917 (1980).

The Rohm and Haas patent was on a process of weed control in rice fields by spreading a prescribed dosage of propanil, a selective herbicide. Propanil has no substantial commercial use other than as a selective herbicide (used mostly to kill the weeds that grow in rice fields while not stunting the rice itself). Rohm and Haas manufactured propanil and sold it in containers with instructions on how to use it to practice the patented farming method, electing of course not to sue its customers. Thus the customers, by buying from Rohm and Haas, got, de facto, a freedom to use the invention (*i.e.,* an equivalent of a license). Farmers buying from other manufacturers of propanil, and the other manufacturers of propanil who also marketed in containers instructing how to infringe the patented farming process, got no license—a clear "conditioning" of the patent license upon the direct infringer's buying from the patentee as approved in *A.B. Dick,* but condemned in *Mercoid* as misuse, and then confused (strange as it seems) rather than resolved by the Congress's 1952 enactment of 35 U.S.C. § 271. Rohm and Haas declined to license competing manufacturers of propanil, asserting its unilateral right to not license.

The trial court found contributory infringement of the classic form condemned in Section 271(c), but nevertheless found misuse under *Mercoid,* which it deemed to be still the law. The court found that *Mercoid* at least required such a patentee to offer licenses to all comers (presumably at a law-determined reasonable royalty) in order to avoid misusing its patent in restraint of trade in the unpatented propanil.

The parties stipulated for purposes of the summary judgment motion on misuse, and in a subsequent trial it was found that propanil was not a staple commodity of commerce with any substantial noninfringing uses. The parties argued the summary judgment motion purely upon contributory infringement under Section 271(c) and (d), though inducing infringement under Section 271(b) is equally applicable to the subject facts.

Given that argument which omitted reference to inducing infringement under Section 271(b), the Supreme Court majority built its conclusion upon the legislative history of Section 271(c) and (d), with only little apparent awareness of Section 271(b). The Court majority rejected the trial court's misuse theme and found that Congress had sent no signal requiring compulsory licenses of patents but instead had sent a signal authorizing suit for contributory infringement.

If the injunctive relief given against contributory infringers results in an anticompetitive effect upon the unpatented good, propanil, that is the unavoidable result of the patent owner's doing what the statute authorizes him to do—just as all other enforcement of patents against direct infringers has an anticompetitive effect—and is not misuse of the patent.

If, now, we meld the clear scope of Section 271(b) into the picture as painted for Section 271(c) and (d), we come to this conclusion:

(1) *Mercoid* partly ~~reversed.~~ overruled. Insofar as a patentee may do business, (i) in a *non*staple commodity of commerce, (ii) with no substantial noninfringing use which (iii) is a material part of the invention, 35 U.S.C. § 271(c) has overturned *Mercoid*. There is no misuse in not granting licenses other than to the patentee's customers and concurrently suing contributory infringers and/or direct infringers who buy from them.

(2) *Mercoid* partly retained. Insofar as a patentee may do business in a commodity which fails any one of the requirements of Section 271(c), that is, which either is a staple commodity of commerce, which has sub-

130

stantial noninfringing uses, or that is not a material part of the invention (like paper is not a material part of a mimeograph machine invention though used in it), Section 271(c) does not reverse the *Mercoid* "its misuse" law.

of Consl

(3) New line by Section 271(b). But if the accused infringer is actively and knowingly inducing infringement with its product, it is clear under any reasonably consistent applications of Section 271(b) that he is liable and suit against him is no misuse, even if the product is a staple with noninfringing uses and not a material part of the invention—as in *A.B. Dick* with respect to knowingly inducing infringements.

That leaves the misuse law of *Mercoid* to apply where:

(1) there is no act of knowing or active inducement of the infringement; and
(2) the product fails one of the Section 271(c) criteria, that is, if it is either a staple, has noninfringing uses, or is not a material part of the invention.

This is not merely what the statute and Supreme Court have said; socially it is good law. This good law extends patent coverage to all those who knowingly contribute to or induce a direct infringement and profit from the direct infringement—which is the proper reward to the patentee, who invested high-risk R&D money to develop the invention. *I am't necessarily su...*

But it also permits no restraint of trade in that portion of the market for any good that is not known to be used in direct infringement; and it lets the manufacturer of staples make and sell on the open market without having to keep track of where its products go when some go into a direct infringement and some do not.

That, of course, is neither the *Mercoid* extreme nor the *A.B. Dick* extreme. It is the kind of middle line that a good Congress ought to have drawn, and which it did in fact draw—says the Supreme Court.

That is one reading of *Rohm & Haas.* Other lawyers express uncertainty as to whether this reading is the only reading in this sophisticated area.

The case then returned to the district court for trial of a myriad of issues, including inducing and contributory infringement and patent misuse. On October 27, 1982, the trial court wrote an opinion of some 268 pages, deciding all misuse issues in favor of the patentee. *Rohm & Haas Co. v. Dawson Chem. Co.,* 557 F. Supp. 739, 217 U.S.P.Q. 515 (S.D. Tex. 1982), *rev'd on other grounds,* 722 F.2d 1556, 220 U.S.P.Q. 289 (Fed. Cir. 1983).

The court found inducing infringement under Section 271(b) and contributory infringement under Section 271(c) and applied a rule of reason to Section 271(d) in that context, to a net effect consistent with the foregoing analysis of the Supreme Court's decision in *Dawson Chem. Co. v. Rohm & Haas Co., supra.*

§ 10.06 Royalties Based on Unpatented Subject Matter

Although not per se illegal, using the leverage of a patent to extort royalties on unpatented subject matter is a patent misuse.

For example, in *Zenith Radio Corp. v. Hazeltine Research, Inc.,* 395 U.S. 100, 161 U.S.P.Q. 577 (1969), Hazeltine offered to license Zenith on the condition that Zenith pay royalties on all television sets manufactured, regardless of whether the set employed any of Hazeltine's patented inventions. Zenith refused the license and was sued for patent infringement. The Supreme Court held that conditioning a license on payment of royalties based on final sales of a product that might not incorporate the patented invention is misuse. *Id.,* 395 U.S. at 135, 161 U.S.P.Q. at 591.

A royalty base broader than the patented subject matter is not objectionable if it serves the mutual convenience of both the licensee and the licensor, and provided the licensor does not condition the granting of the license on the broad base royalty while refusing to license on any other terms. *Id.,* 395 U.S. at 133–41, 161 U.S.P.Q. at 590–93.

In considering whether such a royalty base is merely a convenience for the parties, one factor is whether the patented component is regularly marketed by itself. If it is not, and if there is no other egregious conduct, an agreement basing royalties on sales of the finished product rather than on the fair market value of the patented component has been held to not be patent misuse. *Western Elec. Co. v. Stewart-Warner Corp.,* 631 F.2d 333, 208 U.S.P.Q. 183 (4th Cir. 1980), *cert. denied,* 450 U.S. 971 (1981).

To determine if there was "conditioning" by the licensor, courts look to see whether the license condition was the result of good faith bargaining between the parties or was imposed on the licensee by the patent holder, and whether the licensee raised objections that were overridden by the licensor. *Glen Mfg., Inc. v. Perfect Fit Indus., Inc.,* 420 F.2d 319, 321, 164 U.S.P.Q. 257, 258–59 (2d Cir.), *cert. denied,* 397 U.S. 1042 (1970); *Magnavox Co. v. Mattel, Inc.,* 24 Pat. Trademark & Copyright J. (BNA) 601 (N.D. Ill. 1982); *Leesona Corp. v. Varta Batteries, Inc.,* 522 F. Supp. 1304, 1341, 213 U.S.P.Q. 222, 253 (S.D.N.Y. 1981).

What can properly be included in a royalty base is limited only by the creativity of the parties, provided the royalty base is chosen for their mutual convenience and there is no conditioning.

If it can be shown that the entire market value of the whole is attributable to the patented component, royalties based on sale of the whole are proper. *See Paper Converting Mach. Co. v. FMC Corp.,* 432 F. Supp. 907, 195 U.S.P.Q. 123 (E.D. Wis. 1977), *aff'd mem.,* 588 F.2d 832 (7th Cir. 1978); *see also Westinghouse Elec. & Mfg. Co. v. Wagner Elec. & Mfg. Co.,* 225 U.S. 604 (1912). Further, it is not patent misuse for a multipatent licensing agreement to base royalties on the sale of all products using any of the inventions covered by the licensed patents, so long as the arrangement is designed to serve the parties' mutual convenience. *Leesona,* 522 F. Supp. at 1341, 213 U.S.P.Q. at 252–53.

The District Court for the Middle District of Tennessee held that a royalty structure based, in part, on sales of unpatented goods does not violate the antitrust laws where the royalty is only triggered by use of the patented process. *Miller Instituform, Inc. v. Instituform of N. Am., Inc.,* 605 F. Supp. 1125 (M.D. Tenn. 1985).

In summary, "the fact that royalties are paid on unpatented goods is not the test of misuse." *General Tire & Rubber Co. v. Firestone Tire & Rubber Co.,* 349 F. Supp. 333, 343, 174 U.S.P.Q. 427, 436 (N.D. Ohio 1972), *pet. denied,* 431 F.2d 1199 (6th Cir. 1970), *cert. denied,* 401 U.S. 975 (1974). "[T]he test for patent misuse is the purpose and effect of the royalty provision." *Id.*

§ 10.07 Price Fixing

Historically, the right of the patent owner to fix prices charged by his licensee for sale of the patented product was lawful. *United States v. General Elec. Co.,* 272 U.S. 476 (1926); *Cummer-Graham Co. v. Straight Side Basket Corp.,* 142 F.2d 646 (5th Cir.), *cert. denied,* 323 U.S. 726 (1944).

However, later cases have whittled away at the broad scope of the *General Electric* expression:

— *United States v. Line Material Co.,* 333 U.S. 287, 76 U.S.P.Q. 399 (1948), held that two or more patent owners could not combine their patents and, with the combination of patents, fix prices.

— *United States v. United States Gypsum Co.,* 333 U.S. 364, 76 U.S.P.Q. 430 (1948), held that all members of an industry may not be licensed under price-fixing licenses.

— *United States v. New Wrinkle, Inc.,* 342 U.S. 371, 92 U.S.P.Q. 158 (1952), elaborated to the effect that a major portion of the members of an industry may not be licensed with license-fixed prices.

— In further expansion, *Newburgh Moire Co. v. Superior Moire Co.,* 237 F.2d 283, 111 U.S.P.Q. 126 (3d Cir.

1956), held that more than one other member of the industry may not be licensed at fixed prices.

When almost the precise *General Electric* case was represented to the Supreme Court, a single manufacturer licensing a single licensee-competitor at fixed prices, the Supreme Court divided in a 4-to-4 split, one justice not sitting. *United States v. Huck Mfg. Co.*, 214 F. Supp. 776, 137 U.S.P.Q. 39 (E.D. Mich. 1963), *aff'd*, 382 U.S. 197, 147 U.S.P.Q. 404 (1965).

Thus, while in some cases an existing price-fixing license may be salvaged, it would be a rare circumstance where an informed lawyer would invite his client into this problem by permitting him to execute a new price-fixing license. *See Edward Katzinger Co. v. Chicago Metallic Mfg. Co.*, 329 U.S. 394, 72 U.S.P.Q. 18 (1947); *MacGregor v. Westinghouse Elec. & Mfg. Co.*, 329 U.S. 402, 72 U.S.P.Q. 21 (1947); *United States v. Masonite Corp.*, 316 U.S. 265, 53 U.S.P.Q. 396 (1942); *Tinnerman Prods., Inc. v. George K. Garrett Co.*, 185 F. Supp. 151 (E.D. Pa. 1960), *aff'd*, 292 F.2d 137, 129 U.S.P.Q. 438 (3d Cir.), *cert. denied*, 368 U.S. 833 (1961); *United States v. Vehicular Parking, Ltd.*, 54 F. Supp. 828, 61 U.S.P.Q. 102 (D. Del. 1944).

A striking contrast is *Broadcast Music, Inc. v. CBS*, 441 U.S. 1, 201 U.S.P.Q. 497 (1979), discussed in § 9.03, in which price fixing was an indirect effect of a licensing structure dictated by other considerations, and the license was sustained as lawful under the rule of reason.

§ 10.08 Quantity Restrictions

Restrictions on the quantity of licensed production have been both sustained and condemned, the condemnations often being justified by other aspects of the situation. *United States v. Studiengesellschaft Kohle m.b.H*, 670 F.2d 1122, 212 U.S.P.Q. 889 (D.C. Cir. 1981); *American Equip. Co. v. Tuthill Building Material Co.*, 69 F.2d 406 (7th Cir. 1934); *Rubber Tire Wheel Co. v. Milwaukee Rubber Works Co.*, 154 F. 358 (7th Cir. 1907), *appeal dismissed*, 210 U.S. 409

(1908); *Baldwin-Lima-Hamilton Corp. v. Tatnall Measuring Sys. Co.,* 169 F. Supp. 1 (E.D. Pa. 1958), *aff'd per curiam,* 268 F.2d 395 (3d Cir.), *cert. denied,* 361 U.S. 894 (1959); *United States v. E. I. duPont de Nemours & Co.,* 118 F. Supp. 41, 99 U.S.P.Q. 462 (D. Del. 1953), *aff'd on other grounds,* 351 U.S. 377 (1956); *Q-Tips, Inc. v. Johnson & Johnson,* 109 F. Supp. 657, 95 U.S.P.Q. 258 (D.N.J. 1951), *modified,* 207 F.2d 509, 99 U.S.P.Q. 183 (3d Cir. 1953), *cert. denied,* 347 U.S. 935 (1954); *United States v. General Elec. Co.,* 82 F. Supp. 753, 80 U.S.P.Q. 195 (D.N.J. 1949).

Those who write for law reviews on this topic seem too often to equate quantity limitations with price fixing and condemn them both. But the rule of reason should support the legality of quantity restrictions in at least a number of situations which can be imagined—like a small appliance manufacturer licensing a major such as General Electric for an electric carving knife and limiting General Electric to not more than twice the production that the licensor is able to produce—thereby to assure (lawful purpose?) that the licensor is able to retain at least *some* competitive place in the market without being totally eliminated by the market might of his own licensee.

§ 10.09   Field of Use Restrictions

Historically, the patent owner was viewed as entitled to license his patent for limited areas of use. *See General Talking Pictures Corp. v. Western Elec. Co.,* 305 U.S. 124 (1938), still being cited with approval in *A. & E. Plastik Pak Co. v. Monsanto Co.,* 396 F.2d 710, 715 (9th Cir. 1968) ("The holder of a patent can validly license it to others on the condition that they use it only for certain purposes."); and *Chemagro Corp. v. Universal Chem. Co.,* 244 F. Supp. 486, 489, 146 U.S.P.Q. 466 (E.D. Tex. 1965) (Patent owner or licensee may limit use in a defined field).

The rule still seems to be applicable, at least when the primary purpose of the restriction is shown to be increased financial return to the inventor for the use of his invention.

However, the licensing pattern must not divide a naturally competitive market.

For example, if the patented invention is in bearings, a license to one full-line electric motor manufacturer like G.E., for bearings to be used in motors of under five horsepower, while to another equally full-line manufacturer, for motors of more than five horsepower, would divide a naturally competitive market; perhaps with no increase in return to the patent owner. In some situations it might be argued that the primary purpose or effect of this licensing pattern was more the illegal one.

On the other hand, to grant an exclusive license to an electric motor manufacturer for electric motors, another license to Pratt and Whitney for aircraft engines, and still another to Johnson for boat motors, when none of the licensed fields of use compete with each other and the grant of exclusive licenses in the subject areas will return more money to the patentee, would not seem to have any anticompetitive effect, and should surely be lawful.

But the "field of use" theme can clearly be carried too far, and into applications where it does not fit. This is seen by the apparent inconsistency between *Chemagro, supra; United States v. Glaxo Group,* 302 F. Supp. 1, 162 U.S.P.Q. 513 (D.D.C. 1969), *rev'd on other grounds,* 410 U.S. 52 (1973); and *Munters Corp. v. Burgess Indus. Inc.,* 450 F. Supp. 1195, 194 U.S.P.Q. 146 (S.D.N.Y. 1977), *on reh'g,* 201 U.S.P.Q. 756 (S.D.N.Y. 1978).

In *Chemagro,* the patent was on an agricultural and lawn and garden insecticide, apparently deemed safe in 10 percent concentrations when used by agricultural professionals but not safe in that concentration when used by the home gardener—for whom a 2 percent concentration was the recommended product. The patent owner produced the 10 percent product, sold it in packages bearing a license restriction that it not be repackaged and resold for the home and garden market in 2 percent concentrations—which is exactly what defendant did. The court there approved the label

137

license restriction, apparently against a weak argument by the defendant.

By contrast, in *Glaxo,* involving a pharmaceutical, a division of the dosage market from the bulk sales market by a licensing pattern was held to be unlawful. *See also United States v. Bristol-Myers Co.,* 82 F.R.D. 655 (D.D.C. 1979), in which pursuant to a consent decree, defendants Beecham Group, Ltd. of England, and Beecham, Inc., were required to sell ampicillin in bulk quantities for the life of the patent. *But cf. United States v. Ciba Geigy Corp.,* 508 F. Supp. 1118 (D.N.J. 1976), in which certain bulk sales restrictions were held legal if for the purpose of protecting the patentee.

And finally, in *Munters,* we see the "exhaustion of patent" theme applied to produce a result inconsistent with *Chemagro.* Munters made and sold patented "Munters Fill," a material used for various purposes, including use in evaporative air cooling units. Munters sold Munters Fill to Buffalo Forge Co., its exclusive licensee for the air cooling field of use. Another customer, Burgess, bought Munters Fill and commenced the same use.

An obvious conflict arose over Buffalo's exclusive field of use license to use in air cooling units, and Burgess's feeling that it was entitled to any use of the commodity sold by the patentee. So Munters filed a declaratory judgment action to resolve its problem of loyalty to its exclusive licensee and customer.

The court held that when the product had once been made and sold under the authority of the patent, the patent right had been exhausted and there no longer existed any patent right to preclude others from use, and no right exclusively to license the field of use. The original opinion found a violation under the per se rule of *United States v. Arnold, Schwinn & Co.,* 388 U.S. 365 (1967). On rehearing after *Continental T.V., Inc. v. GTE Sylvania, Inc.,* 433 U.S. 36 (1977), the court again found the license to be a violation, this time under the rule of reason.

The facts surrounding exploitation of process inventions of course do not fit these cases squarely, and to license a patented process of manufacture for use in making one product only, and again for making another product only, would at least commonly be lawful. *But see United States v. Bandag, Inc.,* No. 77-210-G (M.D.N.C. May 6, 1977), in which the legality of a lawsuit settlement involving a process patent and an allocation of markets thereunder was challenged, but subsequently dismissed by stipulation because the allegedly anticompetitive provisions had been abandoned.

Restrictions on use of the products produced by the patented process and then sold would be only rarely distinguishable in result from that of *Glaxo* and *Munters,* in which the right to restrain use was held to be exhausted by the first sale under the authority of the patent owner and the alleged field of use restriction was held to be improper.

Some other cases of interest relative to field of use licenses include *Hensley Equip. Co. v. Esco Corp.,* 383 F.2d 252 (5th Cir. 1967); *Armstrong v. Motorola, Inc.,* 374 F.2d 764, 152 U.S.P.Q. 535 (7th Cir.), *cert. denied,* 389 U.S. 830 (1967); *Bela Seating Co. v. Poloron Prods., Inc.,* 297 F. Supp. 489, 160 U.S.P.Q. 646 (N.D. Ill. 1968), *aff'd,* 438 F.2d 733, 168 U.S.P.Q. 548 (7th Cir.), *cert. denied,* 403 U.S. 922 (1971); *Barr Rubber Prods. Co. v. Sun Rubber Co.,* 277 F. Supp. 484, 156 U.S.P.Q. 374 (S.D.N.Y. 1967), *aff'd in part and rev'd in part,* 425 F.2d 1114, 165 U.S.P.Q. 429 (2d Cir.), *cert. denied,* 400 U.S. 878 (1970); *Benger Laboratories, Ltd. v. Laros Co.,* 209 F. Supp. 639, 135 U.S.P.Q. 11 (E.D. Pa. 1962), *aff'd,* 317 F.2d 455, 137 U.S.P.Q. 693 (3d Cir.), *cert. denied,* 375 U.S. 833 (1963); *Eversharp Inc. v. Fisher Pen Co.,* 204 F. Supp. 649, 132 U.S.P.Q. 423 (N.D. Ill. 1961); *Baldwin-Lima-Hamilton Corp. v. Tatnall Measuring Sys. Co.,* 169 F. Supp. 1 (E.D. Pa. 1958), *aff'd per curiam,* 268 F.2d 395 (3d Cir.), *cert. denied,* 361 U.S. 894 (1959); *Deering, Milliken & Co. v. Temp-Resisto Corp.,* 160 F. Supp. 463, 116 U.S.P.Q. 386 (S.D.N.Y. 1958), *rev'd on other grounds,* 274 F.2d 626, 124 U.S.P.Q. 147 (2d Cir. 1960); *United States v. Birdsboro Steel Foundry & Mach. Co.,* 139 F. Supp. 244, 108 U.S.P.Q. 428 (W.D. Pa. 1956); *Carter-Wallace, Inc. v. United States,* 449 F.2d 1374 (Ct. Cl. 1971); *Lanova Corp. v. Atlas Imperial*

Diesel Engine Co., 55 A.2d 272, 75 U.S.P.Q. 225 (Del. Super. Ct. 1947); *see also Atlas Imperial Diesel Engine Co. v. Lanova Corp.,* 79 F. Supp. 1002, 78 U.S.P.Q. 319 (D. Del. 1948).

Analogizing field of use restrictions, the court in *Ciba-Geigy Corp. v. Bolar Pharmaceutical Co.,* 212 U.S.P.Q. 712 (E.D.N.Y. 1981), held that a patentee may refuse to license a patented drug in combination with an unpatented product. Ciba owned a patent for the compound hydrochlorothiazide (HCT), and granted individual licenses to manufacture, use, and sell HCT in straight dosage form and in any combination dosage form except in combination with hydralazine, the subject of an expired patent.

Ciba argued that this licensing practice did not attempt to condition the licensing of HCT upon the use of hydralazine or any other product and hence was not a tying arrangement. Rather, Ciba was excepting from the license grant one use of HCT, namely use in combination with hydralazine—a limited license similar to the field of use restriction upheld in *General Talking Pictures Corp. v. Western Elec. Co.,* 305 U.S. 124 (1938). The court held:

> If Ciba has a valid patent for HCT, it has a monopoly in HCT. . . . Ciba may if it chooses, license some but not all uses for HCT. . . . To hold otherwise would mean Ciba would be forced either to license all uses of the [HCT] patent or to forego licensing altogether. . . . [The effect of Ciba's licensing practices in the market] is a direct result of the HCT monopoly created by [Ciba's] patent.

212 U.S.P.Q. at 713.

§ 10.10 Territorial Restrictions

Unlike trade secret, know-how, and trademark law, *statutory* patent law specifically provides for territorial restrictions. Section 261 of United States Code, Title 35, states that:

> The applicant, patentee, or his assigns or legal representatives may in like manner [*i.e.,* by instrument in writing] grant and

convey an exclusive right under his application for patent, or patents, to the whole *or any specified part of the United States.*

35 U.S.C § 261 (emphasis added).

This statutory approval for territorial restrictions within the United States in patent licenses seems to be anathema to many judges, and not infrequently you will find a judicial expression that goes directly into the teeth of this solid pronouncement of congressional policy. Even so, territorial limits in patent licenses to manufacture are clearly lawful in the United States. *Dunlop Co. v. Kelsey-Hayes Co.,* 484 F.2d 407, 179 U.S.P.Q. 129 (6th Cir. 1973), *cert. denied,* 415 U.S. 917 (1974); *Brownell v. Ketcham Wire & Mfg. Co.,* 211 F.2d 121, 100 U.S.P.Q. 338 (9th Cir. 1954); *Blohm & Voss AG v. Prudential-Grace Lines, Inc.,* 346 F. Supp. 1116, 174 U.S.P.Q. 484 (D. Md. 1972), *rev'd on other grounds,* 489 F.2d 231, 180 U.S.P.Q. 165 (4th Cir. 1973), *cert. denied,* 419 U.S. 840 (1974).

But the lawful right to grant an exclusive patent license to manufacture, use, and sell, for example, in California, does not also include the right to specify the territory for resale after the patented product has passed out of the hands of the patent owner and/or the licensed manufacturer. *United States v. Bausch & Lomb Optical Co.,* 321 U.S. 707, 61 U.S.P.Q. 61 (1944); *Ansul Co. v. Uniroyal, Inc.,* 306 F. Supp. 541, 163 U.S.P.Q. 517 (S.D.N.Y. 1969), *aff'd in part and rev'd and remanded in part,* 448 F.2d 872, 169 U.S.P.Q. 759, 170 U.S.P.Q. 549 (2d Cir. 1971), *cert. denied,* 404 U.S. 1018 (1972); *United States v. Serta Assocs. 296 F. Supp. 1121, 160 U.S.P.Q. 142 (N.D. Ill. 1968), aff'd,* 393 U.S. 534, 160 U.S.P.Q. 142, *reh'g denied,* 394 U.S. 967 (1969); *United States v. National Lead Co.,* 63 F. Supp. 513, 66 U.S.P.Q. 141 (S.D.N.Y. 1945), *aff'd,* 332 U.S. 319, 73 U.S.P.Q. 498 (1947).

While there are many variations of the "restrictions on resale" theme, the issue of whether the product involved is patented or not does not seem to be a controlling one. *See United States v. Arnold, Schwinn & Co.,* 388 U.S. 365 (1967), later modified by *Continental T.V., Inc. v. GTE Sylvania, Inc.,* 433 U.S. 36 (1977); *see also Adolph Coors Co. v. A & S Wholesalers, Inc.,* 561 F.2d 807 (10th Cir. 1977); *Hensley Equipment Co. v. Esco Corp.,* 383 F.2d 252, 155 U.S.P.Q. 183 (5th Cir. 1967); *American Industrial Fastener Corp. v. Flushing Enters., Inc.,* 362 F. Supp. 32, 179 U.S.P.Q. 722 (N.D. Ohio 1973). The mere fact that territorial restrictions are imposed upon licensees cannot form the basis of an antitrust claim when the party asserting the claim lacks standing under Section 4 of the Clayton Act. *Reinke Mfg. Co. v. Sidney Mfg. Corp.,* 446 F. Supp. 1056, 199 U.S.P.Q. 401 (D. Neb. 1978), *aff'd,* 594 F.2d 644, 201 U.S.P.Q. 344 (8th Cir. 1979) (antitrust counterclaim cannot be maintained by defendant when license agreements in question were executed and terminated before defendant entered the market since these restrictions could not have injured defendant's business or property).

Schwinn, as interpreted by other courts, did not outlaw location clauses restricting a retailer or distributor to sell out of only one specified place of business, but did declare that any restriction by a manufacturer upon a distributor or dealer to whom title, dominion, and risk had passed was a per se antitrust violation if it restricted either the class of customers to whom resales could be made (*e.g.,* no sales to other retailers) or restricted the territory into which the product could be delivered upon resale. If the manufacturer transaction with the distributor or dealer was one of consignment in which title, dominion, and risk were retained by the manufacturer, the per se rule did not apply under *Schwinn.*

In *Continental T.V. v. Sylvania,* the Supreme Court expressly reversed the distinction between transactions in which title, dominion, and risk all passed and those in which all, or some of them, did not. Further, the Court expressly held that vertically imposed locations clauses are subject to the rule of reason, leading any reader to believe that as applied to the Sylvania distributorship it was reasonable.

From there on, the ultimate meaning of the opinion becomes more obscure. But the total reversal of *Schwinn's* per se rule, in favor of rule of reason, as applied to all true vertically imposed territorial restrictions, is at least one logical construction of *Sylvania*. And while it appears that the Court may have restored restrictions as to class of customers to the rule of reason category, both from this opinion and others of recent vintage one can draw no less than a hesitant attitude toward class-of-customer restrictions. For examples of the impact of *Sylvania, see Eiberger v. Sony Corp. of Am.,* 622 F.2d 1068 (2d Cir. 1980); *Eastern Scientific Co. v. Wild Heerbrugg Instruments, Inc.,* 572 F.2d 883 (1st Cir.), *cert. denied,* 439 U.S. 833 (1978); *General Beverage Sales Co. v. East-Side Winery,* 568 F.2d 1147 (7th Cir. 1978); *Donald B. Rice Tire Co. v. Michelin Tire Corp.,* 483 F. Supp. 750 (D. Md. 1980), *aff'd per curiam,* 638 F.2d 15 (4th Cir. 1981), *cert. denied,* 454 U.S. 864 (1981).

Query: In view of 35 U.S.C. § 261 quoted above, has *Sylvania* any application to patent or know-how license situations? It seems clear that territorial restrictions in the patent license are legitimized by Section 261 when applied to territory of manufacture, use before first sale, or first sale.

In know-how or trade secret licenses, one guess is that the rule of reason would apply, with bias in favor of legality in roughly direct proportion to the strength, confidentiality, and general viability of the know-how and trade secrets. *Cf. Shin Nippon Koki Co. v. Irvin Indus. Inc.,* 186 U.S.P.Q. 296 (N.Y. Sup. Ct. 1975). A word of caution—the territorial restrictions in such a license probably ought to expire with or soon after the expiration of secrecy of the information— which is a contract often hard to draft.

But after the first sale under the authority of the patent owner (or the know-how or trade secret owner or the authority of that owner's licensee), further restraint on either territory or class of customers would be subjected to a rule of reason examination at best. And given the doctrine of exhaustion of the patent monopoly discussed elsewhere, the rule of reason analysis is likely to result in a conclusion of illegality of the restraints after first sale.

For further treatment of territorial restrictions in international technology agreements, the reader's attention is directed to papers by Richard H. Stern, formerly of the Department of Justice, appearing in Les Nouvelles, The Licensing Executive Society Newsletter, Volume 5, No. 5, November 1970 issue, at page 221; also Stern's parallel paper, July-August 1970 APLA Bulletin; and by Ford F. Farabow, Jr., and Brian G. Brunsvold, appearing in Licensing Law and Business Report, Volume 1, No. 1, May 1978 issue, at page 1. *See also Robintech, Inc. v. Chemidus Wavin, Ltd.,* 450 F. Supp. 823, 198 U.S.P.Q. 466 (D.D.C. 1978), *aff'd,* 628 F.2d 142, 205 U.S.P.Q. 873, 879 (D.C. Cir. 1980) (export limitation clause of license agreement restricting export of staple product made in U.S. by patented process to any part of the world except Great Britain constitutes a patent misuse); *Van Dyk Research Corp. v. Xerox Corp.,* 631 F.2d 251, 254–55 (3d Cir. 1980), *cert. denied,* 452 U.S. 905 (1981) (even if defendant may be in violation of antitrust law by virtue, *inter alia,* of participating in an international cartel, plaintiff must prove that the illegality was a material cause of its injury); *Mannington Mills, Inc. v. Congoleum Indus. Inc.,* 610 F.2d 1059, 203 U.S.P.Q. 81, 83 (3d Cir. 1979) (allegation that Congoleum conspired with certain of its foreign licensees to terminate Mannington's foreign sales licenses states a claim on which relief may be granted under Section 1 of the Sherman Act).

In *Dunlop Co. v. Kelsey-Hayes Co.,* 484 F.2d 407 (6th Cir. 1973), *cert. denied,* 415 U.S. 917 (1974), the court held that territorial restrictions in a foreign patent license prohibiting exportation of patented goods from foreign manufacturers into the U.S. did not violate the antitrust laws. In dicta, the court stated that if 35 U.S.C. § 261 permits a patentee to grant territorial licenses in the United States, then clearly a patentee could do the same thing with foreign licenses without violating the antitrust laws of this country. *Id.* at 417.

And particularly note the decision in *Zenith Radio Corp. v. Hazeltine Research, Inc.,* 395 U.S. 100, 161 U.S.P.Q. 577 (1969). The facts there interrelate patent pools, package licensing, royalties on gross sales of both patented and unpatented goods, and territorial restrictions.

A group of Canadian companies, mostly subsidiaries of United States companies, formed a pool of about 5,000 patents, granted only package licenses, and refused to license imported goods. The Supreme Court found that the clear purpose of this arrangement was to exclude concerns like Zenith from the Canadian market unless they were willing to manufacture there. In this context, the territorial limitation that Zenith would be granted a license only if it manufactured in Canada was held to be a treble damages antitrust violation.

It is noteworthy that the patent statute authorizing territorial restrictions to parts of the United States does not address territorial market lines between the United States and Canada, the United States and Europe, and so forth.

An interesting twist on this theme is *Sanofi, S.A. v. MedTech Veterinarian Prods.,* 565 F. Supp. 931, 220 U.S.P.Q. 416 (D.N.J. 1983). Sanofi granted American Home Prods. (AHP) an exclusive license under its U.S. patent to sell acepromazine maleate for use in treating animals in the veterinary field. Sanofi also supplied the patented drug to a German company, which in turn resold it to a company in Kansas. Sanofi and AHP sued for infringement and moved for a preliminary injunction.

The court held that the patentee's unrestricted sale abroad constituted a waiver of its right to exclude the patented product from the U.S. However, such a sale by the patentee does not preclude an exclusive licensee from keeping the product out of the country because the foreign purchaser could acquire no more rights to make, use, and sell in the U.S. than the patentee that sold the product. The court granted AHP a preliminary injunction.

In *United States v. Westinghouse Elec. Corp.,* 471 F. Supp. 532, 200 U.S.P.Q. 514 (N.D. Cal. 1978), *aff'd,* 648 F.2d 642 (9th Cir. 1981), the government attacked territorial market lines effected by Westinghouse's refusal to license its U.S.

and Canadian patents while licensing its other foreign patents to the Mitsubishi companies.

Drawing an analogy to the Second Circuit Court of Appeals decision in *SCM Corp. v. Xerox Corp.*, 645 F.2d 1195, 209 U.S.P.Q. 889 (2d Cir. 1981), *cert. denied*, 455 U.S. 1016 (1982), the Ninth Circuit Court of Appeals rejected the government's contention, stating:

> To find an antitrust violation because Westinghouse, having licensed its foreign patents to Mitsubishi, has thereby helped them to become potential competitors in the United States, but has not granted them licenses of its United States patents, which they need in order to compete here, would severely limit the protection extended by Congress in the laws under which Westinghouse's United States patents were granted. The antitrust laws do not grant the government a roving commission to reform the economy at will. Just as "[n]o court has ever held that the antitrust laws require a patent holder to forfeit the exclusionary power inherent in his patent the instant his patent monopoly affords him monopoly power . . .," *SCM Corporation v. Xerox Corporation*, 2 Cir., 1981, 645 F.2d 1195, 1204, so, too, no court has held that a patentee must grant further licenses to potential competitors merely because he has granted them some licenses. Just as "[t]he patent system would be seriously undermined . . . were the threat of potential antitrust liability to attach upon the acquisition of a patent at a time prior to the existence of the relevant market and, even more disconcerting, at a time prior to the commercialization of the patented art," *Id.* at 1206, so too would the patent system be undermined if a licensing agreement, perfectly legal when signed, might later form the basis of an antitrust violation because the licensee had flourished under the agreement.
>
> We agree with the district court that the government's theory "[t]aken to its logical limits . . . would find almost every patent licensing agreement to be illegal."

648 F.2d at 648.

In *United States v. Sealy, Inc.*, 388 U.S. 350, 153 U.S.P.Q. 763 (1967), and again in *United States v. Topco Assocs. Inc.*, 405 U.S. 596, 173 U.S.P.Q. 193 (1972), the Supreme Court found a horizontal conspiracy to be the underlying purpose of the arrangement for territorial restrictions in trademark licenses. So finding, the Court held that the territorial restrictions under cover of a trademark license were per se illegal, even though the trial court had found the arrangement to be pro-competitive in the given industry involved in *Topco.*

Furthermore, the allocation of markets may not be accomplished with the use of otherwise legal devices such as pass-over payments, rights of first refusal, exclusive manufacturing licenses, and areas of primary responsibility, at least when the arrangement is essentially a horizontal one. And an arrangement will be considered horizontal if the party imposing the restriction is not truly independent from the party restricted. *Ohio Sealy Mattress Mfg. Co. v. Sealy, Inc.,* 585 F.2d 821, 200 U.S.P.Q. 337 (7th Cir. 1978), *cert. denied,* 440 U.S. 930 (1979).

In *JBL Enters., Inc. v. Jhirmack Enters., Inc.,* 509 F. Supp. 357, 210 U.S.P.Q. 438, 441–43 (N.D. Cal. 1981), *aff'd,* 698 F.2d 1011 (9th Cir.), *cert. denied,* 464 U.S. 829 (1983), the court assumed *arguendo* that defendant imposed customer and territorial restrictions on the sale of its trademarked products by its distributors, performed a rule of reason analysis, and found plaintiff failed to demonstrate that defendant's conduct had an impact on competition in the relevant market. Plaintiff merely demonstrated injury to a single competitor, rather than to competition, and that injury was found to have resulted from an increase in competition, rather than a restraint on competition.

There remains some authority that a territorial restriction in a vertical trademark license may be lawful, but those cases are not the most recent and must now be reevaluated in light of *Sealy, Topco, Schwinn,* and *Sylvania* and the particular facts involved in the given market situation and license.

For example, in *In re Coca-Cola Co.,* 91 F.T.C. 517 (1978), *rev'd sub nom. Coca-Cola Co. v. FTC,* 642 F.2d 1387 (D.C. Cir. 1981); and *In re PepsiCo, Inc.,* 91 F.T.C. 680 (1978), *rev'd sub nom, Coca-Cola Co. v. FTC,* 642 F.2d 1387

(D.C. Cir. 1981), the FTC decided that certain exclusive territories in the soft drink industry were illegal. Applying the rule of reason, the Commission distinguished between drinks sold in nonrefillable containers and drinks in refillable containers. Rejecting the argument that such restrictions were necessary for quality control as well as the administrative judge's finding that such restrictions were pro-competitive, the Commission found the restrictions unreasonable as applied to nonrefillable containers because there was no adequate justification for the substantial adverse effects these restraints had in the industry. The Commission also looked at intrabrand and interbrand competition to conclude that elimination of intrabrand competition had adverse effects on interbrand competition.

As applied to refillable containers, the commission held the territorial restrictions to be permissible because of the bottler's need to anticipate the number of reusable bottles that might be returned.

During appeal of the FTC determinations in *Coca-Cola* and *PepsiCo,* after oral argument but before an opinion issued, Congress responded to these FTC determinations by enacting the Soft Drink Interbrand Competition Act, 15 U.S.C. §§ 3501–3503 (1980) "to clarify the circumstances under which territorial provisions in licenses to manufacture, distribute, and sell trademark soft drink products are unlawful under the antitrust laws." S. Rep. No. 645, 96th Cong., 2d Sess. 1 (1980); H. R. Rep. No. 1118, 96th Cong., 2d Sess. 1 (1980), *both reprinted in* 1980 U.S. Code Cong. & Ad. News 4391.

Section 3501 of the Act provides:

Nothing contained in any antitrust law shall render unlawful the inclusion and enforcement in any trademark licensing contract or agreement, pursuant to which the licensee engages in the manufacturer (including manufacture by a sublicensee, agent, or subcontractor), distribution, and sale of a trademarked soft drink product, of provisions granting the licensee the sole and exclusive right to manufacture, distribute, and sell such product in a defined geographic area or limiting the licensee, directly or indirectly, to the manufacture, distribution, and sale of such product only for ultimate resale to consumers within a defined geographic area: *Provided,* That such product is in substantial and effective competition with other products of the same general class in the relevant market or markets.

All parties to the appeal agreed that the Act controlled. Accordingly, the court dismissed the complaints and set aside the FTC orders. *See also First Beverages, Inc. v. Royal Crown Cola Co.,* 612 F.2d 1164 (9th Cir.), *cert. denied,* 447 U.S. 924 (1980).

§ 10.11 Package Licensing; Uniform Royalties; "Conditioned" Terms

Voluntary package licensing designed for the convenience of the parties to the license agreement and involving no element of coercion and no extension of the scope of the licensed patents still appears to be lawful. *Well Surveys, Inc. v. Perfo-Log, Inc.,* 396 F.2d 15, 158 U.S.P.Q. 119 (10th Cir.), *cert. denied,* 393 U.S. 951 (1968); *Automatic Radio Mfg. Co. v. Hazeltine Research, Inc.,* 339 U.S. 827, 85 U.S.P.Q. 378 (1950). For example, in *Playskool, Inc. v. Famus Corp.,* 212 U.S.P.Q. 8, 16 (S.D.N.Y. 1981), the court upheld a license agreement that included all past, present, and future trademarks and patents against a claim of compulsory packaging absent a showing of coercion. The same principles apply to a trademark licensing agreement. *Ohio-Sealy Mattress Mfg. Co. v. Sealy, Inc.,* 585 F.2d 821, 200 U.S.P.Q. 337 (7th Cir. 1978), *cert. denied,* 440 U.S. 930 (1979).

Further, the licensor is under no obligation to renegotiate for an individual licensing scheme if the licensee later becomes dissatisfied with the package license. *Hull v. Brunswick Corp.,* 704 F.2d 1195, 218 U.S.P.Q. 24 (10th Cir. 1983).

In such a package license, it appears to remain lawful for the royalties to be at a constant level for the life of the last to expire of the patents, so long as this was not coerced out of the licensee by the use of leverage (in the nature of a tie-in).

Hull v. Brunswick Corp., supra; *Beckman Instruments, Inc. v. Technical Dev. Corp.,* 433 F.2d 55, 167 U.S.P.Q. 10 (7th Cir. 1970), *cert. denied,* 401 U.S. 976 (1971); *GAF Corp. v. Eastman Kodak Co.,* 519 F. Supp. 1203, 213 U.S.P.Q. 356 (S.D.N.Y. 1981); *Cohn v. Compax Corp.,* 87 A.D. 2d 364, 451 N.Y.S. 2d 171, 1982–2 Trade Cas. (CCH) ¶ 64,800 (N.Y. App. Div. 1982).

Compulsory package licensing is, of course, an illegal tying of one patent license to others in the package. It is a patent misuse and in context of other elements may also be an antitrust violation. *Duplan Corp. v. Deering Milliken, Inc.,* 444 F. Supp. 648, 197 U.S.P.Q. 342 (D.S.C. 1977), *aff'd in part, rev'd in part on other grounds,* 594 F.2d 979, 201 U.S.P.Q. 641 (4th Cir. 1979), *cert. denied,* 444 U.S. 1015 (1980). However, a license to use a process covered by multiple patents does not create a package licensing problem because the licensee is not required to take a license under any patent that does not apply to the process. *Binks Mfg. Co. v. Ransburg Electro-Coating Corp.,* 122 U.S.P.Q. 74 (S.D. Ind. 1959), *modified,* 281 F.2d 252, 126 U.S.P.Q. 318 (7th Cir. 1960), *cert. dismissed,* 366 U.S. 211 (1961).

"Conditioning" the license of one patent on the taking of a license and paying royalties for a license under others, or conditioning the license upon a charge of royalties for the total sales of unpatented as well as patented wares, is equally offensive under the antitrust laws. *Zenith Radio Corp. v. Hazeltine Research, Inc.,* 395 U.S. 100, 161 U.S.P.Q. 577 (1969); *Beckman Instruments, Inc. v. Technical Dev. Corp.,* 433 F.2d 55, 167 U.S.P.Q. 10 (7th Cir. 1970), *cert. denied,* 401 U.S. 976 (1971); *Glen Mfg. Inc. v. Perfect Fit Indus. Inc.,* 420 F.2d 319, 164 U.S.P.Q. 257 (2d Cir.), *cert. denied,* 397 U.S. 1042 (1970); *Rocform Corp. v. Acitelli-Standard Concrete Wall, Inc.,* 367 F.2d 678, 151 U.S.P.Q. 305 (6th Cir. 1966); *McCullough Tool Co. v. Well Surveys, Inc.,* 343 F.2d 381, 145 U.S.P.Q. 6 (10th Cir. 1965), *cert. denied,* 383 U.S. 933 (1966); *American Securit Co. v. Shatterproof Glass Corp.,* 268 F.2d 769, 122 U.S.P.Q. 167 (3d Cir.), *cert. denied,* 361 U.S. 902 (1959); *Sheller-Globe Corp. v. Milsco Mfg. Co.,* 206

U.S.P.Q. 42, 67–68 (E.D. Wis. 1979). *But see Broadcast Music Inc. v. CBS,* 441 U.S. 1, 201 U.S.P.Q. 497 (1979).

Query: Does the licensor have the burden in a subsequent patent infringement suit of proving no coercion of his licensee or conditioning of his license? Or does the defendant have the burden of proving that there was conditioning or coercion?

This becomes a very real and practical issue in many situations, as Mr. Justice Harlan intimated in his dissent in *Zenith v. Hazeltine, supra.* The patent owner may have wanted such a license but not have insisted on it, and the licensee may have graciously—even overanxiously—"given in" for the deceitful purpose of fabricating a later attack based on a viciously false charge of "coercion."

Or the attack of "coercion" may be by a third party defendant who seeks to justify his plagiaristic patent infringement by proving that the license offer was "conditioned" upon the licensee's taking the license under the package and paying royalties on gross sales. It may well have been that the licensor really wanted to license only one of his patents, and to enforce the others by injunctive remedy, but in the spirit of generosity of alternative choice wrote, "What would you think about a package license under all of our patents at a constant royalty rate?" That is a phrase likely to be used as a veiled threat or condition, and equally likely to be used by a good faith offerer of "take your choice." But if the license was in fact consummated in package license form with a uniform royalty on gross sales for the life of the last patent to expire, any lawyer worth his salt stands a chance of persuading a court to give the license offer the malevolent construction.

Historically, patent owners felt secure in charging a uniform royalty for use of any or all of the patents licensed in a package until the expiration of the last of the patents in the package. But now it seems that failure of the licensor to give separate royalty rates on each of the licensed patents, or failure of the royalties to decrease during the term of the license upon the expiration of some of the licensed patents,

151

may suggest coercion in the packaging adequate to support a conclusion of antitrust violation. *Zenith, supra; American Securit Co. v. Shatterproof Glass Corp.,* 268 F.2d 769, 122 U.S.P.Q. 167 (3d Cir. 1959), *cert. denied,* 361 U.S. 902 (1959). *See also Motorola, Inc. v. Kimball Int'l, Inc.,* 601 F. Supp. 62 (N.D. Ill. 1984) (a licensing scheme, which proposed a higher royalty rate for companies taking a license after patent infringement suit was brought against them than royalties required of a company that took a license without being sued, was held to be a valid affirmative defense of patent misuse even though the royalty scheme was merely proposed and had not been executed).

Here again, let us take time to develop the insidious evil of this concept through an example.

Royalties are never, in the real world of industry, set merely by the number of patents involved in the license. Royalties are set by a multitude of other factors, the primary one being the spread between cost of a product embodying many inventions, and what the market will pay without being unduly biased to the cheaper substitute.

If every patent used in the manufacture of your color television set were licensed at a minimum of 1 percent, you would likely prefer the radio because the cost of the television would be too high. By operation of the marketplace retail price, RCA cannot collect more than X percent royalties for licensing its many color television patents. But if it can extend the market-set maximum royalty level for all of its patents, until the last of them expire, it has an extra incentive to continue new developments and get new patents, thereby serving the public's interest in advancing the useful arts.

Not uncommonly, three patents are, as a practical matter, inherently used together in even a single component, such as a cathode, and failure to use all three is to destroy the commercial acceptability of the other two. Patents of a group may thus, on occasion, be viewed as "blocking patents" in that any one blocks the commercial use of the others in a particular application.

In these situations, neither licensor nor licensee may talk about separate licenses—all correspondence may concern the royalty rate based not on the number of patents, but what the licensee can afford to pay for the best integrated structure. Fortunately, the last case involving blocking patents held that, at least in that situation, the hindsight review of the negotiations should not be viewed with malevolent eyes, and that there was no antitrust violation in the license. *North Am. Phillips Co. v. Stewart Eng'g Co.,* 319 F. Supp. 335, 166 U.S.P.Q. 477 (N.D. Cal. 1970).

The complexities of the legitimate complaint against coercion, in the context of royalties and the nature of the package license negotiation, do not permit complete treatment here. But the practical conclusion is this: The unwary, innocent license negotiator may trap himself, or he may be trapped by his adversary, into a written or implied record that will lead a court to conclude illegal conditioning or coercion existed when in fact there was none. Hence, we find that the innocent are almost as likely to be convicted of the wrong as the guilty.

The mix of legal theory and judicial performance is such that here again we find antitrust waters working away at the footings of the patent system—in significant part because the judicial actions are unnourished by the realities of patent licenses in the commercial world.

§ 10.12 Discriminatory Royalties

Historically, patent owners have felt that they could charge different royalties to different licensees. There are a number of reasons why this is often sound economic practice, and often it may encourage rather than restrict competition.

For example: The first licensee may have assumed the expense and risk of getting Food and Drug Administration approval of foods produced by use of a patented, arsenic-base agricultural chemical. The second licensee may have assumed the burden of talking to every county agriculture agent in five states, and of educating them to educate farmers as to the value and use of the new chemical, and thereby develop the market. The third licensee may seek his license at a time when the market has already been proven and developed and sterilized of risk. Are nonuniform royalties justified?

Further, the first licensee may have honored the patent without litigation, while the second licensee may have forced the patent owner to spend $300,000 in litigation expense before taking the license.

One licensee may be primarily interested in high priced, low-volume applications of an invention, while a second licensee may be primarily interested in a low priced, high-volume market. A first licensee may have sales power in markets the patent owner cannot reach, while a second licensee may be strongest in the market of the patentee's own back yard.

These and a number of other factors often bias the patent owner either to license at variant royalties or to grant no second license at all.

Congress has spoken in the Robinson-Patman Act, 15 U.S.C. § 13(a), to the effect that *commodity* price discrimination, as between competitors, is unlawful. You will all agree that price discrimination in *legal services* is lawful. Why not also in patent licenses? A license to make, use, and sell is an intangible right, no more a commodity than legal services and, therefore, not within the ambit of Robinson-Patman. *Allen Archery, Inc. v. Browning Mfg. Co.,* 1982–2 Trade Cas. (CCH) ¶ 64,736 (D. Utah 1982).

Note that any two licensees could not compete in the licensed product but for the patent owner's waiver of his right to preclude others from use of his invention. Nevertheless, we find holdings that discriminatory royalty rates among licensees competing with each other that result in injury to competition among the licensees may be both patent misuse and an unfair method of competition in violation of Section 5 of the Federal Trade Commission Act. *LaPeyre v. FTC,* 366 F.2d 117, 151 U.S.P.Q. 79 (5th Cir. 1966);

Allied Research Prods., Inc. v. Heatbath Corp., 300 F. Supp. 656, 161 U.S.P.Q. 527 (N.D. Ill. 1969); *Peelers Co. v. Wendt,* 260 F. Supp. 193, 151 U.S.P.Q. 378 (W.D. Wash. 1966); *Laitram Corp. v. King Crab, Inc.,* 244 F. Supp. 9, 146 U.S.P.Q. 640 (D. Alaska), *modified,* 245 F. Supp. 1019, 147 U.S.P.Q. 136 (D. Alaska 1965); *see also Solvex Corp. v. Freeman,* 459 F. Supp. 440, 199 U.S.P.Q. 726 (W.D. Va. 1977) (the patentee gave more favorable license terms to licensees who purchased an unpatented product from the licensor for use in the patented process); and *Motorola, Inc., v. Kimball Int'l, Inc.,* 601 F. Supp. 62 (N.D. Ill. 1984) (Affirmative defense of patent misuse could be raised in an infringement action even though the alleged misuse pertained to a discriminatory licensing scheme that was merely *proposed* and not yet executed. The licensing scheme allegedly involved charging a company a higher royalty rate if a patent infringement action had been filed against it; substantially lower royalties were required of a company that took a license before being sued for infringement.).

Certainly, if the nature of the royalty discrimination pattern can be shown to have been intended or to have the inherent effect of substantially restraining competition, we must view the discrimination critically even though we might not so view other discriminations not so afflicted.

Happily, in one case on this particular point, *Bela Seating Co. v. Poloron Prods., Inc.,* 438 F.2d 733, 168 U.S.P.Q. 548 (7th Cir. 1971), *aff'd* 160 U.S.P.Q. 646 (N.D. Ill. 1968), *cert. denied,* 403 U.S. 922 (1971), the court took a significant swipe at *Allied Research Prods., Inc. v. Heatbath Corp., supra,* and *Laitram Corp. v. King Crab, Inc., supra,* and sustained the legality of discriminatory royalties, at least when valid reasons are shown. In *Honeywell Inc. v. Sperry-Rand Corp.,* 180 U.S.P.Q. 673, 763 (D. Minn. 1973), the court stated that a finding of patent misuse or a Sherman Act violation for discriminatory licensing requires a showing of the following:

(1)   the plaintiff took a license;

(2)   the royalty rate charged the plaintiff and that charged a competitor were unequal;

(3)   in all particulars relevant to equality of rates plaintiff and its licensed competitor were similarly situated; and

(4)   the royalties were an important expense factor in the production costs, and the discriminatory rate caused substantial impairment of competition in the relevant market.

See also USM Corp. v. SPS Technologies, Inc., 694 F.2d 505, 216 U.S.P.Q. 959 (7th Cir. 1982), *cert. denied*, 462 U.S. 1107 (1983) (no patent misuse when differential royalties charged for purpose of erecting economic barriers to sublicensing of licensees and maximizing profits); *Carter-Wallace, Inc. v. Otte*, 1978–1 Trade Cas. (CCH) ¶ 61,976 (E.D.N.Y. 1978); *LaSalle Street Press, Inc. v. McCormick & Henderson Inc.*, 293 F. Supp. 1004, 160 U.S.P.Q. 222 (N.D. Ill. 1968); *Carter-Wallace, Inc. v. United States*, 449 F.2d 1374 (Ct. Cl. 1971).

But why should the burden be upon a patent owner to show "valid reasons" for waiving part of his total right to preclude others for one consideration and another part of his right to preclude others for another consideration? And by what measure do we determine the "validity" of the reason, when no waiver of his right to preclude others can be as anticompetitive as the total nonwaiver, the total nonlicense?

We who practice law by foresight instead of by judicial hindsight find that discriminatory royalty rates are one of the many areas of per se uncertainty of the law.

§ 10.13   Graduated Royalties

Recall here the graduated royalty used as an example in the rule of reason discussion in § 9.02, *supra*. The context of the graduated royalty, not the fact of graduated royalty, determined its legality.

Patent royalty escalation is not, by itself, misuse. *In re Yarn Processing Patent Validity Litigation*, 541 F.2d 1127,

192 U.S.P.Q. 241 (5th Cir. 1976), *cert. denied,* 433 U.S. 910 (1977). Normally a patent holder may charge whatever it likes for a license. *Brulotte v. Thys Co.,* 379 U.S. 29, 143 U.S.P.Q. 264 (1964); *American Photocopy Equip. Co. v. Rovico, Inc.,* 257 F. Supp. 192 (N.D. Ill. 1966), *aff'd,* 384 F.2d 813, 155 U.S.P.Q. 119 (7th Cir. 1967), *cert. denied,* 390 U.S. 945 (1968).

Royalty rates that decreased when a stated minimum royalty had been paid were upheld in *Eversharp, Inc. v. Fisher Pen Co.,* 204 F. Supp. 649, 132 U.S.P.Q. 423 (N.D. Ill. 1961). This decrease encouraged a "larger volume of manufacture and sales and, in turn, . . . encourage[d] competition." *Id.* at 204 F. Supp. 669, 132 U.S.P.Q. at 439. A downward sliding scale royalty rate was also upheld in *Arthur J. Schmitt Found. v. Stockham Valves & Fittings, Inc.,* 292 F. Supp. 893 (N.D. Ala. 1966), *aff'd per curiam,* 404 F.2d 13 (5th Cir. 1968), *cert. denied,* 398 U.S. 965 (1970), against charges that the royalty rate was discriminatory, violated the antitrust laws, and constituted patent misuse.

Ascending royalty rates have on occasion been used to force licensees to abide by territorial or quota limitations. Thus, it can be argued that a decision whether such a limitation violates the antitrust laws does not involve a clash between patent and antitrust law. *Pfotzer v. Aqua Sys., Inc.,* 162 F.2d 779, 74 U.S.P.Q. 199 (2d Cir. 1947); *see also United States v. E.I. duPont de Nemours & Co.,* 118 F. Supp. 41, 99 U.S.P.Q. 462 (D. Del. 1953), *aff'd on other grounds,* 351 U.S. 377 (1956).

A royalty rate for a package of patent licenses, with the rate per patent decreasing as the number of patents goes up, may also escape the antitrust laws and the misuse doctrine. Further, refusal to grant a royalty reduction through grant-back licensing when a potential licensee seeks a license under one patent while allowing a royalty reduction if the licensee takes a license under a package of patents did not constitute patent misuse or violation of an antitrust consent decree in *Western Elec. Co. v. Stewart-Warner Corp.,* 631 F.2d 333, 208 U.S.P.Q. 183 (4th Cir. 1980), *cert. denied,* 450

U.S. 971 (1981). This holding is based on the fact that the prospective licensee was given a choice—take a license under one patent alone or on a combination of patents at a different royalty rate. *Id.* at 338–39.

In one case, *Laitram Corp. v. Depoe Bay Fish Co.,* 549 F. Supp. 29 (D. Or. 1982), the alleged infringer amazingly accused the patentee of misuse in charging a uniform license fee throughout the country. The fee for a license on the patentee's process for peeling cooked shrimp was based on pounds of unpeeled shrimp. Depoe contended that this uniform rate base discriminated against Northwest peelers because Northwest shrimp lose more of their weight in the cooking and peeling process than other shrimp. The court rejected this argument, pointing out:

> If Laitram were to adjust its royalty rate to account for the generally lower yields of the Northwest, it could also be required to adjust its rate for higher quality shrimp which command a higher price in the marketplace.

Id. at 35.

A "value-in-use" pricing practice was upheld in *Akzo N.V. v. International Trade Comm'n,* 808 F.2d 1471 (Fed. Cir. 1986), *cert. denied,* 107 S. Ct. 2490 (1987). DuPont allowed its customers to use the patented aramid fibers for whatever purpose they chose but based the royalty on the ultimate end-use. Akzo alleged that the program violated the antitrust laws. The Federal Circuit held that value-in-use pricing is not per se an anticompetitive restraint on trade within the meaning of the antitrust laws and found that DuPont's practice actually had a procompetitive effect of increasing the volume of aramid fibers sold.

§ 10.14   Post-Expiration Royalties

Post-expiration royalties do not seem to fit as neatly into the per se format as price fixing. Nevertheless, the Supreme Court called these provisions "unlawful per se" in *Brulotte v. Thys Co.,* 379 U.S. 29, 143 U.S.P.Q. 264 (1964), and pointed out the analogy to tie-ins. *See also Agrashell, Inc. v.*

Hammons Prods. Co., 479 F.2d 260, 177 U.S.P.Q. 501 (8th Cir.), *cert. denied,* 414 U.S. 1022 (1973); *Duplan Corp. v. Deering Milliken, Inc.,* 444 F. Supp. 648, 197 U.S.P.Q. 342 (D.S.C. 1977), *aff'd in part, rev'd in part on other grounds,* 594 F.2d 979, 201 U.S.P.Q. 641 (4th Cir. 1979), *cert. denied,* 444 U.S. 1015 (1980).

Indeed, post-expiration royalties are in the rough nature of a tie-in in that they are royalties on unpatented goods. They are often an exercise of "leverage"—and the more you study trends in antitrust law the more leverage gravitates to front stage center. Hence, it may seem appropriate to apply here the same rationale discussed with respect to tie-ins and require a "not insubstantial" amount of commerce in the formerly patented product before these misuses will become violations of the Sherman Act.

There is yet another problem, however, in carrying tie-in law over to post-expiration royalties. Under *Brulotte* these royalties are uncollectable, and the licensees need merely decline to pay them when the time comes. The patentee at that time has no more patent leverage to exert—the patent is expired.

What we really have is a situation in which the contract obligation to pay post-expiration royalties is a nullity. There will be great difficulty in proving direct damage. But beyond that, we have with post-expiration royalties a situation of zero patent leverage, since no one need fear an infringement suit after the patent expires. The foregoing leads us to conclude that a post-expiration royalty provision, while a patent misuse, is probably not in normal circumstances an antitrust violation.

Of course the more patent sympathetic point of view is that the consideration of any contracted-for covenant or privilege can be a time payment, not paid contemporaneously with the running of the privilege. Under such a theory the grant of license could relate to any period and payments could be in that or any subsequent period—it being a matter of free and proper contract negotiation whether there be payments after the patent has expired, either in amount absolute or based upon production. In *Brulotte, supra,* the Court characterized the post-expiration royalties as *not* being deferred payments for use of the patented machine during the pre-expiration period. Several cases have distinguished *Brulotte* on these grounds, or because continuing R&D services were being rendered.

In *Riker Laboratories, Inc. v. Gist-Brocades, N.V.,* 636 F.2d 772, 208 U.S.P.Q. 777 (D.C. Cir. 1980), a license agreement was involved that granted the right to make, use, and sell a patented therapeutic composition and the right to use a trademark in connection with the sales. Plaintiff alleged that trademark licensing fees, which were required to be paid after expiration of the patent, constituted post-expiration royalties. Without reaching this issue, the court remanded the case for trial.

Aronson v. Quick Point Pencil Co., 440 U.S. 257, 201 U.S.P.Q. 1 (1979), merits consideration on this issue of royalties. The Court held that the federal patent law did not preempt state contract law so as to preclude enforcement of a contract for a "reduced royalty" on the sale of an "invention," for which a patent was sought but not issued, for as long as the contracting party continued to sell the "invention."

Brulotte was distinguished on the basis that that decision was premised on the use of a patent monopoly as leverage, in effect, to extend the life of that monopoly, while in the present case, the parties clearly contemplated in their agreement that no patent might issue and structured their royalty arrangement on that possibility. The Court recognized that leverage might also be drawn from a pending application for patent and suggested that abuse of this "leverage" might vitiate a license. However, on the stipulated record of this case, the Court decided the patent application was not proved to have played any part in the contract to pay indefinitely the reduced royalty. Enforcement of the contract was not found to be inconsistent with any of the purposes of the patent system (i.e., to encourage and reward invention, promote disclosure, and ensure that ideas in the public domain remain there for free use of the public).

The result in this case may be misleading, because it will commonly be possible to show that a leverage of the possible patent was used to extract the promise to pay royalties for indefinite terms, and the premise of the case may dissipate. But in *Stanfield v. Osborne Indus., Inc.,* 7 Kan. App. 2d 416, 643 P.2d 1115 (1982), *modified,* 232 Kan. 197, 654 P.2d 917, 217 U.S.P.Q. 853 (1982), the court cited *Aronson* to enforce a license agreement requiring payment of a royalty for as long as the licensee uses the invention, despite rejection of the required patent application.

Thus, *Brulotte* controls with regard to royalty payments projecting beyond the expiration date of the underlying patents when the agreement is solely a patent license, and *Aronson* appears to control with regard to royalty payments when the agreement is solely a trade secret or know-how agreement. But, when the agreement is a hybrid granting exclusive rights both to trade secrets and know-how and to claims of patents, the law is not so clear.

In *Pitney-Bowes, Inc. v. Mestre,* 517 F. Supp. 52, 211 U.S.P.Q. 681 (S.D. Fla. 1981), *aff'd in part and dismissed in part,* 701 F.2d 1365, 218 U.S.P.Q. 987 (11th Cir.), *cert. denied,* 464 U.S. 893 (1983), the trial court concluded, in light of *Aronson* and *Kewanee Oil Co. v. Bicron Corp.,* 416 U.S. 470, 181 U.S.P.Q. 673 (1974), that "given a hybrid trade secret and patent agreement providing clearly separate forms of protection, the trade secret protection might have a separate legal viability and might survive the expiration of the patent," and that the issuance of a patent on a machine that is the subject of a trade secret agreement and that is mentioned in descriptive terms by reference to its patent application, but the issuance of which patent is not a condition of the agreement, does not transform the agreement into solely a patent license. 517 F. Supp. at 61–62, 211 U.S.P.Q. at 689.

The court held, however, that the agreement must contain explicit language differentiating between the trade secret protection and the patent protection underlying the royalty obligation and allocating the royalties between the two forms of protection. Absent these provisions, the agreement on its face would be contrary to the decision in *Brulotte. Id.*, 517 F. Supp. at 63, 211 U.S.P.Q. at 690; *accord, Veltman v. Norton Simon, Inc.*, 425 F. Supp. 774, 194 U.S.P.Q. 168 (S.D.N.Y. 1977). On appeal, however, the *Pitney* court followed *Brulotte* and held the hybrid agreement unenforceable.

In *Boggild v. Kenner Prods.*, 776 F.2d 1315, 228 U.S.P.Q. 130 (6th Cir. 1985), *cert. denied,* 106 S. Ct. 3284 (1986), the court reversed the trial court decision to uphold an agreement requiring the licensee to pay royalties beyond the expiration of patents covering the licensed device. One of the controlling factors was that the parties entered the agreement with a clear expectation that a valid patent would issue.

In *Meehan v. PPG Indus., Inc.*, 802 F.2d 881, 231 U.S.P.Q. 400 (7th Cir. 1986), *cert. denied,* 107 S. Ct. 1301 (1987), the court upheld a trial court summary judgment holding that the royalty provisions of a contract were unenforceable where they required payments beyond the expiration of the U.S. patent. The contract provided that the licensee was to make payments until the last patent expired. The agreement included a Canadian patent that expired almost two years after the U.S. patent. The court held that because the terms of the agreement demonstrated that the plaintiff used his right to obtain a patent to project his monopoly power beyond the patent period, the agreement was per se unlawful.

§ 10.15 Settlement of Patent Interferences and Patent Infringement Litigation

Settlement agreements are normally favored by the courts. This is also true in patent litigation. *Aro Corp. v. Allied Witan Co.*, 531 F.2d 1368, 190 U.S.P.Q. 392 (6th Cir.), *cert. denied,* 429 U.S. 862 (1976).

But settlements in patent litigation and patent interference proceedings can be something more than merely a compromise between parties. Unlike other types of cases, those involving patents, by definition, involve the public interest. These settlements invite scrutiny for anticompetitive effects.

If the agreement itself transcends what is necessary to protect the patent monopoly, it may be found to violate the antitrust laws. *Standard Sanitary Mfg. Co. v. United States*, 226 U.S. 20 (1912).

Even if the agreement on its face does not violate the antitrust laws, the conduct of the parties before and after its execution may reveal the true anticompetitive intent of the settlement agreement.

Intent behind a settlement agreement in the patent litigation context is of utmost importance to the court. In *Duplan Corp. v. Deering Milliken, Inc.*, 444 F. Supp. 648, 197 U.S.P.Q. 342 (D.S.C. 1977), *aff'd in part, rev'd in part on other grounds*, 594 F.2d 979, 201 U.S.P.Q. 641 (4th Cir. 1979), *cert. denied*, 444 U.S. 1015 (1980), the court found that an agreement to settle patent litigation was, in reality, a scheme to stabilize and maintain royalties and to monopolize the U.S. market. The scheme was proven by the following conduct of the parties:

(1)   The patentee sold his device without royalty prior to the agreement but charged a royalty after the agreement.

(2)   After the agreement the royalty rates of the settling parties were substantially the same.

(3)   The parties challenging the patentee's priority knew the patents were weak and believed they were invalid.

(4)   The agreement contained cross-convenants not to sue.

(5)   The parties after settlement cooperated in fixing royalties and keeping out competition.

If the motive behind previous settlement agreements represents no more than compromises of the patentee's claim for royalties, then refusal to settle a lawsuit with one defendant on the same terms as the patent owner had settled with other defendants is not patent misuse. *Western Elec. Co. v. Stewart-Warner Corp.*, 631 F.2d 333, 208 U.S.P.Q. 183 (4th Cir. 1980), *cert. denied*, 450 U.S. 971 (1981).

The concern over settlement of patent interference proceedings also comes from the judiciary's concern regarding motive for settlement. Settlement to prevent a fight over validity is sometimes not palatable while settlement as to the issue of priority may be. *United States v. Singer Mfg. Co.*, 374 U.S. 174, 137 U.S.P.Q. 808 (1963) (White, J., concurring).

Agreements made in connection with or in contemplation of termination of an interference between two patent applications must be filed with the Patent and Trademark Office. 35 U.S.C. § 135(c). Failure to so file renders unenforceable both the agreement and any patent involved in the interference or subsequently issued on an application so involved. *Id.* Moreover, the government has standing to seek a declaratory judgment that such a patent is unenforceable. *CTS Corp. v. Piker International Corp.*, 727 F.2d 1550 (Fed. Cir.), *cert. denied*, 105 S. Ct. 221 (1984); *United States v. FMC Corp.*, 514 F. Supp. 1166, 210 U.S.P.Q. 486 (E.D. Pa. 1981).

If the agreement does not on its face violate the antitrust laws, the antitrust claimant may not always find it easy to prove the requisite conduct of the parties to show violation of the antitrust laws.

In *Honeywell, Inc. v. Sperry-Rand Corp.*, 180 U.S.P.Q. 673 (D. Minn. 1973), the court considered plaintiff's allegations that settlement of some interferences violated Sections 1 and 2 of the Sherman Act. Sperry-Rand and IBM settled eleven interferences by cross-licensing agreements, six of them concerning the patent-in-suit. IBM thereafter had no reason to pursue a possible public use proceeding and a possible allegation of fraud on the Patent Office against Sperry-Rand.

Despite finding suppression of the facts concerning the interference settlement agreements and despite finding that IBM possessed evidence of and believed in the invalidity of the patent, the court held there was no violation of the antitrust laws and no proof of injury. *Id.* at 757–58. Proof of the parties' anticompetitive conduct was not enough to overcome the facial validity of the agreements. But recall that this was the case where the technological merger effected by the settlement of the interferences was condemned.

§ 10.16   Copyrights; Blanket Licensing, *Broadcast Music, Inc. v. CBS*

A unique mix of conditioned blanket or block licensing, price fixing, and other business practice characterizations came together in *Broadcast Music, Inc. v. CBS,* 441 U.S. 1, 201 U.S.P.Q. 497 (1979).

Thousands of composers found that their works were being performed by thousands of performers in taverns and other places and found that they could not police the infringement of their copyrights on music. As a result, in 1914 they organized the American Society of Composers, Authors and Publishers (ASCAP). ASCAP and a similar organization, Broadcast Music, Inc. (BMI), have been subject to past antitrust scrutiny and now operate under a consent decree, in which the present operation is characterized as follows:

(1)   Each organization has nonexclusive licenses to grant nonexclusive licenses to perform thousands of musical compositions. These are *performance,* not publication, licenses.

(2)   Essentially all currently performed copyrighted music is subject to one or the other of these licenses.

(3)   ASCAP and BMI grant only blanket licenses under all of their licensed compositions. For example, they will not grant a license at a different price solely to Gershwin compositions, or any other sub-part of their repertoire.

(4)   Persons wishing to perform music retain the legal right to negotiate individual licenses with composers. However, the prices obtained through ASCAP and

BMI are so low, and the cost of individual license negotiations are relatively so high, that no one undertakes to negotiate individual licenses even though the only license available from ASCAP or BMI is a blanket license, covering all of their compositions. So the legal right to individual licenses is rendered illusory by the fact that the blanket license is available at costs below the mere cost of negotiating a single performance license.

(5) The money paid by the licensee may be on a per-program or per-performance basis, or may be an annual subscription rate for all programs and performances during the course of a year, but the sum is not directly related to either the quality or the quantity of music used.

(6) The money collected by ASCAP and BMI is divided among composers according to a formula determined by periodic surveys reflecting the character and frequency of use of each composer's music and other factors.

(7) At least insofar as the blanket mechanism is concerned, no new and unknown composer has an opportunity to seek to introduce his music into the marketplace by offering it at a lower price than a big name, popular composition. Further, the practicalities dictate that a new composer seeking individually to license the performance of his music has no opportunity to indulge in price competition as between his music and other music, in part owing to the circumstance that the blanket license of even the best and most desirable music is at a cost per performance lower than the cost of an individual license negotiation.

Obviously, "conditioned" package licensing existed in that the licensor would not license one piece of music without licensing all in its repertoire. Price fixing existed in that all music in a repertoire was licensed to the buyer for a fee that was unrelated to the quality or quantity of music used by the buyer, or in the case of annual subscriptions from ASCAP or BMI, unrelated even to the frequency of use of the music.

However, after a significant amount of background study and analysis, including consideration of the Justice Department amicus brief, which expressed the view that the blanket license should not be flatly prohibited, the Court eventually arrived at the "purpose and effect" analysis, and concluded that the court of appeals had been wrong in finding a per se violation.

Although the Supreme Court remanded the case for determination of lawfulness under the rule of reason, the Court's justification for finding no per se violation was supported by many arguments of reasonableness under the circumstances of this particular marketplace, and thereby seemed to dictate a conclusion of reasonableness by the Court below on remand.

Mr. Justice Stevens, in dissent, agreed that the per se rule should not apply, but felt that the determination of whether the licensing practice was lawful under the rule of reason was properly before the Supreme Court and he would decide that it was unreasonable, and thereby unlawful.

The lesson of the case illustrates once again the importance of a "purpose and effect" analysis in the context of the particular market involved, and the unreliability of conclusionary rules such as "price fixing is illegal" and "forced package licensing is per se illegal." For here, two classical examples of per se illegalities, found in the presence of the unique circumstance of the marketplace for music performances, were considered not to be per se illegal and were strongly implied by the majority to be lawful under the rule of reason.

On remand, the court of appeals held that CBS failed to prove that the blanket license was an unreasonable restraint of trade. *CBS v. ASCAP,* 620 F.2d 930, 205 U.S.P.Q. 880 (2d Cir. 1980). Blanket licenses of copyrighted musical compositions have also been upheld in other contexts. *See F.E.L. Publications, Ltd. v. Catholic Bishop,* 214 U.S.P.Q. 409 (7th

167

Cir. 1982), *rev'g*, 506 F. Supp. 1127, 210 U.S.P.Q. 403 (N.D. Ill. 1981) (blanket license of copyrighted hymns to Catholic parishes upheld under rule of reason analysis); *Broadcast Music, Inc. v. Moor-Law, Inc.,* 527 F. Supp. 758, 212 U.S.P.Q. 873 (D. Del. 1981), *aff'd,* 691 F.2d 490 (3d Cir. 1982) (blanket license to individual nightclub owner survived antitrust challenge under rule of reason); *Buffalo Broadcasting Co. v. ASCAP,* 744 F.2d 917 (2d Cir. 1984), *cert. denied,* 469 U.S. 1211 (1985) (blanket license of copyrighted music to local television stations not unreasonable restraint of trade).

§ 10.17 Trade Secret, Know-How, and Show-How Licenses

Know-how, being in the nature of results of previously performed engineering services, and show-how, being in the nature of a teaching service or the "shipping cost" of know-how, may properly be couched in terms of personal service undertakings, the money considerations for which are not defeasible upon the event of patent expiration or invalidity or loss of secrecy of discrete secrets.

A few recent decisions recognize a licensor's right to collect royalties for these assets or services, despite the failure of an element such as the patent, as long as the contract is clear.

Timely Prods. Inc. v. Costanzo, 465 F. Supp. 91, 201 U.S.P.Q. 567 (D. Conn. 1979), illustrates one court's desire for specificity in the contracts. In this case a license agreement failed totally when the subject patent was invalidated, despite the agreement's intended coverage of other ongoing services and know-how. The court reached that conclusion because the agreement did not (explicitly or implicitly) provide for severability of the royalty rates between the patent and other services.

Often because of negotiative compromises, engineering reasons, or even tax law reasons, the parties do not wish to carve out the consideration attributable to each intellectual property or engineering service treated in the contract. It seems clear that the parties ought to have this much freedom to contract, with all elements of the contract enforceable in spite of the occurrence of foreseeable events like patent invalidity or expiration, loss of secrecy of trade secrets, or the like. If that is their desire, the contract should include a clause stating that the parties agreed for their own convenience and fully contemplated not to allocate and yet be bound by royalty and other money clauses. But *Timely Products, supra,* may be argued by some as suggesting that failure to allocate what money is to be paid for each value, which the court later perceives to have been separable, may be risky.

In *Robintech, Inc. v. Chemidus Wavin, Ltd.,* 450 F. Supp. 823, 835, 198 U.S.P.Q. 466, 478 (D.D.C. 1978), *aff'd,* 628 F.2d 142, 205 U.S.P.Q. 873 (D.C. Cir. 1980), the court specifically indicated that a "know-how" component of a licensing agreement would survive a determination that the underlying patent was invalid, that those provisions may have continued vitality, and that they may be independently enforceable.

In *Pitney-Bowes, Inc. v. Mestre,* 517 F. Supp. 52, 211 U.S.P.Q. 681 (S.D. Fla. 1981), *aff'd in part and dismissed in part,* 701 F.2d 1365, 218 U.S.P.Q. 987 (11th Cir.), *cert. denied,* 464 U.S. 893 (1983), discussed earlier with regard to post-expiration royalties, the trial court held regarding a hybrid trade secret and patent agreement, which clearly provided separately for both trade secret and patent protection, that the trade secret protection survived the expiration of the patent, and that the post-patent expiration rights of the parties to the trade secrets were a matter of contract law left for agreement between the parties. On appeal, however, the court found an illegal extension of the patent because royalties remained the same even after the patents had expired.

Proper focus on each of the elements given in a license agreement, including the patent, discrete trade secrets, confidential know-how, and show-how, *with royalties appropriately apportioned,* can sometimes be quite helpful.

The application of antitrust principles to trade secret and know-how licenses is beyond the scope of this paper. However, an excellent, though dated, paper on this topic is Mac-Donald, "Know-How Licensing and Antitrust Laws," 62 Mich. L. Rev. 351 (1964). MacDonald observes that the position of trade secrets and know-how with respect to the antitrust laws is approximately comparable to that of patents. This conclusion is based on the realistic considerations that trade secrets and know-how are often greater in economic value than technology embodied in patents and that the owner of technology has no meaningful patent protection in many foreign markets.

Even though a full discussion of antitrust aspects of trade secret and know-how licensing is impossible in this paper, two cases appear to characterize much of the applicable law and point out some very important considerations.

First, consider *A. & E. Plastik Pak Co. v. Monsanto Co.*, 396 F.2d 710 (9th Cir. 1968). In *Plastik,* Monsanto's patent, directed to a clear type of plastic sheet, had expired when Plastik hired a key Monsanto engineer in aid of Plastik's effort to begin its own production of the material. Monsanto complained of wrongful appropriation by Plastik of confidential technology. Plastik protested that the technology was in the public domain by operation of the expired patent. That controversy was settled by a license covering the confidential technology known to the defecting employee and providing that Monsanto would purchase large amounts of Plastik's initial production, supposedly to allow Plastik the economics of large-scale production while refraining from competition with Monsanto. When the parties disagreed about certain obligations under the agreement, arbitration was initiated. Plastik then filed suit to avoid the arbitration, alleging that there were no trade secrets or know-how protectable at law, and hence that the restraints of the license were an antitrust violation.

The court indicated that the agreement was not prima facie invalid, but rather that invalidity depended upon whether the technology fairly supported the ancillary restraints.

However, it should be pointed out that the court's decision reflected no appreciation of the fact that manufacturing plant design and associated operating know-how and experience, which is not and realistically cannot be disclosed in a patent, is of great and critical value to an undertaking such as Plastik's. Often this know-how is very expensive and is impossible to come by from public sources. Monsanto had spent large amounts of money and effort to develop a package of know-how, and it rightfully had an important and expensive property right, irrespective of broad concepts of process or product being disclosed fully and claimed in a patent.

For example, half a billion dollars were spent to develop the jumbo jet J-59 aircraft engine years after patents on the concepts of the jet engine had expired. If a party who must spend large amounts of money to create this property has no protection of the results from that expenditure, then the money will not be spent and society will be deprived of its values—like jumbo jet airplanes of the Boeing 747 and Douglas DC-10 class.

In any event, the court in *Plastik* held that the determination of "the existence and extent of technology within the knowledge of [the defecting Monsanto employee] which Monsanto can rightfully claim as privately controlled" and Monsanto's purpose for granting the Plastik license "is the crucial factual antitrust issue, for without such technology as a basis no restriction on competition [as contained in the license] could be valid as an ancillary restraint. . . . Such issues the parties cannot, by stipulation or otherwise, exclude from the area of judicial scrutiny and determination. We conclude that it was abuse of discretion for the [trial] court to make this issue available for arbitration." 396 F.2d at 716. The important concepts illustrated in *Plastik* can be summarized as follows:

—For the most part, the principles of antitrust and misuse that are applied to patents will be applied in trade secret and know-how licenses insofar as they fit. But neither trade secrets nor know-how enjoys a presumption of validity.

—An important special focus must be given to the question of whether the trade secret and/or know-how can be proved up in court to be of sufficiently great importance, substance, and confidentiality as to give rise to a lawful primary purpose.

—If the license is a license of technology that is truly in the public domain (knowledge readily available from public sources), in reality it is no more than a cover story for the restraints in the license.

A more recent decision relating to restraints in know-how licenses is *Shin Nippon Koki Co. v. Irvin Indus., Inc.*, 186 U.S.P.Q. 296 (N.Y. Sup. Ct. 1975). In *Shin Nippon*, territorial limitations on the sales of machines manufactured by a licensee using the know-how were expressly upheld. Recognizing that there were few recent decisions on this point, Judge Frank followed the reasoning of *Dr. Miles Medical Co. v. John D. Park & Sons*, 220 U.S. 373 (1911) and *Fowle v. Park*, 131 U.S. 88 (1889), and expressly rejected recent personal views of employees of the Justice Department, advocating these limitations to be illegal restraints.

As in the prior cases, *Shin Nippon* required that the restraints be "ancillary" to the grant of the technology itself. In determining that the limitations were ancillary, the court considered "(1) the subject matter of the license is substantial, valuable, secret know-how; (2) such restraint is limited to the 'life' of the know-how; *i.e.*, the period during which it retains its secrecy, and (3) such restraint is limited to those products only which are made by the use of the know-how." 186 U.S.P.Q. at 298.

Thus, the territorial restraint appears to be valid and enforceable when incorporated in a license of substantial, valuable, secret know-how, as long as the restraint is limited in time (expressly or impliedly) to the "life" of the know-how, and to those products made by use of the know-how.

Consider again *Aronson v. Quick Point Pencil Co.,* 440 U.S. 257, 201 U.S.P.Q. 1 (1979). A simple invention was disclosed in a contract negotiation that matured into a contract to pay one royalty rate if a patent issued, and another royalty rate for as long as the invention was used if a patent did not issue. The court sustained the contract for indefinitely continuing royalties even though all secrecy in the invention was by its nature terminated within weeks of, if not as of, the marketing date.

Compare, however, the case of *CVD, Inc. v. Raytheon Co.,* 769 F.2d 842, 227 U.S.P.Q. 7 (1st Cir. 1985), *cert. denied,* 475 U.S. 1016 (1986). In *CVD,* the Court of Appeals for the First Circuit held that attempts to restrain competition, by imposing a trade secret license on former employees under the threat of litigation for the alleged disclosure of those secrets, was a bad faith violation of the antitrust laws when public disclosure of those secrets had already been made.

It seems that perhaps in connection with licenses of know-how, both lawyers and courts often miss the understanding of certain true and important social values and how to build correctly from them. Cannot a know-how license be used as a cover story for illegal restraints? But recognize that they give real life commercial viability to transactions in know-how, even theoretically available nonsecret know-how; and without legal stature for packages of know-how, society suffers grievously.

Chapter *11*

Purgation

Patents, when misused as in licenses that violate the antitrust laws, are unenforceable even when valid.

The granddaddy of patent misuse cases was perhaps *Carbice Corp. of Am. v. American Patent Dev. Corp.*, 283 U.S. 27 (1931), which was a suit by the patent owner against the manufacturer of a staple commodity of commerce, dry ice, charging contributory infringement by the sale of dry ice with the knowledge that it would be used in patented refrigeration cartons. The judgment for the defendant on grounds that the suit was an effort to monopolize an unpatented product, dry ice, did not contain any reference to the term of the patent owner's disqualification to maintain suit.

The idea of purgation, whereby a patent though once misused becomes again enforceable, seems to have slipped unnoticed into the law, perhaps beginning with *American Lecithin Co. v. Warfield Co.*, 105 F.2d 207, 42 U.S.P.Q. 180 (7th Cir.), *cert. denied,* 308 U.S. 609 (1939). There, the patent owner effectually granted implied licenses (under its patent on mixing lecithin with chocolate to preserve the chocolate) only to customers of its lecithin, and in this case sued a direct infringer, having previously lost a suit against a contributory infringer under the *Carbice* rule. *See J.C. Ferguson Mfg. Works v. American Lecithin Co.*, 94 F.2d 729 (1st Cir. 1938), *cert. denied,* 304 U.S. 573 (1938).

The court implemented the *Carbice* theory in this case against the direct infringer, pointing out that the method of doing business, in which no licenses were granted to chocolate manufacturers to use lecithin from other sources, resulted in an unlawful monopoly effect with respect to unpatented lecithin. (Contrast the modern law of misuse under 35 U.S.C. § 271(b) and (c) in *Dawson Chem. Co. v. Rohm & Haas Co.,* 448 U.S. 176, 206 U.S.P.Q. 385, *reh'g denied,* 448 U.S. 917 (1980).)

The *American Lecithin Co. v. Warfield Co.* opinion made special mention of defendant's request for "an affirmative penalty upon plaintiff, such as a forfeiture of the patent or an implied license for the statutory period," and responded: "In the discussions above, we believe we have shown that the defendant's theory is really unsound." 105 F.2d at 211, 42 U.S.P.Q. at 184. No suggestion of purgation in any of the words used, only in the refusal to forfeit the patent, which would be a null refusal unless the patent document had some form of potential life left in it.

Then came a pair of cases, *B.B. Chem. Co. v. Ellis,* 314 U.S. 495, 52 U.S.P.Q. 33 (1942), and *Morton Salt Co. v. G.S. Suppiger Co.,* 314 U.S. 488, 52 U.S.P.Q. 30 (1942), decided the same day. *B.B. Chemical* seemed on its facts to be identical to the Seventh Circuit *American Lecithin Case, supra,* and petitioner suggested to the Supreme Court that it was entitled to relief because it was now (prior to Supreme Court review) willing and offering to give unconditional licenses to manufacturers on a royalty basis. Said the Court:

> It will be appropriate to consider petitioner's right to relief when it is able to show that it has fully abandoned its present method of restraining competition in the sale of unpatented articles and that the consequences of that practice have been fully dissipated.

314 U.S. at 498.

On the same day, in *Morton Salt,* 314 U.S. at 493, 52 U.S.P.Q. at 33, the time phrase took the form:

> at least until it is made to appear that the improper practice has been abandoned and that the consequences of the misuse of the patent have been dissipated.

Nobody thought *Morton Salt* had been purged, but the time frame had been set down, and the necessary events of (1) abandonment of the practice, and (2) dissipation of its consequences, had been set down as guides for future practice. This evolution occurred in cases closely related in misuse concept, contributory infringement, and implied licenses only to purchasers of the unpatented commodity; and it occurred in dictum.

The foundation stone of these particular misuse cases was shattered (though it seems not destroyed) by the Patent Act of 1952's new Section 271, which restores causes of action for induced and contributory infringement. *Dawson Chem. Co. v. Rohm & Haas Co.,* 448 U.S. 176, 206 U.S.P.Q. 385, *reh'g denied,* 448 U.S. 917 (1980). But the law of purgation seems to have been established, and the 1952 Patent Act does not seem to have caused a ripple in the law of purgation.

Further cases, largely in dictum, have developed the finer points of purgation, which concern patent lawyers more than antitrust lawyers. *See Shea v. Blaw-Knox Co.,* 388 F.2d 761, 156 U.S.P.Q. 481 (7th Cir. 1968); *Hensley Equip. Co. v. Esco Corp.,* 383 F.2d 252, 155 U.S.P.Q. 183 (5th Cir. 1967); *McCullough Tool Co. v. Well Surveys, Inc.,* 343 F.2d 381, 145 U.S.P.Q. 6 (10th Cir. 1965), *cert. denied,* 383 U.S. 933 (1966); *Pet Inc. v. Kysor Indus. Corp.,* 404 F. Supp. 1252, 193 U.S.P.Q. 492 (W.D. Mich. 1975); *Kearney & Trecker Corp. v. Cincinnati Milacron, Inc.,* 403 F. Supp. 1040, 184 U.S.P.Q. 134 (S.D. Ohio 1975), *aff'd,* 562 F.2d 365, 195 U.S.P.Q. 402 (6th Cir. 1977); *Stewart v. Mo-Trim, Inc.,* 192 U.S.P.Q. 410 (S.D. Ohio 1975); *In re Yarn Process Patent Validity & Anti-Trust Litigation,* 398 F. Supp. 31, 182 U.S.P.Q. 323, 185 U.S.P.Q. 334 (S.D. Fla. 1974), *vacated,* 401 F. Supp. 673, 189 U.S.P.Q. 598 (S.D. Fla. 1975); *Jack Winter, Inc. v. Koratron Co.,* 375 F. Supp. 1, 181 U.S.P.Q. 353 (N.D. Cal. 1974); *Congoleum Indus., Inc. v. Armstrong Cork Co.,* 366 F. Supp. 220, 180 U.S.P.Q. 40, 180 U.S.P.Q. 264 (E.D. Pa. 1973), *aff'd,* 510 F.2d 334, 184 U.S.P.Q. 769 (3d Cir.), *cert. denied,* 421 U.S. 988 (1975); *Blohm & Voss AG v. Prudential-Grace Lines, Inc.,* 346 F. Supp. 1116, 174 U.S.P.Q. 484 (D. Md. 1972), *rev'd on other grounds,* 489 F.2d 231, 180 U.S.P.Q. 165 (4th Cir. 1973), *cert. denied,* 419 U.S. 840 (1974); *Dubuit v. Harwell Enters.,* 336 F. Supp.

1184, 171 U.S.P.Q. 550 (W.D.N.C. 1971): *Sonobond Corp. v. Uthe Technology, Inc.,* 314 F. Supp. 878, 165 U.S.P.Q. 731 (N.D. Cal. 1970); *Ansul Co. v. Uniroyal, Inc.,* 306 F. Supp. 541, 163 U.S.P.Q. 517 (S.D.N.Y. 1969), *aff'd in part and rev'd and remanded in part,* 448 F.2d 872, 169 U.S.P.Q. 759, 170 U.S.P.Q. 549 (2d Cir. 1971), *cert. denied,* 404 U.S. 1018 (1972); *Valmont Industries, Inc. v. Yuma Mfg. Co.,* 296 F. Supp. 1291, 161 U.S.P.Q. 567 (D. Colo. 1969); *McCullough Tool Co. v. Scherbatskoy,* 283 F. Supp. 486, 159 U.S.P.Q. 106 (N.D. Okla. 1968); *Columbus Automotive Corp. v. Oldberg Mfg. Co.,* 264 F. Supp. 779, 153 U.S.P.Q. 97 (D. Colo. 1967), *aff'd per curiam,* 387 F.2d 643, 156 U.S.P.Q. 488 (10th Cir. 1968).

But purgation law is very largely rhetorical dictum, with no more thought or analysis behind some of the expressions we rely upon than exists behind a parrot's unthinking repetition of what it has heard. It follows that little of the law is, in and of itself, reliable authority. Still, the fabric is there, and it is strong enough for a good lawyer to reasonably base his advice in most situations.

For the patent owner: When a misuse has occurred, be biased to purge and purge with a public flare. Advocate that the plagiarist who is a parasite upon industry's effort to progress the arts has the burden of proof of nondissipation of consequences, but carry the burden of proving dissipation as fully as you can. Assume you'll have to smell like a rose to get the court to permit purgation after litigation commences; but if caught in the box, purge, replead, and with a little bit of luck the defendant may lose his case to you.

The converse types of arguments, of course, fit the infringer's view of the same circumstances. But when trying to evaluate what the court will do, read carefully all the judge's prior opinions. If he was brought up on Nader economics, he will be for defendant almost independently of the evidence. If he was brought up on property morals and concepts and feels a businessman is not only entitled to profits but generally *must* enjoy them if business is to provide an abundance of jobs, goods, and services for the people to enjoy, he will tend, when the evidence permits, to find a way around most all the plagiarist's arguments of nondissipated consequences. *See, e.g., White Cap Co. v. Owens-Illinois Glass Co.,* 203 F.2d 694, 97 U.S.P.Q. 192 (6th Cir. 1953), *cert. denied,* 346 U.S. 876 (1953).

And the law, after all, is what the judge does, even if it is for his own subjective reasons.

Chapter 12

Current Thinking and Likely Enforcement Policy of the Antitrust Division Regarding Patent Licensing Practices

In the 1970s, officials of the Antitrust Division cataloged patent licensing practices viewed by the Department of Justice as being per se antitrust violations. The catalog, the infamous Nine No-No's, listed practices characterized as being "pretty clearly unlawful," and became the subject of talks intended "to dispel some of the alleged doubts and reported uncertainty concerning the law in this area." *See* Remarks of Bruce B. Wilson, Deputy Assistant Attorney General, Antitrust Division, before the Michigan State Bar Antitrust Trust Law Section and the Patent, Trademark and Copyright Law Section, Detroit, Michigan, September 21, 1972, Trade Reg. Rep. (CCH) ¶ 50,146 (1972); Remarks of Ky P. Ewing, Jr., Deputy Assistant Attorney General, Antitrust Division, before the San Francisco Patent Law Association, Pebble Beach, California, May 5, 1979, Trade Reg. Rep. (CCH) ¶ 50,398 (1979).

But in the 80s the patent licensing practices formerly declared "pretty clearly unlawful" have been recognized by the Department as being not so "clearly unlawful," and the Nine per se No-No's have been criticized as over-inclusive, lacking economic rationality, and being per se where the rule of reason should apply. *See* Remarks of Abbott B. Lipsky, Jr., Deputy Assistant Attorney General, Antitrust Division, before the American Bar Association Antitrust Section,

Licensing

Washington, D.C., November 5, 1981, Trade Reg. Rep. (CCH) ¶ 50,434 (1981).

In 1984 statements of Justice Department policy toward patent licenses, both the Chief of the Intellectual Property Section of the Antitrust Division, Roger Andewelt, and the Assistant Attorney General of the Antitrust Division, J. Paul McGrath, repudiated the Nine No-No's and hostile court decisions as, in McGrath's words, "antiquated antitrust doctrines that unreasonably restrict [American firms'] ability to secure efficiencies through patent licensing." Mr. McGrath noted the decline of America's investment in R&D compared to that of its competitors, Japan and West Germany, and the importance of technology licensing to give the R&D investor a fair chance to reap from his investment. He pointed to two licensing practices, tie-ins and field of use restrictions, which often have procompetitive effects. Mr. McGrath reiterated the Department's position that the lawfulness of patent licenses should be based on a factual economic analysis; only when the overall effect of a license is anticompetitive should it be held unlawful. *See* Remarks of Roger B. Andewelt, Chief, Intellectual Property Section Antitrust Division, before the National Institute On Industrial & Intellectual Property, Philadelphia, Pennsylvania, October 11–12, 1984, 53 Antitrust Law Journal, Issue 3, p. 206 (1985), and remarks of J. Paul McGrath, Assistant Attorney General, Antitrust Division, before the Seminar Services International Conference on U.S. Patent Practice, Arlington, Virginia, April 5, 1984, 27 Pat. Trademark & Copyright J. (BNA) 624 (April 12, 1984).

Charles F. Rule, Deputy Assistant Attorney General, Antitrust Division, remarked before the legal conference sponsored by the World Trade Association and the Cincinnati Patent Law Association, October 21, 1986, 33 Pat. Trademark & Copyright J. (BNA) 18 (Nov. 6, 1986) that over the last six years the Justice Department has sought to debunk the Nine No-No's, indicating that they no longer represented the Department's policy. He also stated: "For each of the nine no-nos, for example, there are *at least* as many potential

182

procompetitive explanations for the restriction as there are anticompetitive excuses for its condemnation. And in the great majority of cases, those benefits will outweigh any anticompetitive threat."

For a summary of the Nine No-No's and the current position of the Antitrust Division, see Appendix B, *infra.*

Unfortunately the courts have not yet revealed such a reversal of thought as has the Department of Justice. And indeed pre-1981 established case law may make it hard to come by such a judicial correction within the decade even if judges of the CAFC are all of the same mind as the Department—which is unlikely.

So licensors and licensees are advised to be extremely cautious in any violations of the Nine No-No's, lest some court find a per se patent misuse in spite of the reversal of view of the Department of Justice.

Chapter *13*

Extraterritorial Jurisdiction of United States Antitrust Law

The conditions under which extraterritorial jurisdiction will be exercised in antitrust actions is beyond the scope of this paper. However, a few general observations will be made.

Restraints on exportation from the United States to a foreign nation affect the export trade of the United States, and restraints on exportations from foreign nations to the United States affect import trade. Apparently, if either the licensee or the licensor is within the jurisdiction of the United States, United States antitrust law could be applicable to such foreign commerce with the United States.

A new Section 7 of the Sherman Act became effective on October 8, 1982, that by its language restricts the extraterritorial reach of the antitrust law.

Sec. 7. This Act shall not apply to conduct involving trade or commerce (other than import trade or import commerce) with foreign nations unless—

(1) such conduct has a direct, substantial, and reasonably foreseeable effect—

(A) on trade or commerce which is not trade or commerce with foreign nations, or on import trade or import commerce with foreign nations; or

(B) on export trade or export commerce with foreign nations, of a person engaged in such trade or commerce in the United States; and

(2) such effect gives rise to a claim under the provisions of this Act, other than this section.

> If this Act applies to such conduct only because of the operation of paragraph (1)(B), then this Act shall apply to such conduct only for injury to export business in the United States.[1]

Just what effect this new provision will have on the antitrust jurisdictional requirements, which were previously stated only in terms of effect on interstate or foreign commerce, has yet to be determined. Section 7 now requires a direct, substantial, and reasonably foreseeable effect on commerce, a standard similar to that recently advocated by the Department of Justice and by some courts. *E.g., Industrial Inv. Dev. Corp. v. Mitsui & Co.,* 671 F.2d 876, 883 (5th Cir. 1982), *cert. denied,* 464 U.S. 961 (1983) (activities that directly or substantially affect flow of commerce into or out of the U.S. fall within the Sherman Act). Thus, Section 7 may in part have adopted a policy already followed by some courts of examining the extent and nature of the effect of the activity in question on U.S. commerce before sustaining jurisdiction. *E.g., Rohm & Haas Co. v. Dawson Chem. Co.,* 557 F. Supp. 739, 217 U.S.P.Q. 515 (S.D. Tex. 1982), *rev'd on other grounds,* 722 F.2d 1556, 220 U.S.P.Q. 289 (Fed. Cir. 1983) (jurisdiction sustained based on an agreement between Rohm & Haas and Bayer that allegedly resulted in curtailment of exports to Costa Rica and Swaziland).

Extraterritorial application of the Sherman Act is subject to numerous exceptions and limitations. Excepted from the general propositions of jurisdiction enumerated above are sovereign immunity, the act of state doctrine, and sovereign compulsion. Limiting the general proposition are comity and conflicts of law. *E.g., Mannington Mills, Inc. v. Congoleum Corp.,* 595 F.2d 1287, 1291–99, 202 U.S.P.Q. 321, 324–30 (3d Cir. 1979).

United States courts, as the courts of any sovereign, have little power when the losing party to a lawsuit is not present in the United States and has no property located in the United States. Unless provided otherwise by treaty, a United

---

[1] 15 U.S.C. § 7.

States judgment will be enforced in a foreign nation only if comity is granted by that foreign nation. However, comity is not readily granted. Indeed, many provisions of United States antitrust law are considered by foreign nations to be detrimental to their own best interests. *See, e.g.,* "British Statute Signed by Queen Elizabeth on March 20, 1980, to Protect British Interests from Foreign Antitrust Judgments," 959 Antitrust & Trade Reg. Rep. (BNA), p. F-1 (April 10, 1980); "Commonwealth Nations Adopt Resolution Criticizing U.S. Treble Damage Judgments," 963 Antitrust & Trade Reg. Rep. (BNA), p. A-10 (May 8, 1980).

Chapter 14

Licensing Considerations in The EEC—The Block Exemptions, January 1985

Although EEC licensing antitrust law will not be fully explored in this paper, a modern decision by the Court of Justice of the European Communities is worth noting because, for the first time, the Court has decided a licensing case.

During the last 24 years, the Commission has been active in developing a body of law in the area of technology licensing. On December 24, 1962, the Commission gave its opinion on numerous patent license provisions that it did not consider to be prohibited by Article 85(1) of the Treaty of Rome. Since that time, the Commission has restricted its notice by decisions on various license agreements.

The facts behind the *Maize Seed* case, Nagesser K.G. and Eisele v. EEC Commission, Case 258/78 (1982) 1 CMLR 278 (1983), involved a French company, INRA, which had developed new maize varieties certified in France under breeders' rights. To extend marketing into the Federal Republic of Germany, INRA entered an agreement with one Eisele, a German, by which Eisele would obtain registration of the breeders' rights in Germany in exchange for an exclusive distributorship. The Commission challenged the agreement, holding that an exclusive license always violates Article 85(1) because it eliminates the licensor as a competitor in that territory as well as preventing any further licenses.

The most important points of the Court's decision addressed two provisions of the license agreement. The first permitted Eisele to claim his breeders' rights to stop all imports of certified INRA maize into Germany (*i.e.,* an exclusive license). The second required INRA to prevent all exports of certified INRA maize into Germany (*i.e.,* an absolute territorial protection provision).

With regard to the first provision, the Court applied what may be equivalent to a rule of reason analysis in holding that *in this case* the exclusivity was necessary to induce Eisele to spend the effort and money to start his business. The Court's decision thus overturned the Commission's ruling to the extent that it invalidated any agreement between INRA and Eisele that prohibited INRA or another licensee of INRA from producing or selling maize in Germany.

Regarding the second provision, the Court agreed with the Commission and held this license restriction to be a violation of Article 85(1).

Apparently, the only firm rule to be derived from the *Maize Seed* case is that a licensor may prohibit its licensees from exporting into another country where the licensor has granted an exclusive license. Thus, any license provisions, such as noncompetition clauses and tie-ins, previously considered to be no-no's by the Commission, should be avoided in any license agreement involving the EEC.

In a more recent decision, the Court of Justice for the EEC considered the legality under EEC antitrust law of various clauses that are often included in licensing agreements. In *Windsurfing Int'l Inc. v. Commission of the EEC,* Case 193/ 83, decided February 25, 1986, the court held several clauses in licenses granted by Windsurfing with respect to sailboards to be illegal.

The court held that the rights under the German patent were limited to only the rig of the sailboard and not the board itself. Nevertheless, a royalty based on both the rig and the board was held to be permissible.

The licenses also provided that a notice stating that the product was manufactured under the patent was to be applied to the board. The court held this to be impermissible, since it gave an improper indication of the actual scope of the patent.

Clauses prohibiting the licensee from challenging the validity of the patent and acknowledging the validity of Windsurfing trademarks were held to be improper.

Provisions with respect to quality control and requiring the rigs to be sold only in conjunction with boards were held to be outside the scope of the patent grant and therefore impermissible.

Finally, limitations with respect to manufacturing localities were held to be improper.

Chapter 15

Recent Trends

In 1970 the then Chief of the Patent Group of the Antitrust Division of the Department of Justice said that with respect to the interface of intellectual property with antitrust there are "no rules of per se legality, there are not any completely safe harbors." Stern, "A Future Look at Patent Fraud and Antitrust Laws," 52 J. Pat. Off. Soc'y 3 (1970). If there are no certainties in the law of antitrust as applied to licensing of intellectual property, and not *any* completely safe harbors, would it surprise anybody that licensing diminishes—to the detriment of competition?

Or would it surprise anyone that investment in intellectual property thereafter diminishes, because when it is not licensed, the return on those investments also diminishes?

Would it surprise anyone that progress of the useful arts and sciences stagnates to great public detriment?

The United States appears to have changed from a manufactured goods exporter to a net manufactured goods importer—owing in major part to the decline of technical superiority of U.S. manufactured goods. This, along with many other economic factors, has led to the decline of United States technological leadership in the world.

Among the many philosophies which have earned a full share of the blame is the egalitarian sophistry of antitrust and misuse law of the 1940s to 1980, as applied to technology transfer contracts.

Both a few decisions since about 1973 and the Department of Justice position since 1980 have reflected a desirable change of trend and an appreciation of the fact that neither "patent" nor "exploitation of a patent" is a four letter word.

Part 3

Protection of Interests in Licensed or Assigned Intellectual Property

Chapter 16

Introduction to Bankruptcy Clauses

A common provision in almost every license or assignment of intellectual property is an "ipso facto" bankruptcy clause. In a license, the clause usually reads:

8. Bankruptcy. In the event of

(a) an appointment of a trustee or receiver,

(b) assignment of assets for the benefit of LICENSEE's creditors,

(c) any levy of execution involving the license herein granted, or

(d) an adjudication of the LICENSEE's bankruptcy, the license herein granted terminates.

In an assignment, the ipso facto bankruptcy clause usually reads:

8. Bankruptcy. In the event of

(a) an appointment of a trustee or receiver,

(b) assignment of assets for the benefit of LICENSEE's creditors,

(c) any levy of execution involving the license herein granted, or

(d) an adjudication of the LICENSEE's bankruptcy, the license herein granted terminates.

Until 1979, some courts reluctantly enforced ipso facto bankruptcy clauses.[1] The Bankruptcy Reform Act of 1978

---

[1] *See Schokbeton Indus., Inc. v. Schokbeton Prods. Corp.,* 466 F.2d 171 (5th Cir. 1972) (debtor in possession could not assume a patent license because the ipso facto bankruptcy clause was enforceable); *In re Diana*

(the Reform Act") obliterated the effectiveness of all such clauses as of its October 1, 1979, effective date.[2]

The Reform Act did more than simply obliterate ipso facto bankruptcy clauses. Under the Reform Act, any royalty or infringement debts that were incurred before a bankruptcy petition is filed may be forgiven and discharged.[3] In fact, a license to a debtor may be transferred to the highest bidder under the Reform Act—a bidder that may be an aggressive, price cutting competitor of the licensor.[4]

Reform went deeper still. The trustee of a licensor in bankruptcy can reject a license *in toto*. The licensor may be left to sue for infringement or to negotiate a license at a reduced royalty.[5]

Finally, the filing of a petition in bankruptcy operates as an "automatic stay,"[6] enjoining any acts, judicial or otherwise, to recover from or dispose of property in which the debtor in bankruptcy may have an interest. Before taking any action against property in which the trustee in bankruptcy claims an interest, a party must formally petition the bankruptcy court for relief from the automatic stay. Failure to obtain the bankruptcy court's permission to act against property of the estate may result in the exercise of contempt power by the court.

Shoe Corp., 80 F.2d 827 (2d Cir. 1936) (deferred license fees, due upon the automatic termination of a patent license and equipment lease, constituted a liquidated contract claim entitling the licensor to a 35 percent payment under the plan); *Lichman v. Moore,* 131 F. Supp. 434 (D.N.H. 1955) (insolvency reversion clause in a patent assignment exchanged for common stock of the assignee). Valid; *In re Michigan Motor Specialities Co.,* 288 F. 377 (E.D. Mich. 1923) clause terminating a license if licensee "discontinues its business through insolvency, ... bankruptcy, ... or any other clause" enforced). These cases have been criticized by a leading bankruptcy authority: *see* Countryman, "Contracts in Bankruptcy," 59 Minn. L. Rev. 479 (1974).

[2] 11 U.S.C. §§ 365(e), 541(c)(1) (1980).

[3] 11 U.S.C. §§ 5601, 502, 727(b), 1141(d)(1)(A) (1980).

[4] 11 U.S.C. §§ 363(b), 365(f) (1980).

[5] 11 U.S.C. §§ 365(a) (1980).

[6] 11 U.S.C. §§ 362 (1980).

Intellectual property transfers often involve at least one party whose finances are less solid than the Rock of Gibraltar. The lawyer representing the more stable party should coach his client on the consequences if the less stable party should file for bankruptcy. After the passage of the Reform Act, a lawyer may seriously mislead his client by including an ipso facto bankruptcy clause in an agreement transferring intellectual property. A default clause inadequately arms a client against a less stable party's potential financial problems. Lawyers must learn to structure licenses and assignments to assure their clients the biggest stick available if and when the client must deal with a trustee[7] or debtor in possession.[8]

---

[7] The trustee acts as the representative of the estate. 11 U.S.C. § 323 (1980). The trustee actually collects and liquidates the estate in a Chapter 7 case. 11 U.S.C. § 704 (1980). Although trustees will not usually be appointed in reorganization cases, a trustee may operate the business. 11 U.S.C. §§ 1104, 1108 (1978). The trustee has many special powers under Chapters 3 and 5 to collect property of the estate and to use, lease, or sell property of the estate. *See Chapter 17, infra* for a more detailed discussion of these powers.

[8] A "debtor in possession" is the debtor in an ordinary Chapter 11 reorganization. 11 U.S.C. § 1101. The Reform Act contemplates that in most cases the debtor in possession will continue to operate the business. 11 U.S.C. § 303(f). The debtor in possession has the same powers as a trustee to recover property of the estate. 11 U.S.C. § 1107. Additionally the debtor in possession has the same restrictions on his ability to liquidate or sell property out of the ordinary course of business as does a trustee. *Id.*

Chapter 17

A Synopsis of Liquidation and Reorganization Proceedings

Bankruptcy is constitutionally sanctioned.[1] A party in serious financial difficulty may seek the protection of the bankruptcy court, make full disclosure of his obligations, give up most of his property to form an estate, and be discharged of almost all obligations. A person coming out of bankruptcy with a discharge is given a fresh start.

The fact that debts can be compromised and forgiven may come as a shock to the uninitiated. A licensing attorney performs a valuable service for his client by advising the client to avoid potential bankruptcy problems.

A client's rights in transferred intellectual property will be most protected in bankruptcy if the right can be characterized as a security interest. The following discussion will reveal the importance of this characterization.

The filing of a bankruptcy petition[2] creates an estate[3] that includes all legal and equitable interest of the debtor in property as of the date that the petition is filed.[4] A legal representative of the estate, normally a trustee or debtor in possession, can avoid certain transfers of property made by the debtor prior to the date that bankruptcy was filed.[5]

In a Chapter 7 liquidation proceeding,[6] a trustee is appointed to collect, classify, and liquidate the estate.[7] The

---

[1] U.S. Const. art. I, § 8, cl. 4.
[2] 11 U.S.C. §§ 301, 302, 303 (1980).
[3] 11 U.S.C. § 541(a) (1980).
[4] *Id.*
[5] 11 U.S.C. §§ 544, 545, 547 (1980).
[6] 11 U.S.C. § 701, *et seq.*
[7] 11 U.S.C. §§ 702, 704 (1980).

trustee labels the assets of the estate as either property sub-ject to a security interest,[8] or as rights under an executory contract.[9] The property of the estate may simultaneously bear both labels: for example, a company can perfect a secu-rity interest in a contractual right to use leased equipment. Two types of property interests are thereby created—an executory contractual right to use the equipment and a secu-rity interest in the right to use the equipment.

The debtor's creditors are ranked in bankruptcy according to the characterization of their interest in the debtor's prop-erty. Secured creditors are at the top of the "totem pole" of creditors when it comes to recovery in a bankruptcy pro-ceeding. Secured creditors normally receive the collateral securing their claims[10] or at least receive proceeds from the sale of that collateral to the extent of any allowed claims.[11] Any estate property that remains after the satisfaction of secured creditors' claims will first be used to pay administra-tive expenses,[12] including lawyer fees. Perhaps six or seven cents on the dollar will be left to reimburse unsecured credi-

---

[8] A "security interest" is a lien created by an agreement. 11 U.S.C. § 101 (37) (1980).

[9] An executory contract is one in which obligations remain unper-formed by both parties. *See* Chapter 20, *infra.*

[10] A proof of claim is filed by the creditor, the trustee, or the debtor. 11 U.S.C. § 501. A claim for which proof has been filed is deemed allowed, unless someone objects. 11 U.S.C. § 502. "Claim" is defined to include:

(A) right to payment, whether or not such right is reduced to judg-ment, liquidated, unliquidated, fixed, contingent, matured, unma-tured, disputed, legal, equitable, secured or unsecured; or (B) right to an equitable remedy for breach of performance if such breach gives rise to a right to payment, whether or not such right to an equitable remedy is reduced to judgment, fixed, contingent, matured, disputed, undisputed, secured, or unsecured.

11 U.S.C. § 101(4). Gone is the distinction between tort claims and contract claims. Provision is made for estimating any contingent or unliquidated claim in order to avoid delay in closing of the bank-ruptcy case. 11 U.S.C. § 502(c)(1).

[11] 11 U.S.C. § 506(c) (1980).

[12] 11 U.S.C. § 506(c) (1980).

tors who stand at the bottom of the totem pole of creditors.[13]

A Chapter 11 business reorganization operates somewhat differently.[14] The debtor in possession or trustee in a business reorganization, if one is appointed, continues to operate the business while the creditors and debtor work out a plan for reorganization. The reorganization plan may impair any obligation[15] and forgive by discharge any obligation of an unsecured creditor.[16] Nonconsenting creditors, including secured creditors, can be forced to accept the plan.[17]

The trustee, debtor in possession, or a committee of creditors can reject unacceptable contracts and leases and negotiate new terms for other contracts and leases. The trustee or debtor in possession also may assume and assign contracts classified as "executory" after certain defaults are cured and adequate assurance of performance is provided.[18]

Although given great leeway in managing an estate, the representative of the estate cannot completely ignore the interest of the estate's creditors. Property of the estate must be handled according to the Reform Act. For example, a lease, sale, or use of property of the estate can only be consummated if such lease, sale, or use occurs in the ordinary

---

[13] Pursuit of an unsecured claim is probably not justified, as unsecured creditors rarely receive a significant portion of their claim. One author notes,

[Y]ear in and year out, less than 15% are "asset cases" in which something is paid to creditors. Another 15% are "nominal asset" cases in which there is nothing for creditors after the allowance of exemptions and the payment of administrative expenses. The balance of about 70% are 'no asset' cases in which there is nothing available to pay administrative expenses. In the less than 15% of cases where something is available for creditors, assets in 1969 . . . produced about $113,000,000, almost one fourth of which was consumed by administrative expenses, and unsecured creditors averaged a dividend of 7 or 8% after payment of priority claims.

Countryman, "A History of American Bankruptcy Law," 81 Com. L. J. 226, 231 (1976).

[14] 11 U.S.C. § 1101, *et seq.*

[15] 11 U.S.C. § 1123(b)(1) (1980).

[16] 11 U.S.C. § 1129(b)(1) (1980).

[17] 11 U.S.C. § 1129 (1980).

[18] 11 U.S.C. § 365 (1980).

course of business.[19] The trustee or debtor in possession may lease, sell, or use property of the estate out of the ordinary course of business only after notice and hearing.[20]

Other sections also limit the authority of the trustee or debtor in possession to use, lease, or sell property of the estate. For example, the trustee may not use, lease, or sell property in a manner inconsistent with an order granting relief from the automatic stay.[21]

One of the primary goals of the trustee or debtor in possession is to collect all property of the estate, including property that has been preferentially or fraudulently transferred by the debtor prior to filing bankruptcy. Unsecured creditors can receive more of a dividend on liquidation of the estate if the value of the estate is increased. Under certain circumstances, the trustee may set aside a transfer of intellectual property by the debtor.

---

[19] 11 U.S.C. § 363(c)(1) (1980).
[20] 11 U.S.C. § 363(b) (1980).
[21] 11 U.S.C. §§ 362(d), 362(e), 362(f), 363(d) (1980).

Chapter *18*

An Assignor with No Security Interest Will Have No Control at an Assignee's Bankruptcy

A hypothetical case will illustrate the plight of an unsecured creditor in bankruptcy. Consider the case of Salt of the Earth Corporation ("Salt of the Earth"), a family-owned corporation with a principal place of business in Muskogee, Oklahoma.

In 1975, an employee of Salt of the Earth invented a new electronic ignition system that could be used in virtually all combustion engines. The employee assigned the invention to Salt of the Earth as required by his employment contract.

Salt of the Earth did not have the capital needed to develop and market the improved electronic ignition. Instead, Salt of the Earth patented the invention and found a buyer for the patent—Big Daddy Corporation ("Big Daddy"). The assignment provided:

(1) a $5000 minimum monthly royalty plus 5 percent of gross receipts on products sold by Big Daddy;

(2) a traditional ipso facto bankruptcy clause—in the event of an act or event of bankruptcy, then all the assigned rights, title, and interests revert to the ASSIGNOR, Salt of the Earth;

(3) a default clause to the effect that if any default by Big Daddy remains uncured for 60 days after notice, then all the assigned rights, title, and interests revert automatically to the ASSIGNOR.

The patented electronic ignition system was extremely successful; however, Big Daddy still faced financial difficulties caused by Japanese imports and a sudden market shift to smaller cars. Big Daddy was forced into involuntary bankruptcy when a group of Big Daddy's creditors filed a petition against Big Daddy. Big Daddy could no longer pay royalties to Salt of the Earth under the assignment.

§ 18.01 An Assignee-Debtor's Interest in a Patent Will Belong to the Bankruptcy Estate

Assume that you are the lawyer who drafted Salt of the Earth's assignment to Big Daddy. Salt of the Earth will first ask you whether Salt of the Earth now owns the patent under the ipso facto bankruptcy clause or under the default clause. How will you answer Salt of the Earth?

Under the Reform Act, Salt of the Earth clearly cannot enforce the ipso facto clause:

[A]n interest of the debtor in property becomes property of the estate . . . notwithstanding any provision[1]

Under the Reform Act, all of Big Daddy's rights at the time of the petition belong to the bankruptcy estate, including "all legal and equitable interest of the debtor in property as of the commencement of the [bankruptcy] case."[2] Nor can Salt of the Earth exercise its rights under the default clause after bankruptcy is commenced. The automatic stay forbids Salt of the Earth from taking any action "to obtain possession of property of the estate or of property from the estate."[3]

[1] The Estate Representative Can Recover Property Transferred by the Debtor Before Bankruptcy Was Filed

Assume that Big Daddy defaulted just before Big Daddy was forced into bankruptcy, and that Salt of the Earth claimed its patent under the default clause before the credi-

---

[1] 11 U.S.C. § 541(c)(1) (1980).
[2] 11 U.S.C. § 541(a)(1) (1980).
[3] 11 U.S.C. § 362(a)(3) (1980).

tors filed their petition. Salt of the Earth still may not own its patent. Salt of the Earth may be forced to reconvey the patent to the estate if the trustee can show that the reversion of the patent to Salt of the Earth was a "voidable" preference.[4]

To be a voidable preference, the reversion of the patent to Salt of the Earth must first have been a "transfer of property of the debtor."[5] The reversion of the patent was a "transfer" by virtue of the default clause in the assignment and the exercise of Salt of the Earth's right of reversion.[6] The contractual right of reversion and the patent rights themselves were "property of the debtor," as defined in the legislative history of the Reform Act and in the cases decided under the predecessor to the act.[7]

To be a "voidable preference," the reversion of the patent to Salt of the Earth additionally must have been a transfer: to a creditor,[8] for or on account of an antecedent debt,[9] while the debtor was insolvent,[10] and within ninety days before the bankruptcy petition was filed.[11] The transfer also

---

[4] A debtor in possession under Chapter 11 may also recover voidable preferences under 11 U.S.C. § 547 (1980). 11 U.S.C. §§ 541(a)(3), 704(1), 1106(A), 1107(a) (1980).

[5] 11 U.S.C. § 547(b) (1980).

[6] The definition sections of the Reform Act provide that "'transfer' means every mode, direct or indirect, absolute or conditional, voluntary or involuntary, or disposing of or parting with property or with an interest in property, including retention of a security interest." 11 U.S.C. § 101(40) (1978). The default clause arguably qualifies as a security interest under 11 U.S.C. § 101(37) (1980).

[7] 11 U.S.C. § 547; *Tatum v. Acadian Prod. Corp.,* 35 F. Supp. 40 (E.D. La. 1940) ("a transfer of property . . . includes the giving or conveying of anything of value which has debt-paying or debt-securing power" (oil and gas rights)); *Comparone v. M. J. Caplan Co.,* 270 Mass. 74, 169 N.E. 667 (1930) (goodwill).

[8] 11 U.S.C. § 547(b)(1) (1980).

[9] 11 U.S.C. § 547(b)(2) (1980).

[10] 11 U.S.C. § 547(b)(3) (1980).

[11] 11 U.S.C. § 547(b)(4)(A). Note that the preference period expands to a year if the transferee is an insider with reasonable cause to believe that the debtor was insolvent at the time of transfer. 11 U.S.C. § 547(b)(4)(B) (1980). An "insider" is defined in 11 U.S.C. § 101(25).

must have created a "preference" whereby Salt of the Earth received property of a greater value than the dividend that it could have realized in a Chapter 7 liquidation proceeding.

Three of these elements are clearly met by the reversion to Salt of the Earth. Reversion of the patent was a transfer to a creditor (Salt of the Earth had a claim for unpaid royalties) for an antecedent debt (the reversion occurred at least sixty days after default) and clearly created a preference because Salt of the Earth could have realized no dividend in a Chapter 7 proceeding. Salt of the Earth's decision to claim its patent, alone, showed that the patent had some value. The reversion of a patent will almost always create a preference where an assignor fails to retain a security interest and actually exercises his termination rights.

With regard to the "transfer while insolvent" requirement, "the debtor is presumed to have been insolvent during the ninety days immediately preceding the date of the filing of the petition."[12] This presumption shifts the burden of producing evidence to the creditor; however, the trustee still has the burden of proof.[13] The trustee must prove, first, that the transfer occurred within ninety days before bankruptcy was filed. The trustee must also be prepared to show that, at the time of the reversion, Big Daddy's debts were greater than all of Big Daddy's property, given a fair market value.

Salt of the Earth's patent will not be deemed to have been transferred until Salt of the Earth could prevail over a contract creditor's judgment lien on the patent. State law determines when Salt of the Earth would prevail over such a judgment lienor. Normally, a reversionary interest will not defeat the rights of a judgment lienor until that reversionary right has been exercised. In order to have a superior right, Salt of the Earth must exercise its reversionary right more

---

Generally the list encompasses relatives, partners, and the partnerships or corporations that an individual debtor controls. In the case of a corporation "insiders" would include officers, directors, control persons, and affiliated business entities.

[12] 11 U.S.C. § 547(f) (1980).

[13] H. R. Rep. No. 595, 95th Cong., 1st Sess. 375 (1977).

than ninety days before a bankruptcy petition is filed. If the patent is a vitally important asset of Big Daddy, Salt of the Earth's exercise of the reversionary right, itself, may trigger Big Daddy to immediately file a petition in bankruptcy.

[2] An Assignor with No Security Interest in a Patent Will Be at the Mercy of the Trustee and the Secured Creditors

If the trustee is trying to find a buyer for Big Daddy, or if Big Daddy is going through business reorganization, the trustee or debtor in possession will keep Big Daddy's business running during the proceedings. The trustee or debtor in possession may use property of the estate in the ordinary course of business regardless of whether Big Daddy has defaulted in contracts for the use of the property.[14] Big Daddy will continue to manufacture and sell electronic ignitions covered by Salt of the Earth's patent even if Big Daddy's estate fails to pay royalties under the patent.

Royalties incurred by Big Daddy after the bankruptcy petition is filed at least have priority as administrative expenses. Even though administrative expenses, Salt of the Earth may receive far less than a full royalty under its patent because secured creditors normally divest all assets of the estate, leaving nothing to pay administrative expenses and unsecured creditors.

[3] The Debtor's Royalty Obligation Will Be Discharged, and a Trustee Can Sell Patent Rights to the Highest Bidder Free of Any Royalties

Not only can the trustee or debtor in possession permit Big Daddy to continue to exploit Salt of the Earth's patent without paying royalties, the trustee can sell the patent for a lump sum to Slick Predatory—Salt of the Earth's major and

---

[14] 11 U.S.C. § 363(c)(1) (1980) authorizes use, sale and lease of property in the ordinary course of business. The automatic stay, 11 U.S.C. § 362 (1980), enjoins a creditor from taking any action on account of a default.

most powerful competitor.[15] Whether Slick Predatory will have to pay royalties to Salt of the Earth depends on the terms of the original assignment to Big Daddy. If the original assignment had a clause making its terms binding on Big Daddy's successors, assigns, and licensees, and if the assignment was properly recorded in the Patent Office, Slick Predatory should be required to pay royalties.

Slick Predatory could argue that the obligation to pay royalties was personal to Big Daddy and that this personal covenant does not run with the patent property. Such an argument has force even though unsupported by case law.

Salt of the Earth could try to avoid a sale to Slick Predatory by bidding on the patent; however, Salt of the Earth is not exploiting the patent and may not be able to bid a high price for the patent. The trustee's incentive is to get the highest price for the patent. Slick Predatory, a large conglomerate, can undoubtedly bid a higher price for the patent than Salt of the Earth.

Salt of the Earth has little hope of recovering unpaid royalties incurred before the bankruptcy petition was filed. Big Daddy's obligation to pay royalties came within the statutory definition of a "claim."[16] Big Daddy's obligation to pay royalties will therefore be "discharged" in the bankruptcy proceeding. "Discharge" will forgive Big Daddy of all debts incurred before the order for relief issues.[17]

Protected solely by the default and reversionary provisions of the assignment, Salt of the Earth may have no rights in the patent at all if Big Daddy files for bankruptcy.

---

[15] 11 U.S.C. § 363(b) (1980).

[16] A claim is defined as "[a] right to payment, whether or not such right is reduced to judgment, liquidated, unliquidated, fixed, contingent, matured, unmatured, disputed, undisputed, legal, equitable, secured, or unsecured." 11 U.S.C. § 101 (4)(A) (1980).

[17] 11 U.S.C. §§ 727(b), 1141(d)(1)(A) (1980).

§ 18.02 An Assignor with an Enforceable Security Interest and a Well-Drafted Default Clause Has More Control

Secured debts are treated much differently in bankruptcy than unsecured debts. Assume now that Salt of the Earth had perfected a security interest in the patent assigned to Big Daddy. Where Big Daddy's business will continue, Salt of the Earth can petition the court for an order prohibiting or conditioning the use, sale, or lease of the secured patent rights as necessary to provide "adequate protection" for Salt of the Earth.[18] The trustee has the burden to prove that Salt of the Earth is "adequately protected."[19]

The Code provides three alternatives as "adequate protection."[20] (1) The trustee can be required to make periodic cash payments to the extent that use, sale, or lease decreases the value of the lienor's interest in the property; (2) the lienor may be provided with an additional or replacement lien; or (3) the court may grant such other relief as will give the lienor the "indubitable equivalent" of the lien.[21]

[1] The Security Interest Runs with the Property

A trustee in bankruptcy cannot sell property of the estate free and clear of any lien unless: (1) applicable nonbankruptcy law permits such a sale; (2) the lienor consents; (3) the value of the property sold is greater than the aggregate obligations secured by the lien; (4) the lien is disputed in good faith; or (5) the lienor could be compelled to accept a money satisfaction of the obligations.[22]

---

[18] 11 U.S.C. §§ 362(d), 363(e), 362(f), 363(d) (1980).

[19] 11 U.S.C. § 362(g) (1980).

[20] 11 U.S.C. § 361 (1980).

[21] *See* Marsari, "Adequate Protection Under The Bankruptcy Reform Act," 1979 Annual Survey of Bankruptcy Law 171; Trost, Business Reorganizations under Chapter 11 of the New Bankruptcy Code," 34 Bus. Law. 1309 (1979), *reprinted in* 1980 Annual Survey of Bankruptcy Law 165, for descriptions of the alternatives and standards not addressed by the Reform Act.

[22] 11 U.S.C. § 363(f) (1980).

Any sale of the patent to Slick Predatory should be subject to Salt of the Earth's security interest. Salt of the Earth could foreclose on the collateral (the patent itself) upon the failure of Slick Predatory, Inc., to pay royalties as agreed in the assignment to Big Daddy. By listing the proceeds from the sale of the patent as additional collateral in the security agreement with Big Daddy, Salt of the Earth could receive the cash paid by Slick Predatory, Inc., for the patent in the event that the trustee somehow managed to sell the patent free and clear of the security interest.

[2] An Assignor with a Security Interest May Bid on the Patent and Deduct from the Purchase Price the Secured Obligations of the Estate

As a secured creditor, Salt of the Earth also has the option to purchase the patent out of the estate and to deduct the purchase price of the patent from the value of the claim against Big Daddy for past and future royalties.[23] This protection may be the most significant available to secured patent assignors under the Reform Act.

[3] The Clout of a Secured Assignor in a Reorganization Case

To understand Salt of the Earth's increased clout as a secured creditor in confirming a business reorganization plan, one must understand how a reorganization plan is formulated and confirmed.[24] Claims of creditors are divided into classes containing substantially similar claims or interests.[25] Of course, every secured claim is distinctly different from every other secured claim; however, the claims of pat-

---

[23] 11 U.S.C. § 363(k) (1980).

[24] *See generally* Klee, "All You Ever Wanted to Know about Cram Down under the New Bankruptcy Code," 53 Am. Bankr. L.J. 133 (1979); Trost, "Business Reorganizations under Chapter 11 of the New Bankruptcy Code," 34 Bus. Law. 1309 (1979).

[25] 11 U.S.C. § 1122 (1980).

ent assignors should not be so dissimilar that each claim will be in a single class.

A reorganization plan can be confirmed only if approved by all classes; however, a class can "approve" the plan even though its members do not approve.[26] Where a claim or an interest is not impaired by the plan, the class asserting such claims is automatically deemed to approve the plan.[27]

Nonconsenting secured creditors can be forced to accept a plan only if the requirements of 11 U.S.C. § 1129(b)(2)(A) are met. The mechanics of that section are very complicated. At a very minimum, the property must remain subject to the security interest, and the secured party must receive secured cash payments equal to the value of the creditor's interest in the collateral as of the effective date of the plan. Where the collateral is sold free and clear of the lien, the security interest must attach to the proceeds, and the secured party must receive deferred cash payments equal to those that the secured party would have received had the collateral not been sold.

Assume that Salt of the Earth retained a security interest in its patent, in any of Big Daddy's inventory covered by the patent, and in any proceeds from such inventory.[28] Salt of the Earth has a good chance of receiving deferred cash payments equal to its expectation of payment under the assignment, provided the value of the collateral at the effective date of the plan covers such payments.

Compare Salt of the Earth's treatment as a secured creditor in reorganization with the treatment that Salt of the Earth will receive as an unsecured creditor. If Salt of the Earth votes to reject a reorganization plan, the plan still can be imposed on unsecured Salt of the Earth if at least one class accepts the plan and the court determines that all rejecting classes are treated fairly and equitably.[29] Salt of the

---

[26] 11 U.S.C. § 1122 (1980).

[27] 11 U.S.C. § 1129 (1980).

[28] Security interest in inventory to secure payment of the royalty will be very desirable; but for business reasons not always possible.

[29] 11 U.S.C. § 1129(b)(1) (1980).

Earth will be deemed to be treated fairly and equitably if it receives property having a value equal to the amount of the claim against Big Daddy at the effective date of the plan, or if any claimant or interest junior to Salt of the Earth receives nothing.[30]

Under the complex provisions for reorganization, Salt of the Earth could conceivably walk away from a reorganization with absolutely no value, while Big Daddy retains title to the assigned patent. Such a harsh result should never occur; however, clients should be advised to retain a security interest in assigned or licensed patents in order to avoid such a result.

---

[30] 11 U.S.C. § 1129(b)(2)(B) (1980). The legislative history states:
As long as senior creditors have not been paid more than in full, and classes of equal claims are being treated so that the dissenting class of impaired unsecured claims is not being discriminated against unfairly, the plan may be confirmed if the impaired class of unsecured claims receives less than 100 cents on the dollar (or nothing at all) as long as no class junior to the dissenting class receives anything at all.
124 Cong. Rec. H. 1109 (daily ed. Sept. 28, 1978) (statement of Rep. Levitas), *reprinted in* 1978 U.S. Code Cong. & Admin. News 6436, 6476.

Chapter 19

The Nonexclusive Licensor's Advantage

§ 19.01 A Trustee Cannot Assume nor Assign a Personal Contract Unassignable by the Licensee

Now consider the situation of Jet Set, Inc., a nonexclusive licensor. Jet Set holds and practices a patent for a process to make a contact cement that bonds to a variety of surfaces. Jet Set also manufactures in bulk one of the major reactants for use in the process. The demand for the glue made by the process is far greater than Jet Set can meet. Jet Set therefore has granted nonexclusive licenses with minimum and running royalties to acceptable manufacturers. Each license contains a promise by Jet Set to supply the unpatented reactant.

Such a license in bankruptcy will be treated as an executory contract under 11 U.S.C. § 365. A contract is executory where there are substantial unperformed obligations on both sides of the contract.[1] In the case of Jet Set, Jet Set's licensees have not yet performed their obligation to pay royalties throughout the term of the license. Jet Set has not yet performed its obligation to further license and to provide the reactant to its licensees.

Section 365 of the Reform Act, 11 U.S.C. § 365, allows the trustee to assume or reject executory contracts and unexpired leases if certain conditions are met. In the case of a patent license, a very strong argument can be made that the trustee cannot assume nor assign the license without the consent of the licensor. Section 365(c) (the "excuse provision") prohibits assumption where:

---

[1] *See* §§ 20.03 through 21.01[1], *infra.*

(1)(A) [A]pplicable law excuses a party, other than the debtor to such contract or lease from accepting performance or rendering performance to the trustee or an assignee of such contract or lease, whether or not such contract or lease prohibits or restricts assignment of the rights or delegation of duty; and (B) such party does not consent to such assumption of assignment.

The excuse provision tilts the scales in favor of Jet Set and other patent licensors. Patent licenses have long been considered contracts of such a personal nature that the license cannot be transferred from the licensee by assignment[2] nor by operation of law.[3] Jet Set has a good chance of persuading a bankruptcy court that the license cannot be assumed without Jet Set's consent.

Because a debtor in possession is "subject to any limitations on a trustee under . . . chapter [11],"[4] the prohibition against assumption of a license by a trustee could similarly restrict a debtor in possession.[5] By definition, however, a debtor in possession is the debtor.[6] If the debtor in possession assumed Jet Set's license, Jet Set would not be accepting performance from anyone other than its chosen licensee. Because any assumption must be approved by the bankruptcy judge, Jet Set would have the opportunity to argue to the judge the personal nature of the license and the frustration of purpose that would result from saddling Jet Set with a licensee so different, except in name, from the original licensee.

---

[2] *Lane & Bodley Co. v. Locke,* 150 U.S. 193 (1893); *Hapgood v. Hewitt,* 119 U.S. 226 (1886); *Unarco Indus., Inc. v. Kelley Co.,* 465 F.2d 1303 (7th Cir. 1972), *cert. denied,* 410 U.S. 929 (1973).

[3] *Oliver v. Rumford Chem. Works,* 109 U.S. 75 (1883); PPG Indus., Inc. v. Guardian Indus. Corp., 597 F.2d 1090 (6th Cir.), *cert. denied,* 444 U.S. 930 (1979).

[4] 11 U.S.C. § 1107(a) (1980).

[5] *But see* 2 *Collier on Bankruptcy* ¶ 365.05 (15th ed. 1979).

[6] 11 U.S.C. § 1101(1) (1980).

§ 19.02 The Code Protects a Nonexclusive Licensor Whose License Is Assumed

If Jet Set's license is a critical asset of a corporation going through a reorganization, the debtor in possession undoubtedly will be allowed to assume the license. Otherwise chances of successful reorganization would be destroyed. For example, where the licensee is in the business of making the glue, cannot easily design around the process, and cannot afford to defend an infringement suit, the licensee-debtor would have to shut down if the contract was not assumed.

Where the debtor is permitted to assume, and there has been a default, the Reform Act provides three protections for Jet Set. The debtor must: (1) cure defaults;[7] (2) compensate for actual pecuniary loss;[8] and (3) provide adequate assurance of future performance.[9] These requirements will provide some protection for Jet Set, but their value should not be overestimated.

Often cure of defaults and compensation for actual pecuniary loss (that is, payment of past due royalties) will be much less important than adequate assurance of future performance. Because a major goal of the Reform Act is to bring bankruptcy law into conformance with commercial standards, adequate assurance could be reasonably defined. Article Two of the Uniform Commercial Code requires that adequate assurance of future performance be reasonable according to commercial standards.[10] The adequate assurance reasonably to be expected of an insolvent debtor, however, will be less than the adequate assurance to be expected of a solvent debtor.

§ 19.03 An Assumed Nonexclusive License Is Assignable

If Jet Set cannot persuade the bankruptcy court that its nonexclusive license is too personal to be assumed, the trus-

---

[7] 11 U.S.C. § 365(b)(1)(A) (1980).
[8] 11 U.S.C. § 365(b)(1)(B) (1980).
[9] 11 U.S.C. § 365(b)(1)(C) (1980).
[10] U.C.C. § 2-609 (1976).

217

tee or debtor in possession may assign the license.[11] The assignment of a nonexclusive license should be a sale of property out of the ordinary course of business. Notice and hearing should be required before the trustee assigns the contract.[12] At the hearing, Jet Set will once again have the opportunity to impress the court with the personal nature of the license; however, the court is unlikely to be any more impressed on a second hearing of the same argument.

Apparently the only way for Jet Set to prevent an undesirable licensee from acquiring the license from the estate is to purchase back the license. Even that alternative may not be available. For example, where the trustee finds an entity willing to purchase the entire estate of a bankrupt with the intent of operating the business, it is doubtful that Jet Set will be allowed to defeat this intent by purchasing back any rights of the debtor under the license.

§ 19.04 When a Nonexclusive License Is Rejected, the Licensee/Debtor Cannot Continue to Practice the Invention

A trustee also can reject Jet Set's nonexclusive license.[13] Where rejection occurs, the nonexclusive license is deemed breached.[14] The Reform Act, in 11 U.S.C. § 365(g), provides a complex formula for determining when the contract is deemed breached upon rejection. The timing of the breach is important to Jet Set's position on the bankruptcy priority ladder.[15] Prepetition claims, in the absence of a security agreement, fall at the bottom of the priority ladder. Claims for administrative expenses, that is, expenses of operating a business after the petition has been filed, are the first expenses paid after the secured creditors are paid.[16]

---

[11] 11 U.S.C. § 365(f) (1980).
[12] 11 U.S.C. § 365(b) (1980).
[13] 11 U.S.C. § 365(a) (1980).
[14] 11 U.S.C. § 365(g) (1980).
[15] 11 U.S.C. § 507 (1980).
[16] *Id.*

As a practical matter, a trustee is unlikely to reject Jet Set's nonexclusive license unless he considers the patent rights worth less than the effort to assume. If the trustee sees no value in Jet Set's license, Jet Set may have a very difficult time interesting someone else in the invention.

Chapter 20

The Executory Nature of an Intellectual Property Transfer: Rejection by Licensees or Licensors

§ 20.01   Pre-Code Law

Almost all intellectual property transfers will be treated in bankruptcy either like the assignment by Salt of the Earth or the license granted by Jet Set, Inc. The debtor's interest under such transfers will be characterized as either "property of the estate" or an "executory contract." The Reform Act grants some protection to executory contracts. The question becomes, when will a transfer of intellectual property rights be classified as an executory contract?

Although the Reform Act fails to define the terms "executory contract" and "unexpired lease," the legislative history indicates that contracts are executory to the extent that "performance remains due on both sides."[1] This definition follows case law under the old bankruptcy act. In *Jenson v. Continental Fin. Corp.,*[2] the Eighth Circuit considered the meaning of an "executory contract" in the context of the old bankruptcy act. An executory contract was said to be:

"[A] contract under which the obligations of both the bankrupt and the other party to the contract are so unperformed that the failure of either to complete performance would constitute a material breach excusing the performance of the other [citations omitted]." Thus, where the contractual obli-

---

[1] H. Rep. No. 595, 95th Cong. 1st Sess. 347 (1977).
[2] 591 F.2d 477, 481 (8th Cir. 1979).

221

gations of the bankrupt and the other contracting party remain at least partially and materially unperformed at bankruptcy, the contract is executory.

Under this "mutuality of unperformed obligations" standard, a client's transfer of intellectual property can be classed by making a list of the continuing obligations set out in the transfer instrument. A contract clearly will be "executory" where each party has promised to supply something tangible. For example, Jet Set, Inc., promised to supply an unpatented reactant for use in the patented process. The licensee agreed to pay a minimum monthly royalty even if the licensee did not practice the invention.

§ 20.02   Under the Bankruptcy Code: The *Lubrizol* Case

Recent decisions have held that a license agreement can be executory even when relatively little performance is due, and that a *licensee* can find itself holding merely an unsecured claim for damages upon rejection by the *licensor*. A widely remarked case is *Lubrizol Enters. Inc. v. Richmond Metal Finishers, Inc.,* 756 F.2d 1043 (4th Cir. 1985), *cert. denied sub nom. Lubrizol Enters., Inc. v. Canfield,* 475 U.S. 1057 (1986).

In *Lubrizol,* the debtor Richmond Metal Finishers (RMF) had licensed Lubrizol, nonexclusively, to practice a nonpatented process in exchange for a running royalty. A patent application had apparently been filed, but no patent ever issued at any time in question. Licensor RMF owed a continuing most-favored-nation duty to Lubrizol, and was further obliged to defend and indemnify Lubrizol against certain losses. *See* 756 F.2d at 1045.

The Fourth Circuit ruled that the license was executory and could be rejected by the licensor, overturning a district court decision, *In re Richmond Metal Finishers, Inc.,* 38 B.R. 341, (E.D. Va. 1984), *rev'd sub nom. Lubrizol Enters., Inc. v. Richmond Metal Finishers, Inc.,* 756 F.2d 1043 (4th Cir. 1985), *cert. denied sub nom. Lubrizol Enters., Inc. v. Canfield,* 475 U.S. 1057 (1986), and reinstating a bankruptcy court holding, *In re Richmond Metal Finishers, Inc.*, 36 B.R. 270 (Bankr. E.D. Va. 1983). It cited its own adoption of Professor Countryman's test that "a contract is executory if the 'obligations of both the bankrupt and the other party to the contract are so far unperformed that the failure of either to complete the performance would constitute a material breach excusing the performance of the other.'" 756 F.2d at 1045.

§ 20.03 Rejection of a "Naked" Immunity from Suit

A more difficult problem arises where the licensor "transfers" a naked promise not to sue the licensee for infringement and makes no affirmative promises. Professor Countryman has persuasively argued that even though a licensor has not promised to supply something tangible, an unperformed obligation still remains.[3] He argues:

[T]here may be an implied undertaking by the licensor which brings all patent licenses within the ambit of an executory contract. It has been held in a patentee-licensor infringement action against a third party that a final judgment adjudicating the patent invalid constitutes a "complete failure of consideration" amounting to an "eviction" which releases the licensee from any further obligation to pay royalties.[313] [fn. 313 *Scherr v. Difco Labs, Inc.*, 401 F.2d 443 (6th Cir. 1968); *Drackett Chem. Co. v. Chamberlain Co.*, 63 F.2d 853 (6th Cir. 1933). Some courts have confined the eviction doctrine to exclusive licenses. *Ross v. Fuller & Warren Co.*, 105 F. 510 (N.D.N.Y. 1900). *Cf. Automatic Radio Mfg. Co. v. Hazeltine Research.* 176 F.2d 799 (1st Cir. 1949), *aff'd on other grounds*, 339 U.S. 827, *reh'g denied*, 340 U.S. 846 (1950); *Thomson Spot Welder Co. v. Oldberg Mfg. Co.*, 256 Mich. 447, 240 N.W. 93 (1931).] Moreover since the death of the doctrine of "licensee estoppel," the licensee can set up the invalidity of the patent as a defense when sued by the licensor for royalties due under the license.[314] [fn. 314 *Lear, Inc. v. Adkins*, 395 U.S. 653 (1969).] Hence, all patentee-licensors

---

[3] Countryman, "Executory Contracts In Bankruptcy: Part II," 58 Minn. L. Rev. 479, 502 (1974).

are now substantially in the position of having warranted to their licensees the validity of their patents. Although the sanction for the breach of such a warranty is only a forfeiture of royalties rather than liability for damages, this continuing undertaking by the licensor is enough to justify the treatment of all unexpired patent licenses as executory.[315] [fn. 315 *See* Countryman, Part I, at 453. [In countryman, "Executory Contracts in Bankruptcy," 57 Minn. L. Rev. 439, 453 (1973), the author considers whether any obligations flow from a lessor to a surety after the lessor has granted the lessee a lease. He concludes that the surety has sufficient interest in whether the lessor performs his continuing obligations to the lessee to consider the surety-lessor contract executory. Thus the surety example demonstrates that a party need not always have a legal remedy for breach in order to have his contract classified as executory.]]

The following argument could be made in answer to Professor Countryman's argument. Theoretically, a warranty of validity would require restitution to the licensee upon eviction. An adjudication of invalidity means that for some reason the patent never should have issued.[4] An adjudication of invalidity, then, means that the parties to the license operated under a mistake of fact. Where the parties have operated under a mistake of a basic fact, and the burden of that risk falls on the transferor, courts have long awarded restitution.[5] The remedy actually afforded a licensee upon eviction, however, is excuse from future performance. Courts simply allow the licensee to consider the license terminated upon eviction.[6] This remedy is inconsistent with the remedy that one would expect for breach of a warranty of validity.

---

[4] Invalidity is often the major defense to a patent infringement lawsuit. A defendant will try to find some error in the patent application or some substantive error in the examiner's allowance of claims. For a general discussion of the area, *see* R. White, *Patent Litigation: Procedure and Tactics* (1979).

[5] *Restatement of Restitution* § 9(3) (1937).

[6] *Zenith Lab, Inc. v. Carter-Wallace, Inc.,* 530 F.2d 508 (3d Cir.), *cert. denied,* 429 U.S. 828 (1976); *Troxel Mfg. Co. v. Schwinn Bicycle Co.,* 465 F.2d 1253 (6th Cir. 1972).

The refusal of the courts to award restitution to a licensee when a patent is held invalid indicates that the licensor has not assumed the risk of invalidity. In other words, both parties are consciously ignorant with respect to the validity of the licensed patent.[7] "No warranty of the validity of the Letters Patent is implied in any license given thereunder."[8] In fact, many licenses today specifically negate any implied warranty of validity.[9] In light of these arguments, the argument that a patent license implies a warranty of validity is unlikely to prevail.

A licensor also should not rely on *Lear, Inc. v. Adkins*[10] to characterize the transaction between an exclusive licensor and his licensee as an executory contract. The Supreme Court in *Lear* specifically recognized that federal courts are bound by state courts' interpretation of patent licenses.[11] The rule in *Lear* that a licensee may raise invalidity as a defense in a suit for royalties and that a licensee cannot be required to pay royalties while the royalty suit is pending represents a cautious preemption of state contract law in the interests of federal patent policy.[12]

The Supreme Court encouraged state courts to establish rules on trade secret licensing that would not conflict with patent policy.[13] Since *Lear,* courts continue to distinguish between a failure of consideration excusing future performance and a breach of warranty entitling the injured party to restitution.[14] Courts reason that the policy of encouraging

---

[7] *Restatement of Restitution* § 10, Comment a (1937).

[8] *Walker on Patents* Deller's edition, § 403 (2d ed. 1965) (citing thirty-seven cases for the well-established proposition).

[9] H. Mayers, *Drafting Patent License Agreements* § 14.01 (1974).

[10] 395 U.S. 653 (1969).

[11] *Id.* at 661–62.

[12] *Id.* at 670 (where the Court said: "Licensees may often be the only individuals with enough economic incentive to challenge the patentability of an inventor's discovery. If they are muzzled, the public may continually be required to pay tribute to would-be monopolists without need or justification. We think it plain that the technical requirements of contract doctrine must give way before the demands of the public interest.").

[13] *Id.* at 674.

[14] *See* note 6, *supra.*

early adjudication of invalidity would not be served by allowing a licensee to wait until the end of a license term to sue for recovery of all royalties.[15]

Whether Salt of the Earth could persuade a bankruptcy court that the assignment to Big Daddy is executory because Salt of the Earth has remaining unperformed continuing obligations is at best close. Salt of the Earth may be wise to include in future exclusive licenses and assignments a specific recital that Salt of the Earth will join in any suit against infringers, or that the exclusive licensor/assignee will sue infringers. Such an obligation should be sufficient to make the contract executory.

§ 20.04   Can a Licensee Continue Its Use of the Technology after the Licensor's Rejection?

Interestingly, the *Lubrizol* appeals court stated, apparently in dicta, that after a rejection a licensee may no longer practice a licensed process. *See* 756 F.2d at 1048. The basis for its observation was its equation of continued use of the process by the licensee with the licensee's "seek[ing] to retain its contract rights in the technology by specific performance," but that specific performance was unavailable under the bankruptcy statute. *Id.* Consequently, the licensee would be left with merely an unsecured claim for damages. *Id.*

A number of arguments could be made criticizing this dictum. It could be said that the licensor's act of disclosing the process to the licensee lets that particular horse out of the barn—the licensee cannot unlearn what it has been taught.[16] Absent a patent, copyright, mask work registration, or design patent, the only constraint on the licensee's use of the process is the licensor's *contractual* right to exclude—

---

[15] *Zenith Lab, Inc. v. Carter-Wallace, Inc.,* note 6, *supra,* 530 F.2d at 513; Troxel, note 6, *supra,* 465 F.2d at 1257.

[16] A different situation will be presented, of course, if continued use depends on continued possession of documents, copies of computer programs, etc., which remain the property of the licensor during the license relationship.

and it could be said that right dies with the rejected contract.[17]

Even if patent or similar exclusionary rights are available to the licensor, it could further be argued that the license constituted an advance settlement of a potential legal dispute, and that as a matter both of public policy and of congressional intent, the licensor's waiver of its exclusionary right is not to be set aside. In any case, the notion that the mere continued use by the licensee constitutes the seeking of "specific performance" of its contract rights appears strained at best.

Looking at the question from another angle, a licensor who rejects and then seeks to prevent the licensee from practicing the technology could be said to be seeking to *rescind* the agreement, and not merely to commit an anticipatory breach and thereby avoid performance.

§ 20.05 Pending Legislation

The *Lubrizol* decision has recently led to congressional consideration of a bill to overturn it. S.B. 1626 was introduced by Senator Dennis DeConcini in August, 1987. As drafted, the bill provides that unless and until the debtor-licensor assumes a license, "the [licensor] may not interfere with the grantee's rights (i) to deal with the intellectual property, as provided in the contract or lease."

At this writing (early November, 1987), the bill was in the Senate Judiciary Committee, which in recent months has been preoccupied with the Bork and Ginsburg Supreme Court nominations.

---

[17] The argument that the obligation of confidence is dissolved upon rejection was suggested by Marilyn Shea-Stonum, appellate counsel for Lubrizol, at an American Bar Association panel discussion in August, 1987.

§ 20.06 Avoiding the *Lubrizol* Problem

Numerous articles have been written on how counsel for licensees can try to protect their clients from a *Lubrizol* rejection by their licensors.[18] No sure solutions have been proposed.

In the case of computer software, various source-code escrow arrangements have been proposed. The concern here, however, is that a trustee would attempt to void any such arrangement.

Other proposals have addressed the possibility of taking a security interest in, or even acquiring outright ownership of, the intellectual property itself. Again, there is considerable uncertainty whether such an arrangement would withstand a bankruptcy petition.

---

[18] *See* 1987 LICENSING LAW HANDBOOK, Chapters 12–14 (articles by Drabkin & Brooks, Engel & Radcliffe, and Haas & Burk).

Chapter *21*

Retain and Perfect a Security Interest in Intellectual Property

The best way to protect Salt of the Earth is to perfect a security interest in Salt of the Earth's patent rights. The question becomes: how can one protect a security interest in patent rights? Patents, patent licenses, copyrights, mask works, trademarks, and trade secrets are classified as general intangibles under the Uniform Commercial Code [U.C.C.].[1] Unfortunately, it is not clear that U.C.C. Article 9 governs the perfection of a security interest in patent rights. The primary ambiguity arises from the uncertainty whether U.C.C. § 9-106 has been preempted by 35 U.S.C. § 261.

Article 9 of the U.C.C. requires the filing of a "financing statement" in the offices of the proper state(s) within the proper time. Article 9 does not apply to security interests to the extent that a federal statute governs the parties' rights.[2] A financing statement is not necessary and is not effective to perfect a security interest "in property subject to (a) a statute . . . of the United States which provides for national registration . . . or which specifies a place of filing different from that specified" in Article 9.[3]

Arguably, 35 U.S.C. § 261 "specifies a place of filing different from that specified" in Article 9. Section 261 provides that an "assignment, grant or conveyance shall be void" against a subsequent *bona fide* purchaser unless recorded in

---

[1] U.C.C. § 9-106. For a discussion of security interests in copyrights, mask works, trademarks, trade secrets, as well as patent rights, *see* G. Engel and M. Radcliffe, "Intellectual Property Financing for High Technology Companies," U.C.C. L. J. 19:3, 3–33 (1986).

[2] U.C.C. § 9-104(a) (1976).

[3] U.C.C. § 9-302(3)(a) (1976).

the United States Patent and Trademark Office (the "Patent Office"). Conflicting comments to various sections of Article 9 of the U.C.C. cloud the issue of whether § 261 preempts Article 9.[4]

Faced with the potential statutory conflict, courts are split on whether a security interest in patent rights is perfected under state or federal law. According to the Bankruptcy Court for the Southern District of California, a security interest in patent rights is perfected by state filing, under U.C.C. Article 9, and an ownership interest is perfected by filing in the Patent Office.[5] Because Salt of the Earth could find itself unprotected against a *bona fide* purchaser without notice if it filed only under the U.C.C., the *Transportation Design* court suggests that Salt of the Earth file under both the state and the federal systems to be completely protected.[6]

This same reasoning, however, was rejected by the bankruptcy court in Kansas.[7] The Kansas court held that a security interest in patent rights is perfected by filing in the Patent Office. The debtor in the Kansas case was trying to set aside a lender's interest in patents on the ground that the lender's security interest was perfected less than ninety (90) days before bankruptcy was filed. The lender's interest in the debtor's patents was set aside because the lender filed in the Patent Office only 87 days before bankruptcy was filed. The lender had filed under U.C.C. Article 9 a full 94 days before bankruptcy was filed.

---

[4] Comment 1 to U.C.C. § 9-104(a) compares the Federal Aviation Act, the Federal Copyright Act, and similar provisions of the Patent Act. According to Comment 1, to the extent that a federal statute does not regulate the rights of parties to and third parties affected by transactions, security interests in such property remain subject to Article 9. The Copyright Act and federal patent statutes are said to be comparable and "would not seem" to contain sufficient provisions to totally preempt Article 9. Comment 8 to U.C.C. § 9-302(3)(a), however, lists the Copyright Act, but not the Patent Act, as an example of a statute that supersedes Article 9.

[5] *In re Transportation Design & Technology, Inc.,* 48 Bankr. 635, 226 U.S.P.Q. 424 (Bankr. S.D. Cal. 1985).

[6] *Id.* at 635.

[7] *In re Otto Fabric, Inc.,* 55 Bankr. 654 (Bankr. D. Kan. 1985).

Because of the current uncertainties, anyone assigning or licensing patent rights should try to file both under Article 9 of the U.C.C. and in the Patent Office. Unfortunately, filing in the Patent Office may not always be possible.

§ 21.01 Perfecting a Security Interest under Article 9

[1] Perfect a Security Interest upon Transfer, or Give New Consideration Later

Ideally a security interest should be retained when patent rights are first transferred. Where contracts already in existence must be renegotiated, however, the same result can be accomplished by paying the licensee for the security interest. Timing the security interest at the beginning of the license or giving new value will eliminate any chance that the transfer will be voidable.[8] A voidable preference will not arise, because there will be no antecedent debt,[9] or because new value was given for the security interest.[10] Similarly, the transfer cannot be fraudulent because the debtor received fair value in exchange for his grant of the security interest.[11]

[2] There Must Be an Enforceable Contract

The first step to create a valid and enforceable security interest for Salt of the Earth is to have Big Daddy sign a security agreement.[12] The security agreement should identify the parties, contain a description of the collateral, and recite that value has been given in consideration for the security interest.[13] The security agreement may be either incorporated into the overall transfer agreement or prepared as a separate document. A security agreement could read as follows:

---

[8] 11 U.S.C. § 547 (1980).
[9] *See* § 18.01, N.3 thru 18.02, N.19, *supra.*
[10] 11 U.S.C. § 547(c) (1980).
[11] 11 U.S.C. § 548 (1980).
[12] U.C.C. § 9-203 (1976).
[13] *Id.*

Big Daddy Corp., a corporation of Delaware with a principal place of business at 123 Wall Street, Wall Street, Colorado, in consideration of ten dollars ($10.00) and other good and valuable consideration, receipt of which is hereby acknowledged, grants to: Salt of the Earth Corp., a corporation of Oklahoma with the principal place of business at One Main Street, Muskogee, Oklahoma, a security interest in the following property (hereinafter called "collateral"):

All right, title, and interest in and to U.S. Patent No. 5,000,000 entitled "Improved Electronic Ignition"; and any products embodying the inventions defined by the claims of that patent while such products remain in Big Daddy's inventory or control; and all proceeds from sales of, use of, or lease of products embodying inventions defined by the claims of that patent to secure performance of all obligations of Big Daddy Corp. as set out in the "Assignment Agreement" entered into today by Salt of the Earth and Big Daddy Co.

Default in performance of any obligations or any default under the above-referenced Assignment Agreement evidencing the obligations of Big Daddy Corp. is a *DEFAULT* under this security agreement. Upon *DEFAULT* Salt of the Earth may declare all obligations immediately due and payable and has the remedies of a secured party under the Colorado Uniform Commercial Code.

The security interest attaches, making the agreement enforceable by Salt of the Earth, as soon as Big Daddy has rights in the collateral.[14] Thus the lien created becomes effective against Big Daddy Corp. contemporaneously with the execution of the assignment.

[3]   Filing a Financing Statement under U.C.C. Article 9

The security interest must be perfected before Salt of the Earth will have rights superior to those of a subsequent judgment or contractual lienor, or over a *bona fide* purchaser of the patent rights. The U.C.C. prescribes no particular format for a financing statement, but the financing statement must

---

[14] *Id.*

comply with certain requirements.[15] The financing statement must be signed by Big Daddy and Salt of the Earth. The address of each party must be given and the collateral must be described precisely enough to put subsequent readers on notice of the security interest.[16] Printed financing statement forms are generally available at any bookstore or stationer that sells other printed legal forms.

[a] Filing Must Be Timely

Filing a financing statement is the only way to perfect a security interest in "general intangibles" and inventory under U.C.C. Article 9.[17] Filing the financing statement within ten days of the effective date of the assignment should give Salt of the Earth priority over preexisting liens in the same collateral.[18] For example, in a contest with a bank holding a security interest in all property of Big Daddy Corp., including after-acquired property, Salt of the Earth has priority in its lien on the transferred patent rights, but not in other collateral, such as inventory.

When Salt of the Earth perfects, the security interest assumes great importance in the bankruptcy context. Perfection under U.C.C. Article 9 generally occurs when a financing statement is filed. However, in the case of a purchase money security interest, perfection "relates back" to the time that the security interest was granted if a financing statement is filed within ten days after the debtor receives the collateral.[19] Relation back is very important in the bankruptcy context. A transfer will not be voidable if there is a substan-

---

[15] U.C.C. § 9-402 (1976).

[16] *Id.*

[17] U.C.C. § 9-302. (1976).

[18] U.C.C. § 9-312(4) (1976). That section gives a "Purchase Money Security Interest" priority over preexisting liens. A purchase money security interest is one that is: (a) taken or retained by the seller of the collateral to secure all or part of its price; or (b) taken by a person who; by making advances or incurring an obligation, gives value to enable the debtor to acquire rights in or the use of collateral in such value in fact so used. U.C.C. § 9-107 (1976).

[19] U.C.C. § 9-301(2) (1976).

tially contemporaneous exchange of value.[20] Since a security interest is transferred, for bankruptcy purposes, at the time of perfection, it is very important that the perfection of the security interest and the transfer of patent rights occur substantially contemporaneously.

[b]   The Proper State(s) for Filing

The state in which the financing statement should be filed is determined according to the requirements of U.C.C. § 9-103. Under U.C.C. § 9-103, filing should take place, in the case of intangible collateral, where Big Daddy is located. Big Daddy is located at its place of business or, if it has more than one place of business, at its chief executive office. If Big Daddy has no place of business, Big Daddy is deemed to be located at its residence. Big Daddy may have two offices that arguably function as its chief executive offices. If so, Salt of the Earth should file in both jurisdictions. State filing will cut off the trustee's voiding powers as a judgment or contractual lienor.

Where products manufactured or to be sold under the license are named as collateral, a financing statement should also be filed according to the laws of the place where the inventory is located.

[c]   Proper Office for State Filing

U.C.C. § 9-401 governs where in the state a financing statement should be filed. In the model code there are three alternatives for U.C.C. § 9-401. Salt of the Earth should check the law of the state where the assignee has his chief executive office and the law of the jurisdiction where tangible collateral is located to verify where Salt of the Earth should file a financing statement. Filing may be required both in the office of the Secretary of State and in the office of the County Clerk where the collateral is located.

---

[20] 11 U.S.C. § 547(c)(1) (1980).

[d] Periodic Renewal of Filings

Filing of the initial financing statement under Article 9 remains effective for five years.[21] The filing may be renewed, and perfection will relate back to the original filing, by filing a continuation statement. The continuation statement must be signed by the secured party, must identify the original financing statement by file number, and must state that the original statement is still effective. The continuation statement should be filed within six months before expiration of the original financing statement. Continuation statements are effective for five years and may be renewed by filing another continuation statement.[22]

§ 21.02 The Problem of Filing under 35 U.S.C. § 261

The only transactions specifically governed by 35 U.S.C. § 261 are "assignment[s], grant[s], or conveyance[s]. A lender who simply takes a security interest in a patent as a collateral for a loan can structure the loan to fall within these categories. For example, the lender can structure the loan as a patent mortgage. Because the Patent Office treats patent mortgages as full assignments, patent mortgages may be filed in the Patent Office.[23] Alternately, the lender can take an assignment of the patent having a grant-back clause that becomes effective when the loan is repaid.[24] Either of these documents can be filed in the Patent Office.

Consider, however, the plight of Jet Set and Salt of the Earth—how can they file in the Patent Office? Theoretically, Salt of the Earth could structure its assignment to Big Daddy in the form of a patent mortgage. A problem could arise, however, because the mortgage has no set value. Jet Set, on the other hand, has no viable way to structure a nonexclu-

---

[21] U.C.C. § 9-403 (1976).

[22] *Id.*

[23] *E.g., Waterman v. Mackenzie,* 138 U.S. 252 (1891); 37 C.F.R. § 1.331.

[24] *See* G. Engel & M. Radcliffe, "Intellectual Property for High Technology Companies, 19 U.C.C.L.J. Pt. 3 at 12 (1986).

sive license as an assignment, grant, or conveyance, nor as a patent mortgage.

§ 21.03   A Proposed Solution

The dilemma of both Salt of the Earth and Jet Set could be solved by an appropriate amendment to 35 U.S.C. § 261. Section 261 already provides that "patents, or any interest therein, shall be assignable in law by an instrument in writing." The current dilemma could be solved by simply amending § 261 to add the following sentence to the last paragraph:

> A security interest in a patent, or in rights granted under a patent, is perfected by filing the security agreement in the Patent and Trademark Office within three months of the date that the security agreement is executed.

The purpose of the amendment could be made clear in the legislative history as follows:

> The purpose of the amendment is to clarify that federal law supersedes Article 9 of the U.C.C. with regard to perfection of a security interest in patent rights.

> *Background*

> Section 261 states that "patents, or any interest therein, shall be assignable in law by an instrument in writing." The only provision for assuring notice of any such assignment is the provision in the last paragraph that an "assignment, grant or conveyance shall be void" against a subsequent *bona fide* purchaser unless recorded in the Patent and Trademark Office within three months from its date or prior to the date of such subsequent purchase or mortgage. This notice provision failed to provide for recordation of the transfer of any other interests in patent rights. The failure led to uncertainty whether § 261 preempted state law governing the perfection of security interests in patent rights. The uncertainty led one court to find that a security interest in patent rights *could not be perfected* under state law, but only by filing in the Patent Office.

Before the amendment, only an assignment or a patent mortgage could be filed in the Patent and Trademark Office. Lienors other than assignees or mortgagors were left with no way to file proof of their interest in the Patent Office. Other types of lienors could not be absolutely sure that they had perfected security interests in their patent rights under the old law.

The current amendment clarifies that security interests are perfected by filing evidence of the security interest in the Patent and Trademark Office.

Chapter 22

Conclusion

A licensor/assignor of patent rights should not rely on an ipso facto bankruptcy clause to protect himself in the event of the insolvency of a licensee/assignee. The licensor/assignor relying on an ipso facto bankruptcy clause may find himself without any rights in his patent, or forced to deal with an unacceptable licensee.

A licensor/assignor can be protected by perfecting a security interest in patent rights. The licensor/assignor should try to structure the transaction so that he can file evidence of his interest both under the U.C.C. and in the Patent Office. Some licensors/assignors, such as a nonexclusive licensor, should try to file in the Patent Office, but may find that they cannot file evidence of their lien in the Patent Office. Hopefully, the courts will recognize this dilemma and find that these lienors have perfected their security interests under the U.C.C. The ambiguity could be resolved, however, by a clarifying amendment to 35 U.S.C. § 261.

Part 4

Sample Technology License and Marketing Representative Agreement (with Explanatory Annotations)

Sample Technology License and Marketing Representative Agreement

Licensing

5.5 Neither Party Shall Condition Access to License upon Using EE Services

5.6 EE Free to Offer Competitive Processes

5.7 EE and OR1+2 to Develop Marketing Plan
   (i) OR1+2 to Support EE's Sales Efforts at Own Expense
   (ii) EE to Diligently Develop Market at EE Expense
   (iii) OR1+2 Engineering and Consultation Service on Compensated Contract Basis
   (iv) OR1+2 to Receive No Commission on EE Engineering, Construction
   (v) Primary Negotiation Responsibility OR2's in the U.S., EE's in Foreign Countries
   (vi) Negotiations for Engineering or Construction, EE's Control and Expense
   (vii) EE to Keep OR1+2 Advised re Sales Prospects
   (viii) EE to Respond to Client Inquiries
   (ix) EE to Do Studies for Clients
   (x) OR1+2 to Be Given Copy of Proposals and Studies and Chance to Suggest Corrections
   (xi) The Process to Be Publicly Identified as "OR1+2 XYZ PROCESS"
   (xii) OR1+2 May Grant Licenses Direct to Licensees

5.8 OR1+2 Agree to Provide Catalyst

5.9 OR1+2 Catalyst Guarantees Per Industry Norm

5.10 OR1+2 Limit Their Warranty for Engineering the Catalyst Type, Quantity and Configuration

6. Royalties
   6.1 Royalties Negotiable
   6.2 Current Royalty Schedule if Convenient to the Client
   6.3 Royalties Payable by Client 40 Percent to OR2, 60 Percent to OR1
   6.4 EE Not Responsible for Client Royalty Payments

7. Improvements by OR1+2
   7.1 OR1+2 Continue R&D
   7.2 Improvements to Be Made
   7.3 OR1+2 to Make Timely Disclosure or Improvements Deemed Commercial
   7.4 Sales Representative, License, and Right to Sublicense Extend to Improvements
   7.5 Royalties Not Changed for Prior Clients; May Change for Others

8. Improvements by EE and Clients
   8.1 Disclosure of Improvements to OR1+2
   8.2 Disclosures of EE and Client Improvements to Be Timely Made
   8.3 Title to EE Improvements and License Back

244

Licensing

1. Consideration; Effective Date

Effective date
_____ 1983

1.1 The effective date of this agreement shall be _____, 1983.

Consideration

1.2 The parties enter into this agreement in consideration of the mutual covenants and terms herein expressed.

2. Parties

OR2

2.1. OR2 Corporation (OR2) is a Texas corporation with principal offices at 000 A Street Houston, Texas 77____

OR1

2.2 OR1 Company (OR1) is a Texas corporation with principal place of business at ___[street address]___, Houston, Texas 77____.

EE

2.3. EE Inc. (EE) is a Delaware corporation with principal offices at _[street address]_ and with Houston offices addressed at ___[street address]___.

[For complete identification of parties and

246

help in locating them for process service, I like the street address of their office locations.]

OR1+2

2.4. OR1 and OR2 are participants in a joint venture relating to _____ ("SVCCRAF") process and equipment including the "OR1+2 XYZ PROCESS" (or merely "PROCESS") which is the subject matter of this agreement; each venture and its two participants are sometimes referred to collectively as OR1+2.

OR1+2

["Whereas" clauses. Many lawyers still use "whereas" clauses. Their deficiencies prove to be significant only so rarely as to be of no real consequence. But some courts have questioned whether the parties really agreed to whereas recitations, or whether they were only one party's representation, and what warranties are to be read into them.

So I have a preference to put the "whereas" subject matter into other forms of "Background" clauses in which we are quite specific as to what is "represented," "believed," "agreed," or "warranted."]

[Definitions, I sometimes put a section of "Definitions" into the contract proper, sometimes into an Appendix. But when the definitions are largely self-evident and few in number, I have a preference for weaving them into the text when the term first appears. That makes the instrument more readable in these more simple cases without the reader's having to turn forward to backward to definitions as much.]

["Slur words." Some words are purr words to a jury; some are counterproductive or "slur" words. Good contracts are readable by judge or jury to purr about your cause. For that reason I have edited out some of the words I found, like "exploiting." That is not a good courtroom word and we don't need it. Some other editing and writing is for the same rea-

247

Licensing

son—to make the contract read sympathetically to judge or jury.]

3. Background

The PROCESS
defined

3.1. OR1+2 represents that it (they) has (have) developed a catalytic, distillation process for the production of _____ (XYZ) by concurrently conducting in a _____. Insofar as used for making XYZ and within the scope of any of OR1's patents or applications for patents that process for making XYZ is hereinafter referred to as the "PROCESS."

Inventions, patents
and know-how

3.2 OR1+2 warrant that it (they) own several patent rights and applications therefor, both domestic and foreign though not in every country of the world, and that they possess certain know-how relating to that PROCESS and the preferred plants and equipment configurations for using the PROCESS.

[It is a significant tactic in a license like this, that the licensed patents not be identified. ALL OR1 patents are licensed, i.e., subject to a covenant not to sue for infringing a licensed user of the PROCESS.]

Titles sufficient for
this agreement

3.3. OR1+2 are not aware of any ownership by another of inventions or patent rights or trade secret or know-how rights in conflict with their own; and OR1+2 believe that they possess such rights, titles and interests in and to the PROCESS and equipment useful therein as is necessary and appropriate to the terms of this agreement.

[Here note that I have used the verbs "not aware" of conflicting rights and "believes" they own the necessary rights, titles and interests—these in lieu of "warrants." There is no way to be absolutely certain that there is no pending patent application that might issue next month and dominate the situation, so I suggest we not warrant something which is beyond our control.]

EE skills

3.4. EE is an engineering and construction company having valuable experience in designing, constructing and selling plants and equipment to the chemical and refining industries. These skills are of value in the marketing of the PROCESS.

Cooperation in bringing the PROCESS into public use

3.5. The parties desire to cooperate with each other to their mutual advantage in bringing the PROCESS into wide public use.

[Article 4, which follows, raises the question: who is to provide the show-how technical service to the clients of EE? How big a chore is that teaching of the operators, etc.?—Particularly as to foreign clients whose workmen may not speak English? And who is to teach workmen for foreign clients whose workmen may not speak English? And who is to (a) negotiate the size of that undertaking, and (b) pay for its performance?]

4. EE Licensed and Appointed Marketing Representative

EE appointed marketing representative

4.1. OR1 + 2 hereby appoints EE its nonexclusive, worldwide, independent marketing representative to help develop the market for the PROCESS.

[Posturing EE as a nonexclusive sales representative lends a bit of aid to some of the arguments that the license does not overreach in misuse of the patents or violation of the antitrust laws.]

EE License to make and sell plants

4.2. In aid of that appointment OR1 + 2 grant to EE a worldwide nonexclusive license to design and erect and sell to its clients plants for use of the PROCESS, including parts, apparatus and equipment and operating know-how therefor.

[Note the addition of reference here to parts, apparatus, equipment and operating know-how.]

Licensing

EE right to grant licenses to the PROCESS

4.3. Further in aid of that appointment OR1+2 grants to EE the right to license its clients both to use the PROCESS and to sell the product thereof anywhere in the world.

EE sublicenses to be acceptable to OR1 and OR2

4.4. No party shall enter into any contracts or make any warranties on behalf of another party; the terms of any license to an EE client shall be acceptable to OR1 and OR2 and such acceptance shall not be unreasonably withheld.

Acceptable license form is attached

4.5. A draft license is attached hereto as Appendix B suggesting terms typical of those which will commonly be acceptable to OR1 and OR2; however, it is contemplated that each contract will have to be individually negotiated at least in part, to accommodate circumstances unique to the time, to the client and its market, engineering, economic and legal environment.

OR1+2 to have right of approval of licenses

4.6. Accordingly, EE will negotiate the sublicenses to its clients generally along guidelines to be provided by OR1+2, and no sublicense can be finalized until a copy has been submitted to and specifically authorized in writing.

[It seems that the license EE is permitted to grant almost must be approved by both OR1 and OR2, and still I'm led to believe that each situation will be sufficiently unique that a single license form for EE to use is not feasible.]
[How can OR2 get an appropriate check on or control of EE-client's credit rating and inject that into EE's negotiations? Or is that necessary? Will any buyer inherently be sound enough that OR1+2, with its relatively low capital commitment to any individual license negotiations, does not need to worry about the licensee's financial strength?]

5. Cooperative Undertakings

OR1+2 to disclose the PROCESS

5.1. Within _____ days after delivery by EE of a fully executed copy of this agreement to OR1 or OR2, OR1+2

OR1+2 to deliver documents

(i) Shall at its own expense deliver to EE documentation deemed by OR1+2 to be appropri-

250

ate for the transfer of its basic knowledge of the PROCESS to EE.

OR1+2 to conduct technical seminar for EE personnel

(ii) Shall seek to arrange early convenient times at which OR1+2 shall conduct seminars for EE personnel as supplement to the documentary disclosure of (i) above—all sufficiently to enable EE to include the PROCESS in its normal marketing program and to design plants for use of the PROCESS.

First disclosure at OR1+2 expense; further disclosure at EE expense.

(iii) Shall pay the cost of such documents and the teaching of such seminars up to _____ sheets of documents, teaching _____ hours; thereafter if EE should request further documents or seminar time EE shall pay document costs and shall pay all such further seminar costs including $_____ per teaching man-hour—provided that OR1+2 shall not be obligated to more than one man-day of seminar teaching in any one month after the first month.

[You will recognize that I am here suggesting a brainstorming session as to how many documents (I've seen document costs come to $50,000 for a polyethylene plant) and how much teaching time is reasonable. We contract for that plus something, perhaps even double that; but we ought not to leave the obligation open-ended to EE or its clients. Blank checks for teaching time and documents can work out to be as big a mistake as a blank check for money.]

Charter facility to be visited

(iv) Upon reasonable advance notice shall endeavor to obtain permission from Oil Company to allow a reasonable number of EE's employees and prospective clients to visit Oil's commercial plant incorporating one version of the PROCESS, thereby to observe its operation.

OR1+2 and EE to exchange sales prospect information and cooperate in developing market

5.2. OR1+2 and EE will exchange sales prospect information (including future prospects as they develop) and other marketing information and OR2 and EE shall cooperate with each other in determining the best course of action to

251

Licensing

develop the market for the PROCESS and for EE's engineering or construction services with respect thereto.

EE free to seek or decline contracts

5.3. Provided however, while EE shall be free to bid or negotiate for engineering and/or construction work on any plant to use the PROCESS and on terms determined solely by EE, and if it so elects EE may also decline any engineering or construction contracts.

Clients free to contract elsewhere

5.4. Clients shall be free if they so elect to seek their engineering and/or construction work from another contractor with whom OR1+2 shall be free to cooperate.

Neither party shall condition access to license upon using EE services

5.5. Consistent with the foregoing neither EE nor OR1+2 shall condition the grant of license under the PROCESS upon the potential client's buying, engineering or construction services from EE in order to get a license under the PROCESS.

EE free to offer competitive processes

5.6. EE shall be permitted to offer processes competitive to the PROCESS in respect of marketing opportunity or prospects which EE identifies or is pursuing at the date hereof, including the following: (1) Black Oil (New Zealand); (2) U.S. Oil (Saudi Arabia); (3) Saints Oil (Lake Charles, LA).

[For EE to be precluded by contract from competitive offerings at any time raises a potential antitrust problem necessitating further study of the engineering and contracting industry as well as the markets for XYZ technology. The clause above is likely lawful depending upon industry structures of which I am not advised; but I find it sufficiently doubtful as to suggest that: either we permit competitive offerings generally, or I be commissioned to do further studies. If the PROCESS is as good as I've been led to believe, there is no need to restrict EE and that is legally much safer.]

EE and OR1+2 to develop marketing plan

5.7. The parties contemplate that within forty-five days of fulfillment of §§ 5.1 and 5.2

252

above, EE will submit to OR1+2 a proposed marketing plan; within forty-five days after receipt of such plan OR1+2 shall submit to EE its response and suggested program for support and assistance of EE; the proposals are expected to be in accord with these preliminary concepts:

[Because of redundancies in the list of OR1+2 and EE activities, some of which were joint efforts, I've attempted a single list in aid of reduction of the redundancies.]

OR1+2 to support EE's sales efforts at own expense

(i) OR1+2 at its own expense to assist and support EE's sales efforts as may be requested by EE or as may be appropriate to the effort to negotiate licenses with clients, up to some reasonable cost-effective expense or effort consistent with sound business practices.

[At this stage of my studies I have not worked out any pattern of expense-sharing by each OR1 and OR2. That must of course be done, but I don't yet even know whether OR2 has paid the full $_____ recited in the original OR2 contract with OR1.]

EE to diligently develop market at EE expense

(ii) EE at its own expense to take an active and leadership role in diligent development of the market for the PROCESS, both domestic and foreign, in a manner that is deemed cost effective in accord with EE's normal business practices consistent with the market opportunities at the time; but this shall not be construed as a commitment of any specific dollars worth of effort for which EE is liable.

OR1+2 engineering and consultation service on compensated contract basis

(iii) OR1+2 to provide an engineering and consulting service generally on a compensated contract basis as EE may request.

[Note the ambiguity in determining which are support services under (i), which are at OR1+2 expense and which are engineering and consultation services under (iii) which are

Licensing

by compensated contract. We need to brain-storm this a bit further.]

OR1+2 to receive no commission on EE engineering, construction

(iv) OR1+2 to receive nothing for any engineering or construction services of EE.

Primary negotiation responsibility OR2's in the U.S., EE's in foreign countries

(v) While the parties will cooperate in any negotiation, it is contemplated that negotiations in the United States for licenses to client will be conducted primarily by OR2 and at OR1+2 expense; and negotiations for licenses to clients outside the United States will be conducted primarily by EE; each party shall bear its own expense of negotiation in either area.

Negotiations for engineering or construction, EE's control and expense

(vi) Negotiations with clients for contracts for engineering and construction shall be solely under EE's control and at EE's expense.

EE to keep OR1+2 advised re sales prospects

(vii) EE to keep OR1+2 advised as to all current sales prospects and progress on pending negotiations, including written quarterly reports showing the status of all sales prospects and marketing efforts.

EE to respond to client inquiries

(viii) EE to respond to all serious inquiries by potential clients for the PROCESS which EE receives directly from clients or from OR2 if OR2 elects to refer an inquiry; and EE to provide technical and commercial information to prospects free of charge, the quantity and detail of such information to be consistent with information EE provides relating to other processes for which it is a licensee who sublicenses others.

[Query: Is this kind of clause necessary to this contract, or is it an inherent part of EE's market and practice? I guess I prefer to keep the clause]

EE to do studies for clients

(ix) Once a project has been identified and a prospective client requests a technical or commercial study incorporating the PROCESS, EE to prepare and submit to the prospective client a commercial proposal for performing the study under terms and conditions determined solely by EE; and if EE is awarded the contract to do the study, its execution and completion will be solely under EE's control but a copy of the final study shall be provided to OR2.

OR1 + 2 to be given copy of proposals and studies and chance to suggest corrections

(x) OR1 + 2 to be provided with an opportunity to review each proposal for a study, and each report on a study, for technical accuracy, and to be normally provided with an opportunity to suggest corrections as they view them, for EE's consideration prior to submission to the client.

The process to be publicly identified as "OR1 + 2 XYZ PROCESS"

(xi) In advertising, promotional literature, proposals to clients and reports on studies, i.e., wherever feasible, the PROCESS shall be referred to as the "OR1 + 2 XYZ PROCESS."

OR1 + 2 may grant licenses direct to licensees

(xii) Nothing herein to be construed as limiting OR1 + 2's right to grant licenses direct to users of the PROCESS.

[I feel more comfortable legally if we can have this clause along with EE's unlimited right to sell competitive processes. But if EE does well, the obvious incentive of both parties is to do most of their business together.]

OR1 + 2 agrees to provide catalyst

[*]5.8. While all of OR1 + 2 patent rights are nonexclusively licensed for use in the PROCESS, including the OR1 patent on the _____ catalyst _____, whereby clients may at no additional royalty buy catalyst from sources of their choice, OR1 + 2 agree at client's request to supply Client(s) original and replacement catalyst requirements for plants that use the PROCESS.

[We don't want any unfortunate choice of language here to suggest an illegal tie—that clients cannot get a license without buying unpatented catalyst from OR1. But is the plan to sell catalyst _____ of independently pat-

---

[*Consider putting all the §§ 5.8–5.10 relating to providing catalyst and warranting it in a separate Article.]

ented character? If so, we may yet play with this clause some.]

[Consider: can we bias the client to buy OR1 catalyst by not warranting performance of the PROCESS unless OR1 catalyst is used?]

[What are our patent rights on the catalyst?]

OR1+2 catalyst guarantees per industry norm

5.9. Insofar as OR1+2 provides catalyst to EE or to a client for use in the PROCESS, OR1+2 will also provide performance and life guarantees as complete as any guarantees which are generally commercially available for catalysts on processes similar to the PROCESS.

OR1+2 limit their warranty for engineering the catalyst type, quantity and configuration

5.10. For each plant engineered and/or constructed by EE or its sublicensees, OR1+2 agrees, in timely manner after being provided with the requisite plant-and-PROCESS performance parameters and being so requested, at its own expense[*] to provide engineering specification on (i) the quantity and type of catalyst required; (ii) the configuration of catalyst required (though EE or its client will design the catalyst containing vessel).

OR1+2 limits its warranty of the correctness of its specification thus: OR1+2 shall do such re-engineering and equipment redesign and shall pay for such equipment modification as is deemed necessary to render the plant operable as per the performance parameters up to a maximum OR1+2 expense equal to the royalty fee contemplated to be earned during the first ____ years of operation of the subject plant.

[John Doe's and your drafts limited this liability to the "royalty fee paid by client" or words to that effect. My question is, paid by when? A contract may contemplate $100,000 per year for fifteen years depending upon many contingencies, and the trigger event may occur after

---

[*Reconcile with § 5.7(iii).]

only $50,000 in payment. What is to be the limit of liability in this clause?]

6. Royalties

Royalties
negotiable

6.1. Royalties to be paid by the client shall be negotiable consistent with the value of the technology and the scope and anticipated term of protection of the PROCESS know-how package as perceived at the time of the license and under the circumstances thereof. No royalties shall be asked for in an illegal manner; no illegal royalties shall be asked for or paid.

[Conditioned package licenses with one royalty for the term independently of patent expiration, etc., is arguably illegal in many circumstances. Sections 6.1 and 6.2 are part of an effort to rebut such arguments.]

Current royalty
schedule if
convenient to the
client

6.2. Given the client's anticipated acute interest in the commercial-earnings value of the know-how package and hoped-for improvements thereof as an ongoing operating process, and given the circumstance that this value is determined primarily by market conditions and not to any significant degree by the number or types of patent or know-how protections of various parts of the plant or process, country by country, the schedule and term of royalties as recited in Appendix C hereto is perceived to be a currently viable schedule, if it is deemed to the client to be a convenient package to it.

Royalties payable
by client 40 percent
to OR2, 60 percent
to OR1

6.3. Royalties are payable by the client 40 percent direct to OR2 and 60 percent direct to OR1, each at the addresses recited in the Article hereinafter.

[John Doe's draft proposed that all royalties be paid to OR1 as recited in the original OR2 contract with OR1. What is the reason for that? Why not contract as above? If we use John Doe's clause, we introduce an ambiguity that perhaps this new three-way contract changes the old 40-60 split. To prevent that we

257

need either to recite the 40-60 split as to be made by OR1 after it received the royalties, or else to let the payments be direct to the parties on the 40-60 split.]

EE not responsible for client royalty payments

6.4. Except as may by subsequent agreement be specifically provided in some particular license to a client, EE has no responsibility or liability for the payment of royalties to either OR1 or OR2.

[In the sample form license agreement, we should remember to recite royalties payable in U.S. dollars; but in some foreign deals a circuitous or barter type payment may be necessary and we must afford flexibility to work that sort of thing out.]

7. Improvements by OR1+2

OR1+2 continue R&D

7.1. It is contemplated that OR1+2 will continue from time to time to do research and/or development in areas relevant to the

[Note that the continuing R&D obligation is addressed to broader technical subject matter than just the XYZ process. Query: For how long and to what extent is OR1 willing to warrant a continued R&D effort in this area?]

Improvements to be made

7.2. It is hoped but not warranted that through this research and development further improvements in the PROCESS and/or equipment therefor will occur.

OR1+2 to make timely disclosure or improvements deemed commercial

7.3. OR1+2 shall make disclosures to EE of any such improvements it deems appropriate and economic for commercial utilization in the PROCESS at such times and frequency as is deemed appropriate to the subject matter but in all events no later than ninety days after both OR1 and OR2 have concluded that the subject matter is appropriate and economical for commercial utilization by EE or its clients.

Sales rep., license and right to

7.4. The sales representation, license and

258

right to grant sublicenses to clients under §§ 4.1 thru 4.3 above shall extend also to any such improvements in the PROCESS or equipment useful therein, and to any patents domestic or foreign which may issue thereon.

7.5. Royalties payable by clients of EE who were licensed prior to the reduction to practice and commercial development of any improvement are in part being paid expressly for access to such improvements and hence royalties are not subject to change upon the availability of any such improvement; however, it is contemplated that the royalty rates may be modified for subsequent licensees in accord with the OR1+2 perceived value in any such improvements.

8. Improvements by EE and Clients

8.1. EE and its clients by the terms of licenses granted to them shall make timely disclosures to OR1+2 writings supplemented orally as requested by OR1+2, of any and all patentable and nonpatentable inventions, discoveries and significant know-how developments made or conceived by it or them or otherwise within their right so to disclose, which is

(a) Within the scope of any claim as written of any present application for or issued United States patent, owned in whole or in part by OR1 or OR2, and which claim covers apparatus equipment, products or methods useful in practice or development of the licensed PROCESS[*]; or

(b) In the nature of improvements in or modifications of methods of and apparatus, equipment and products for concurrently conducting catalytic _____.

[Note the foregoing paragraph calls for a

[*If we don't identify the patents, the scope of that obligation will be unknown to the licensee who must perform it.]

259

grantback disclosure of certain technical scopes, but not a license or title grantback. As to its time the disclosure grantback as recited in § 8.2 is flexible but fairly explicit. Note the adoption in §§ 3 and 4 below of this same scope of technology in the title grantback. I will want to discuss with you the various considerations for the same or different disclosure grantbacks and license or title grantbacks.]

[John Doe's grantback of improvements merely "to the licensed process" is much less precise than what I am suggesting and his version could turn out better. Still, overreach in grantback clauses is dangerous from a patent misuse and antitrust point of view and we ought to kick around both these efforts before fixing on one.

Also, I think we want grantback of rights in apparatus improvements as well as process improvements—although might we take only license grantbacks on that? And we want grantbacks from EE clients as well as from EE—both to the full extent we feel is lawful.

Finally, John Doe suggests grantback of nonexclusive license with right of sublicense which is legally safer than my proposed grantback of title subject to a reserved paid up license in the party granting back.]

Disclosures of EE and client improvements to be timely made

8.2. Such disclosures shall be made as often and at such times as seem both timely and appropriate to the nature of the improvement/modification/development, but in all events (i) not more than 180 days after first use of the improvement/modification/development; (ii) not more than one year after the development of the improvement/modification/development; (iii) not more than forty-five days after the submission to the management or counsel of the client or EE, by one or more of its employees, of an invention disclosure submitted or considered in contemplation of possible application(s) for patent thereon; (iv) if the improvement/modification/development is potentially patentable, then not less than 180 days prior to the deadline for filing any application for patent thereon, domestic or foreign. (This criteria contemplates that in some instances acts which would bar later applications for patents, such as uses and offers for sale, etc., may have to be delayed for up to 180 days until OR1 + 2 either gets applications for patent on file or else indicates its intent not so to file whereupon EE and the client shall be relieved of any obligation to delay such acts of use, offers for sale, etc.)—whichever occurs first.

Title to EE improvements and license back

8.3. All improvements/modifications/developments under § 8.1 above which are conceived by EE during the term of EE's marketing representation and license under §§ 4.1, 4.2 and 4.3 shall be the property of OR1 + 2 subject to a retained perpetual royalty-free license in EE to make, use and sell the improvement/modification and to be able to license its clients so to do.

[Could you suggest an acceptable time limit on this grantback of title?]

Title to client improvements and license back

8.4. All such improvements/modifications/developments under § 8.1 above which are conceived by clients of EE within five years of the date of the license to that client, shall be the property of OR1 + 2 subject to a retained perpetual royalty-free license in such client to make, use and sell the improvement/modification for its own account.

[The law is vague and uncertain on the point of the length of time for grantbacks in different contract contexts. I urge upon you a five-year limit on any title grantback from an operating licensee. From a sales representative nonoperating licensee we might be more bold if you feel it is important to be more bold with EE.]

261

Licensing

EE to cooperate in enforcement

8.5. If OR1+2 so requests, EE and/or its client, as may be appropriate, shall execute any lawful and proper instruments of title or title-conveyance consistent with §§ 8.3 and 8.4 above, and shall at OR1+2 expense cooperate with all lawful and proper efforts of OR1+2 to obtain, maintain and enforce patent protection thereon in any and all countries of the world.

[We must discuss how to divide the expenses and control of litigation to enforce OR1+2 patent and know-how rights.]

Division of income out of EE improvements

8.6. In the event any improvement/modification/development by EE is of such value and nature as reasonable to afford a charge of a distinct royalty or license fee for that addendum, and in the event any EE client takes a license including such a distinct royalty or license fee, then the gross receipts of such royalty or license fee shall be divided one-half to EE and one-half to OR1+2.

[This provision is one of the provisions giving me a feeling of reasonable safety in asking for title grantback from EE for the life of the EE marketing representative relationship. But note I've suggested no royalty split with clients for the grantbacks from the clients.]

Improvements included in license package

8.7. All improvements/modifications/developments by EE or EE clients, which become the property of OR1+2, shall insofar as used for the manufacture of XYZ by the PROCESS thereupon automatically become part of the package of know-how licensed to EE and its prior clients whereby such prior clients may automatically get the benefit of such improvements/modifications/developments—and this license shall be at no extra charge to the prior licensees excepting in the case of a EE invention of the class where § 8.5 above applies.

262

9. Licensee Infringement of Patents Belonging to Third Parties

OR1 + 2 believe PROCESS not infringe patents of others

9.1. OR1 + 2 believe that the PROCESS does not infringe any valid scope of any patent or know-how right anywhere in the world, but by virtue of the unavoidable impossibility of performing perfect patent searches, and the like, OR1 + 2 cannot warrant that as fact.

OR1 + 2 to provide updated information re any infringement

9.2. As requested from time to time by EE or a potential client-licensee OR1 + 2 agree to provide their best updated information on any possibility of an infringement of patents of others resulting from the erection or use of plants practicing the PROCESS; but OR1 + 2 suggest that such potential client-licensee be encouraged also to get its own legal opinions on this exposure to liability.

Advise re any charge of infringement

9.3. In the event of any charge of infringement of any patent rights of third parties by either the erection or use of plants embodying the PROCESS, OR1 + 2 shall both be promptly advised in writing.

Advise re any suit for infringement

9.4. In the event of any suit for infringement of any patent rights of third parties by either the erection or use of plants embodying the PRO-CESS, OR1 + 2 shall both be promptly advised both by telephone and in writing.

If a claim for infringement, parties will cooperate within guidelines

9.5. It is inherent that the facility for settlement, the economics of possible designing around the offended patent, and the economics and uncertainties of litigation as well as nonlitigation solutions to any such controversy are unique to each such claim and impossible fully to plan for in detail in advance of any third party's charge or suit for infringement of its patents; however, the parties agree to cooperate fully with each other and shall require cooperation also of any offended client(s) to effect the most practical overall solution to such a contingent event within the parameters of the following guidelines:

(i) OR1 + 2 is only permitting EE and its cli-

263

ents to use OR1+2 technology and by the nature of things cannot warrant immunity from charges by others of infringement of their patents.

(ii) OR1+2 shall each contribute up to 50 percent, as needed, of the royalties it has received from any particular client (or does receive from time to time as they are collected from that client) to the various forms of defense by that client against any claim of infringement, including litigation expenses, conceptual engineering efforts to design around the offended patent, royalties payable to the claimant in a license settlement deemed to be the most realistic and overall practical for the parties hereto, etc.

(iii) OR1+2 shall in no event be liable to pay to the claimant, EE or the client collectively, any sum more than 80 percent of the royalties theretofore paid to OR1+2 or for which the client remains liable to pay to OR1+2 after final adjudication and settlement, whether this shall be for adjudicated infringement liability or other purposes outlined in (i) above.

(iv) Any liability adjudicated for any infringements or inducing infringements of rights of others, beyond the sum available therefor under (ii) above, shall be paid by the client or EE as may be adjudicated or agreed upon between them but not by OR1+2.

(v) OR1+2, EE and the client shall each bear its own expense of legal services, design-around efforts and settlement negotiations among themselves and with the claimant.

[Infringement of patents, now unknown, belonging to others, is unlikely. But that contingency is very important owing to the cost of defense of such suits (ranging between $_____ and $_____ most commonly but with 20 percent of the cases outside that range), and owing to the size of the potential

liability. The size of the exposure is much too great for any general assumption by the licensor of liability for his licensee's infringement.

If OR1+2 are to pay an important share of the defense or liability funds, who should select the counsel and otherwise control the defense? Normally the party with the bigger potential liability, the licensee, here.

Contracts now to agree later on "cooperation" as here suggested, are notoriously poor vehicles—except that other vehicles seem to prove out to be even more poor in these situations for a variety of reasons I can discuss with you in person.

There is reason to leave the control of the litigation and its cost—subject to the contributions here recited—in the accused infringer with whom OR1+2 agree to cooperate. There is also reason for the licensor to assume control so as to be sure that the first suit is not lost thereby to make a bad precedent for suits against other licensees who may be in line for suit.

If there is only one licensee I'd be inclined to leave the control and unlimited costs and liabilities in the licensees. But if you have a number of licensees in the same country I would think it better tactics for OR1+2 to assume control—but for the potential liabilities that are likely to far exceed royalty payments.

So as drafted, I have not provided for OR1+2's assumption of control of litigation against its licensees for infringement of rights of others.]

10. Infringement of OR1+2's Patents, Etc.

Parties to advise of infringements

10.1. In the event that any party shall become aware of any perceived infringement or misappropriation of OR1+2's patent, trade secret or know-how rights on the PROCESS or equipment, products or materials useful therein, the

265

Licensing

party shall give notice thereof to the other parties hereto.

EE to cooperate with enforcement of OR1+2 rights

10.2. EE as nonexclusive marketing representative agrees to cooperate with any lawful efforts that OR1+2 may undertake to seek legal remedies for any such infringements or misappropriations, but any expenses so incurred shall be paid by OR1+2.

[What ideas do you have as to whom among OR1 and OR2 should control infringement suits? Who should pay for them—at unpredictable costs ranging between $_____ and $_____ for 80 percent of the cases? Who should recover what portion of the damages?]

11. Indemnities for Malfeasance, Liability for Personal Injury or Property Damage

The license is a sharing of technical information

11.1 The license herein granted to EE and to be granted to clients of EE is primarily in the nature of a sharing of information and of a covenant not to sue for infringements of OR1+2 rights and is not in the nature of a specification of activities required of the licensees or of equipment or process details required to be used by them.

Operation and plant are responsibility of EE and its clients

11.2. Process operation, plant and equipment safety shall be the responsibility of EE and/or its clients.

OR1+2 not liable for personal injury or property damage

11.3 Accordingly, OR1+2 shall not be liable for any personal injury or property damage resulting from the design, construction or use of the licensed PROCESS or any plant or equipment or products used in connection with the PROCESS except to the very limited extent expressly recited herein.

EE indemnifies OR1+2

11.4. Further, EE indemnifies and holds OR1 and OR2 harmless from any and all claims, demands or causes of action and all costs of defense incurred by OR1 or OR2 (including court costs and reasonable attorney's fees actually incurred) which claims, demands or causes of action are asserted by any third party or EE client and are caused or alleged to be caused by reason of any faulty design, construction or operation of any licensed PROCESS or plant or equipment therefor or by reason of any alleged negligence or act or failure to act of any employee, agent or representative of EE (other than OR1 or OR2) or any misrepresentations or alleged misrepresentations by EE to third parties including EE clients which misrepresentations or alleged misrepresentations are not in good faith accord and compliance with information furnished by OR1 or OR2 to EE.

[The law and practice with respect to personal injury and property damage liabilities based on negligence or other strict product liability theories, now may possibly catch even a technology licensor even when the wrong was in the vessel design or fabrication material. So, something like this is desirable.

Since licensees commonly cannot cover the kind of catastrophe that occurred at Bhopal, India, consideration must be given to a requirement of insurance of an appropriate amount.

Then, contrast the next two clauses which may give rise to a need for licensor insurance in favor of the licensee.]

OR1 indemnifies
EE and OR2

11.5. OR1 indemnifies and holds EE and OR2 harmless from any and all claims, demands or causes of action and all costs to EE or OR2 of defense (including court costs and reasonable attorney's fees actually incurred) which claims, demands or causes of action are asserted by any third party or EE client and are caused or alleged to be caused by reason of any alleged defect in the PROCESS as such or processing capacity or percent conversion or an OR2 design or by reason of any alleged negligence or act or failure to act of any partner, employee, agent or representative of OR1 other than OR2 or EE.

267

Licensing

OR2 indemnifies
OR1 and EE

11.6. OR2 indemnifies and holds OR1 and EE harmless from any and all claims, demands or causes of action and all costs of defense to OR1 or EE (including court costs and reasonable attorney's fees actually incurred) which claims, demands or causes of action are asserted by any third party or EE client and are caused or alleged to be caused by reason of any alleged negligence or act or failure to act of any employee, agent or representative of OR2, other than OR1 or EE, or any misrepresentations or alleged misrepresentations by OR2 to third parties including EE clients which misrepresentations or alleged misrepresentations are not in accord with information furnished by OR1 or EE to OR2.

12. Arbitration

[The trend toward poor quality, expensive and untimely performance of the judiciary, particularly in complex and technical cases, suggests an effort to find other mechanisms for dispute resolution.

I do not necessarily urge arbitration under the rules of the American Arbitration Association.

Rather, I suggest we draft a page or so of our own suggestions for resolution of disputes under this contract, if OR1+2 are so inclined.]

13. Transferability

Agreement
assignable with
entire assets of
party

13.1 Each party hereto may assign this agreement and its benefits to any assignee of the entirety of the assets of the party including the personnel normally working in subject matter areas related hereto, provided that the assignee shall first deliver to the parties a written assumption of all the duties and obligations of the assignor.

Assigning party
shall give 30 days
notice and audience

13.2. Thirty days notice of intent to assign shall be given by any assigning party to the other two parties hereto, including the name of the

268

assignee and a general expression of the circumstances of the assignment; and the assignor and assignee shall give the other parties hereto such audience as they request prior to the effective date of the assignment.

Agreement
assignable with
written consent of
parties

13.3. Subject to §§ 1 and 2 above, this agreement may not be assigned by any party without the written consent of the other two parties.

Inures to benefit of
successors

13.4. If assigned as aforesaid, this agreement shall inure to the benefit of and be binding upon the parties hereto and their successors.

[It seems to be legitimate for each party to hang in with the idea that the entire business can be sold as a whole to responsible parties assuming the duties, the short term termination clause being the primary protection.]

14. Confidentiality

Prior secrecy
agreement replaced

14.1 Prior to the effective date of this Agreement EE entered into a Secrecy Agreement with OR1 and OR2 on February 31, 1981; insofar as that Agreement concerns that which is hereinafter defined as CONFIDENTIAL INFORMATION it is merged into and replaced by this agreement.

[I have a bias for this agreement to be complete, and a bias against multiple agreements in related areas because in litigation work we see that the interface between two related agreements is a frequent source of litigious problem.

Also, I'm suggesting to you a bit of a modification of the prior agreement which will be a mite tighter if we can get EE to accept it. I feel EE should because it is not in the chemical or catalyst business itself.]

EE to keep
information
confidential

14.2 Subject to other terms herein EE agrees to maintain in confidence and to treat as confidential trade secret information ("CONFIDENTIAL INFORMATION") all drawings, data, concepts, specifications, flow sheets, designs,

269

parameters, catalysts and catalyst formulations and structures, and other technical know-how and all sales leads and marketing plans and tactics and other business information disclosed to EE by OR1 or OR2.[*]

14.3. Excepting as specifically exempted below, the obligation to treat OR1 + 2 information confidentially shall include information which may be duplicative of similar information in the public domain—for it is desired that competitors not know which of the publicly available information has been selected by OR1 + 2 for its PROCESS, equipment, catalyst and marketing uses.

14.4. Except as specifically exempted below, EE shall make no disclosures or use of any such CONFIDENTIAL INFORMATION; and shall take all appropriate steps to prevent the unauthorized disclosure thereof by its employees and its clients and licensees including the requirement that all disclosees of CONFIDENTIAL INFORMATION execute appropriate obligations of confidence relating thereto and consistent with §§ 4.2 thru 4.3.

14.5. EE shall by contract require of its employees and its sublicensee clients or prospective clients that with respect to any catalyst supplied to them from or at the direction of OR1 or OR2, they: (i) shall not analyze or have analyzed any such catalyst; (ii) shall not sell or give to anyone other than OR1 + 2 any charge or sample or part of any catalyst; (iii) shall dispose of any used catalyst only in accord with arrangements approved in advance by OR1 in a manner designed to prevent the accidental disclosure thereof; (iv) in the event of government request for disclosure of any information about

---

[*Information on the XYZ process is very useful in many other petrochemical product manufacturing processes. Hence this clause is much more broad than merely the "PROCESS"].

the catalyst such as safety or pollution considerations, shall notify OR1 of such requirement and OR1 shall thereupon disclose the necessary information under appropriate obligation of confidence or other protection as may be bound feasible.

EE may make disclosures to clients who agree to protect the confidence

14.6. All provided however: EE may make such disclosures to its clients and prospective clients who have entered into obligations of confidence with their employees and with EE or OR1+2 consistent herewith, as may be necessary and appropriate to the conduct of the business of developing the market for the PROCESS.

Exemptions from obligation of confidence

14.7. And all provided further: EE shall be free to use for its own account and to disclose to others (though without reference to OR1+2 or their PROCESS or catalyst) particular items of technology as to which:

Info generally known to technologists

(i) Such item and its application or use by EE is essentially unrelated to SVCCRAF or OR1 catalysts and without direct or indirect sponsorship by EE is disclosed in any manner making EE's application or use of it generally known to technologists in the petrochemical industry.

[It is important not to merely exempt information "in the public domain" because that phrase is legally vague and indefinite and in many courts biased in favor of the party seeking freedom to use. So here we seek to define with more specificity.]

Info disclosed to EE by third parties

(ii) Such item and its application of use by EE is essentially unrelated to the SVCCRAF or to OR1 catalysts and without direct or indirect sponsorship by EE is disclosed to EE by some outside third party source having the knowledge independently of OR2, OR1 or EE.

Info in EE possession

(iii) Such item or a reasonably complete equivalent thereof shall be shown to have been already conceived or otherwise in the possession of and its value in application to the PRO-

CESS appreciated by EE and reduced to either drawing, writing or physical embodiment prior to the disclosure by OR1+2.

Info disclosed in printed publications or U.S. patents

(iv) Without direct or indirect sponsorship by EE, such item or a reasonably complete equivalent thereof shall be shown to have been disclosed in a printed publication (including U.S. patents) at any time published in the United States or circulated substantially in the petrochemical industry of the United States, which publication as it would be understood by persons in the art not having knowledge of SVCCRAF would suggest its application to the PROCESS or to catalyst structure, manufacture or efficacy.

General info not basis for exemption of specific

14.8. Specific technical information disclosed by OR1+2 to EE or its clients shall not be deemed to be within any of the exemptions of § 14.6 merely because it is embraced in more general information within one of the exceptions.

Info re parts not an exemption re combination

14.9. In addition, any combination of features shall not be deemed to be within any of those exceptions merely because individual features of the combination are within any of said exceptions; rather only if the combination itself and its principle of operation are within an exception shall any combination of features be deemed exempted.

Use of OR1+2 disclosure as guide and screen for searcher does not constitute an exemption

14.10. If it is necessary for persons of ordinary information in the art to use the disclosure by OR1+2 as a guide to a searcher in the art and/ or as a screen to separate the useful ideas or compatible parameters from those not applicable to any viable SVCCRAF process or equipment, then the compilation of information by a searcher shall not constitute an exemption within § 14.6.

15. Controlling Law

Texas law applicable

15.1. All questions relating to the validity, interpretation, performance or enforcement of this agreement, whether by arbitration or otherwise, shall be determined in accord with the laws applicable in the State of Texas, U.S.A.

No party required
to violate any law

15.2. Neither EE nor OR1 nor OR2 shall be required to supply technology, catalyst, apparatus or other value to any sublicensee, if such action would be a violation of any law, regulation or executive order of any country.

16. Force Majeure

Force majeure

16.1 Each party shall be excused from any nonperformance of this agreement which is proximately caused by government regulation, war, strike, act of God, or other similar circumstance normally deemed outside the control of well managed businesses.

[Force majeure clauses are only rarely needed, hence are often forgotten. But I feel that they are as important as many insurance policies you buy.]

17. Notices

Notice in writing

17.1. All notices required herein shall be in writing.

Deliveree

17.2. Written notices may be delivered personally to the president of the subject party or to the officer specified in § 17.3.

Notices effective 3
days after specified
certified mail

17.3. Written notices shall be deemed to have been effective three days following the date of due mailing by certified mail, postage prepaid, return receipt requested, addressed as follows:

Addressed to OR1 as follows:
OR1 Company
P.O. Box _____
Houston, Texas 77_____

Addressed to OR2 as follows:
OR2 Corporation
000 A Street
Houston, Texas 77_____
Attention: President

Addressed to EE as follows:
EE Inc.
P.O. Box _____
Houston, Texas 77____
Attention: Sr. Vice President
and Technical Director.

Change of
addresses

17.4. Each party shall have the right to change the effective address for notice by a notice in writing directed to the other party above.

18. Entire Agreement; Amendments; Headings

Entire agreement

18.1. This agreement together with its appendices constitutes the entire agreement between the parties and supersedes any prior communications whether oral or written.

[Does the prior secrecy agreement have any application after this contract? Reconsider this clause if you retain the prior draft's confidentiality clause rather than my new one.]

Amendments in
writing

18.2. This agreement may be amended or modified only by an instrument in writing signed by duly constituted officers of the parties.

Waivers are not
permanent

18.3 No waiver, no matter how long continuing or how many times extended, shall be construed as a permanent waiver or as an amendment to this instrument.

Marginal headings
not used to
construe text

18.4. The marginal headings herein are for purposes of convenient reference only and shall not be used to construe or modify the terms written in the text of this instrument.

19. OR1 + 2 Contract Unchanged

OR1 contract with
OR2 unchanged

19.1. Excepting insofar as there may be clear and positive expression to the contrary, this instrument shall not be construed as changing the contractual relationship between OR2 and OR1 expressed in instruments of January 0, 1978, August 32, 1978, December 33, 1978 and October 34, 1979.

20. Term and Termination

Termination on
ninety days written
notice

20.1 The appointment of EE as marketing

274

representative under § 4.1, the grant of license under § 4.2, the grant of right to sublicense under § 4.3, together with the relevant undertakings recited in Article 5 and the rights and duties under §§ 8.1 thru 8.3 and 8.7, all of Article 9 and Article 10 may be terminated as a group without reason by any party hereto upon ninety days appropriate written notice to the other parties.

[Some draftsmen say that "the agreement" terminates in this event or that, but certain rights like confidentiality survive termination "of the agreement." I strongly prefer that the "agreement" be perpetual, and that by that agreement certain rights terminate at this time or that.

Further, the bankruptcy clause that is in John Doe's draft and your draft is not effective. It is void by law—the licensee's license continues in the hands of the trustee in bankruptcy regardless of this contract clause. We can, if need be, get the desired result by perfecting a lien interest under the UCC, but that is burdensome and not to be undertaken unless we feel it is really worth it.]

OR1 COMPANY

By: _____

Title: _____

Date of execution: _____

OR2 CORPORATION

By: _____

Title: _____

Date of execution: _____

EE INC.

By: _____

Title: _____

Date of execution: _____

Appendix A

Principles and Guidelines for the Safe Transfer of Technology*

I. PREAMBLE

1.1 Background

Transfer of Technology, in its different forms, is a key element in worldwide economic and social development. Its contribution to the improvement of the social and physical welfare of the world populations and of harmonious relations within the world community is generally recognized.

In a transfer of technology, questions of safety, health and protection of the environment are an important issue. Both suppliers and receivers of technology as well as the other parties involved have a vital interest in ensuring the safety of the technology transferred.

Between countries of different levels of development, a transfer of technology can entail a risk to the less developed community, whose skills, knowledge, experience or socio-administrative framework may not be appropriate to handle adequately the new processes, technologies or products.

The issue is receiving more and more attention, in particular from International Organisations. For example, in September 1985, the World Bank issued "Guidelines for Identifying, Analysing and Controlling Major Hazard Installations in Developing Countries" and in October 1986, the International Labour Office drafted a "Code of Practice on Safety and Health and Working Conditions in the Transfer of Technology to Developing Countries". Further initiatives are expected.

In September 1985, CEFIC issued a Position Paper, "Principles for Safe Transfer of Technology" which is reproduced in section 2 of the present document and is an integral part of it. This position

---

*Counseil Europeen des Federations de l'Industrie Chimique, Avenue Louise 250. Btd 71, B–1060, Bruxelles (April 15, 1987).

277

paper presents the principles which should be considered and agreed upon by the various parties concerned in providing the conditions for a safe transfer of technology. It highlights that any transfer of technology requires a joint, co-ordinated effort by the parties and particularly the supplier and the receiver of technology. This requires a clear allocation of responsibilities and duties amongst the various parties, essentially based on the reality of the powers exercised; it is essential that the responsible party at each stage has effective management control.

1.2 CEFIC Guidelines

The present Guidelines aim at ensuring that the degree of safety of new installations employing the transferred technology are of an internationally accepted level and equivalent to that achieved in the country of origin.

They do not establish which party is responsible for the execution of the various phases in the transfer of technology. This has to be determined and agreed upon by the parties in accordance with the Principles in section 2.

They are primarily for the use of technology suppliers, licensors and contractors in the European Chemical Industry although they may also serve as terms of reference to other parties involved within their own area of responsibility.

In any transfer of technology, good design, engineering, construction and management practices must be followed in order to ensure a high level of safety; however these Guidelines mainly concern "Major Hazard Installations". These installations, which are conveniently identified as being those falling under Article 5 of the Directive 82/501/EEC on Major Accident Hazards, require the use of various methods of hazard assessment and risk management. The Guidelines suggest the application of these same procedures to any transfer of such installations and technologies.

In section 3 of the document Guidelines are developed for each of the various phases in a transfer of technology, from inception to operation. In view of the diversity of the installations transferred and of the types of agreement, these guidelines have to be applied with the necessary flexibility.

1.3 Definitions

In this document:

—The term "safety" is used in its broad sense, i.e. prevention of physical or economical losses as well as accidental damages to life and health of people inside the plant and outside populations and to the environment.

—Hazard means: a physical situation with a potential for human injury, damage to property, damage to the environment or some combination of these.

—Risk means: the likelihood of a specified undesired event occurring within a specified period or in specified circumstances.

II. PRINCIPLES FOR THE SAFE TRANSFER OF TECHNOLOGY

2.1 Introduction

The transfer of technology between countries whether they have the same or different socio-economic regimes, or levels of development, is an important factor for improving and strengthening economic developments and social welfare. It is generally recognised as one of the key factors of harmonious relations within the world community.

In a transfer of technology questions of safety are an important issue. Both providers and receivers of technology and the other parties involved have a vital interest in safety, for ethical and social reasons as well as economic ones. This implies a high level of awareness of the issues at stake and a proper allocation of responsibilities between the parties involved.

Possible safety problems are neither limited to multinationals nor to market economy states and in fact all industrial sectors are confronted with them and not just the chemical industry. However, as recent accidents have shown, this issue is of particular importance to the chemical industry.

This paper presents the principles which should be considered and agreed upon by the various parties concerned in providing the conditions for a sale transfer of technology.

The appendix outlines what is meant by "transfer of technology" in this document as well as the "parties" which can be involved.

Licensing

2.2 Basic Principles

It is a fundamental principle that the highest degree of safety reasonably practicable according to the current stage of knowledge is pursued when considering the transfer of a technology which offers a level of safety and health protection equivalent to that achieved in the home facilities of the technology supplier. Safety should be independent of political, social, economic or commercial factors, but in the transfer of technology, one has also to take into account local requirements and circumstances.

Factors like geographical and climatic conditions, the cultural and socio-economic environment, the infrastructure including emergency services, the legal and administrative framework, including the local intellectual property situation, land use/development control policies, technical constraints, local materials of construction and of equipment as well as the availability of competent operators should be duly taken into account. The process should be chosen and the plant designed with the needs and the capabilities of the host country and the technology receiver in mind.

In addition, parties envisaging such an operation should always consider the international framework, including relevant treaties and conventions as well as existing non-mandatory codes and guidelines.

A careful consideration and evaluation of these local and international factors—and the satisfactory solution of possible problems arising therefrom—are the basis and condition "sine qua non" of any transfer of technology.

2.3 Allocation of Responsibilities Between Parties

2.3.1 General considerations

The allocation of responsibilities and the reality of the decision making and control powers exercised by the various parties in the agreement, including the effective control of operations affecting safety are key elements in a transfer of technology. Equity involvement is not necessarily linked with operational control and each situation has to be considered on its own merits, taking into account the specific context.

The respective duties of the parties involved in the various stages of a transfer of technology should be clearly defined at a preliminary stage and certainly before such transfer takes place.

The main responsibilities lie with the supplier and receiver of the technology, yet the host state must establish the necessary framework for a safe transfer of technology.

In general terms, responsibility must be linked to effective operational control: it must be clear that no party can be held responsible or legally liable if, for reasons beyond its control, its role in conducting and controlling matters affecting safety is limited or non-effective.

2.3.2 Responsibilities of technology suppliers

In principle the responsibility for safe process design, the initial technical training, the supervision of commissioning, start-up assistance and information for safe operation and handling of products used or manufactured should be part of the technology suppliers' duties. The extent of these duties and the period during which they apply can vary depending on the type and context of the specific contract such that, for example, commissioning could be the responsibility of the technology receiver.

2.3.3 Responsibilities of technology receivers

Responsibility for detailed engineering, plant erection, process operation, plant maintenance and modifications, provision of information to local authorities on safety issues, training and supervision of the work-force, and establishment of safety and security check systems should normally be part of the technology receiver's responsibilities, except where a specific contractual provision requires the technology supplier to exercise a control over such tasks.

2.3.4 Division and sharing of responsibilities

In addition to the above principles, the transfer of technology contract should clearly define and regulate the division and sharing of responsibilities between parties.

In particular, once the plant as built according to the specified design and as operated according to specified procedures, has demonstrated its capability to be operated safely in the acceptance test run, a handover document should be signed by all parties involved, including contractors and suppliers.

Thereafter, safety must be seen as an ongoing integral part of the management of the plant at local level. The technology receiver should be responsible for any alteration to the initial process or design, or to the operating procedures, unless the modification was requested by or agreed upon by the technology provider in an amendment to the initial contract.

Even in cases of equity involvement, contracts should be concluded between technology provider and technology receiver on an arms-length basis, i.e. as separate entities, and, likewise, the above measures should be duly documented both by the parent company and local management.

2.4 Framework of Duties of Host Countries Involved in Technology Transfer

Local states and their competent authorities should take the necessary steps in order to adopt and to enforce legal provisions, and administrative and related measures concerning safe operation.

Authorities of the host state should particularly have the duty of:

—evaluating the technical information presented by the local company and its partner in the transfer of technology, giving special consideration to the siting proposed in relation to its national land use planning;

—ensuring that the appropriate regulatory and medical authorities are in possession of adequate information concerning the technical, toxicological, medical and other relevant aspects of the technology due to be received, and that the personnel involved have been adequately and appropriately trained to carry out their duties;

—providing the necessary legal and practical flexibility in order to enable the selection of the contractors, suppliers and equipment best fitting safety requirements;

—giving the necessary import licenses for safe equipment and for original spare parts;

—developing the external emergency plan, including the provision of information to the local authorities and population, as well as the provision of medical resources;

—ensuring compliance of the actual working conditions with local regulations;

—ensuring that the initial conditions of the operating permit are maintained inside the plant;

—exercising development control to avoid inconsistent land uses in the vicinity;

—granting working and residence permits for the required foreign technical permanent or temporary staff;

—providing exit permits for local key personnel to obtain training at the technology providers' facilities;

—guaranteeing the necessary exchange of experts and experience;

—improving professional training of local staff;

—and, in general:

- ensuring that the information provided to them is used for the purposes for which it is disclosed and having due regard to commercial confidentiality;
- enabling the parties to the transfer of technology contract to comply with all contractual duties which fall upon them according to a contract made up in accordance with applicable laws and internationally accepted commercial practice.

III. GUIDELINES

3.1 The Initiation Phase

The elements motivating the transfer of a certain technology to a particular country are generally speaking of an economic nature. But simultaneously with the collection of the feasibility data, a "fact finding" phase should take place to collect information on the factors influencing the various environments of the planned installation:

—*The regulatory environment.* The laws and regulations of the receiving country must be examined, as some of them may have a direct impact on the health and safety aspects. In particular, legal restrictions on sources of supply (equipment, replacement parts, etc.), on location of the installation in relation to housing and effective control of housing around the installation, or on acceptability of expatriate managers or employees should be considered from the very beginning of the study, and the necessary exceptions must be clearly identified. Consideration should also be given to the regulatory constraints of the exporting country and of the international community (banned or severely restricted processes or products, internationally agreed conventions, etc.).

—*The socio-cultural environment.* It is essential that the capability of the local workforce to safely operate the planned technology is assessed. This requires a realistic review of the general level of education and of the availability of technologically trained workers, of competent supervisors and managers, of professionals in the fields of safety, environment, occupational medicine, hygiene and toxicology, educated either domestically or abroad. Problems of communication (languages, symbols) and of mentality (attitude to risk) should not be overlooked. Above all, it is essential to satisfy oneself that the highest management levels are committed to the importance of operating safely so that safety is an integral part of the management of the business.

—*The technological environment.* The capability of the technology receiver and of the domestic or foreign contractors and suppliers to safely build, maintain and operate the installation should be assessed. Also the level of technological culture of the local industry (maintenance, spare parts, etc.) and local transport facilities should be reviewed. Special consideration should be given to the availability of competent waste disposal contractors.

—*The physical environment.* The effects of local climatic conditions, such as temperature, humidity, likelihood of natural events such as hurricanes or floods, as well as geophysical ones such as earthquakes and soil stability, on the proposed installation should be considered. The impact of the proposed installation on the environment, including the inhabited areas, should be considered.

The final decision whether to transfer the technology or not should be guided by the degree of satisfaction achieved from the answers obtained to the questions raised in the fact-finding phase.

3.2 The Negotiation Phase

As highlighted in section 2—the Principles—this is a crucial phase as it governs the clear allocation of duties and responsibilities of the various parties during all stages of the transfer, from its inception to the routine operation.

The various points highlighted in sections 3.3. to 3.7 should be considered by the party who is contractually responsible for the phase involved.

3.3 The Design and Engineering Phase

The installation based on the transferred technology should achieve a degree of safety equivalent to that of the installation of the technology supplier from which it is normally derived. But because of the differences in the local environments identified earlier, some features of the plant installed may differ from those of plants where the technology was originally developed.

This should be kept in mind when performing the various steps of the design and engineering phase:

3.3.1 The basic process

Only processes for which sufficient experience has been gained by the technology provider should be transferred. In addition, the level of competence of local operators, the degree of availability and reliability of critical components (computers, analysers) and of local supply of good quality raw materials, intermediates and utilities should be considered when selecting the process.

Minimization of inventories of hazardous materials also should be considered at this stage.

3.3.2 Design

The installation based on the transferred technology should be designed according to the good engineering practices used for any installation of the same nature. Relevant codes and standards, whether national, international or industrial should be observed. Specific conditions imposed by the local environments should be given consideration. The presence in the design team of a suitably qualified representative of the technology receiver is strongly recommended.

3.3.3 Hazard assessment

At the different stages of development of the design, a hazard assessment of the elements of the planned installation should be carried out. The party responsible for making the assessment should use the techniques currently accepted for the identification of hazards and evaluation of consequences for safety, health or the environment and have access to the necessary information. When justified, quantitative methods of risk assessment may be used for some parts of the installation for comparative purposes.

Results of the various assessments should be taken into account in developing siting, engineering or organisational measures in order to minimize the residual hazards.

3.3.4 Process and specifications manuals

These are a key element of the transfer package. The reference manuals should include:

—a description of the process, including all necessary data on the substances handled, on the chemical reactions involved, their limits of stability, the possible deviations, products of runaways, etc.;
—the flow-sheets, P and I diagrams, drawings, and where relevant, design and construction specifications of components of the installation;
—a summary of any hazard assessments carried out;
—the operating instructions for both routine and non-routine (including emergency) conditions;
—the health and safety aspects of the installation and necessary controls;
—the maintenance instructions and schedules, including instrument testing and calibration;
—the sampling and monitoring procedure;
—a training manual.

The manuals should be written in a language agreed upon by the parties, to reduce the possibility of any misunderstandings.

3.4 Procurement and Erection Phase

Special care should be taken to ensure that all components of the installation are purchased, built, delivered and erected according to the design and engineering specifications. This requires the establishment of stringent procedures for inspection, quality assurance, testing and commissioning of all items of equipment, as well as thorough surveillance and testing of the civil, piping, mechanical, electrical and instrument work. This aspect is of special importance when national regulatory constraints impose the use of local suppliers or contractors.

286

When appropriate, outside help and expertise, for example from the technology provider or any other organization which may be recommended or approved by the technology provider should be sought.

A full survey of the plant should be carried out as designated in the contract at the end of the erection phase and before commissioning the installation. Its results should be incorporated in the process and specifications manuals, together with the "as-built" drawings.

3.5 Emergency Plans

Before the introduction of any hazardous materials, it is essential that an adequate emergency plan has been established, both for the installation and the local community. According to local law and practice, the external emergency plan may be established by the authorities, on the basis of information supplied by the manufacturer. The population in the vicinity of the installation should be informed of what action to take in case of an emergency. It is important to make sure that the internal and external emergency plans are fully coordinated and involve the public emergency services.

The emergency systems and equipment including those for fire-fighting and combating the release of toxics should be duly tested before the build-up of any significant inventory of hazardous materials. In addition, the availability of medical facilities and supplies suitable for the materials handled should be ensured.

3.6 Commissioning

Before the plant is commissioned, the workforce in charge of its operation should have been trained, either locally or at the premises of the technology supplier. This training should involve all levels of staff, embracing operators, supervisors and managers, and should give special consideration to the safety, health and environmental aspects of the process.

It is fundamental that a sufficient number of competent specialists provided by the technology supplier should be available to give assistance to the technology receiver's workforce throughout the commissioning phase.

Any technological and operational modifications agreed and carried out during the commissioning of the installation should be recorded in the Process and Specifications manuals.

Licensing

3.7 The Operation Phase

When the installation, which has been designed, built and started-up according to the above principles, is put on routine operation, its safety is mainly dependent on three factors:

3.7.1 The management

The local management is responsible for the safe operation of the installation. This includes all aspects of good management practices, in particular:

—full understanding of the process safety information upon which the plant is designed;
—periodic hazard reviews of the installation to ensure that the initial level of safety is maintained;
—modifications procedure for hardware, software and process conditions;
—management of rules and procedures for safety and emergency response, including periodic testing and medical facilities and supply;
—training, retraining and qualification for process, mechanical and technical operators;
—accident/incident investigation and reporting;
—routine inspection of plant and equipment, in particular pressure systems, pipework and relief systems and testing of key trip and alarm systems;
—safety auditing procedures.

Whether the technology supplier may assist the local management in fulfilling its duties depends on the type of agreement but in any case it is essential that an organization with clear accountabilities is established to ensure that these duties are carried out and that process safeguarding systems, including emergency shut-down systems, are maintained continuously operational.

3.7.2 The modifications

Process and installations are occasionally modified in accordance with technical progress. However no changes from the initial specifications of the process or design should be permitted without the formal consent of local management. Any modification or adaptation likely to have a significant impact on the safety of the operation should be preceded by a hazard assessment:

whether this will be done by the local manufacturer, the technology supplier or an outside consultant depends on the capacity available and the type of contract. At least the advice of the technology supplier should be sought.

3.7.3 The up-dating of information

New data on the safety aspects of the process or the materials involved may be generated either by the technology supplier or by the technology receiver. It is necessary that such information should be passed on to the other party and provision for this should be made in the agreement between the parties.

APPENDIX

1. Types of Transfer of Technology

Transfer of technology not only means the actual transfer but also the application of the technology as well as the operation of the plant.

A great variety of cases are involved but despite this diversity the key elements are the allocation of responsibilities and the reality of the powers exercised.

With this essential consideration in mind, it is useful to distinguish between:

—a contract for a transfer of technology between independent partners (non-equity involvement), and

—a transfer of technology within the framework of a relationship between companies (equity involvement). Situations here can be extremely variable from minority participation with one or several local partner(s) to majority share-holding or full ownership.

2. Parties Involved in the Transfer of Technology

Having in mind the variety of situations, the possible parties can be described as follows:

a) The technology supplier: this embraces not only large companies, but often also small or medium-sized companies which have developed advanced or specialised technology. This can also involve an engineering company acting on behalf of or in conjunction with the technology provider;

Licensing

b) The technology receiver: may be a company in which the technology provider holds a minority or a majority stake, or a totally independent company (private or state-owned);

c) The contractors, either from the home country or other countries;

d) The host state, i.e. the authorities of the country of the technology receiver.

In addition to these parties who have a direct interest in, and responsibility for, the transfer of technology, other bodies which may be involved are:

e) The commercial banks, private or state-owned which lend funds for the projects;

f) The non-commercial financing institutions, such as the World Bank, or other international or national institutions providing grants for development.

Finally, it should be observed that other bodies like inter-governmental organisations and national or international jurisdictions have an interest in an international consensus on issues related to safety in the transfer of technology.

Appendix B

The "Nine No-No's" of the 1970s

Freely borrowing from remarks of Abbott B. Lipsky, Jr., Deputy Assistant Attorney General, Antitrust Division, before the American Bar Association Antitrust Section, 5 Trade Reg. Rep. (CCH) ¶ 50,434 (1981), the current thinking and likely enforcement policy of the Antitrust Division of the Department of Justice* can be summarized as follows:

No-No Number 1: It is clear that it is unlawful to require a licensee to purchase unpatented materials from the licensor. *Current Position:* "[W]hile it is conceivable that patent tie-ins might be anticompetitive under peculiar conditions, a general rule prohibiting them is almost certainly counter productive." *Id.* at 55,987.

No-No Number 2: The Department views it as unlawful for a patentee to require a licensee to assign to the patentee any patent which may be issued to the licensee after the licensing arrangement is executed. *Current Position:* "The troublesome aspect of this practice is its tendency to reduce the incentives of licensees to engage in their inventive activity, and to guarantee the licensor that its licensee-competitors will obtain no unique advantage over it. . . . [O]ur approach must necessarily constitute a fact-sensitive and careful evaluation of the risk that the incentives to invent have been sacrificed to a degree unnecessary for adequate exploitation of the patentee's monopoly rights." *Id.* at 55,988.

No-No Number 3: The Department believes it is unlawful to attempt to restrict a purchaser of a patented product in the resale of that product. *Current Position:* "Restrictions on resale are to be judged by the same general standards as those that ought to be in use outside the patent field." *Id.*

No-No Number 4: A patentee may not restrict his licensee's freedom to deal in the products or services not within the scope of the patent. *Current Position:* "[T]he analysis of this practice should

---

*Courts never completely adopted the Nine No-No's and also have yet to adopt the Department's change of view.

start with an attempt to determine whether the relationship between the patentee and the licensee is vertical or horizontal. Where the relationship is vertical, the analysis should proceed on the same basis as the analysis of vertical exclusive arrangements outside the patent field. Unless the practice threatens to preempt an entire rung in the distribution ladder, and unless the patentee's advantage is so overwhelming as to make this a credible threat, there is no competitive reason to prohibit exclusive distribution arrangements." *Id.* at 55,988–89.

No-No Number 5: The Department believes it to be unlawful for a patentee to agree with his licensee that he will not, without the licensee's consent, grant further licenses to any other person. *Current Position:* "[Generally] licensees will not undertake the practice of some patents without assurances that the level of activity by other licensees will not rise to the point where the licensee's return falls below that required to justify his investment. It is therefore easy to imagine situations in which the imposition of this fifth rule will prevent the procompetitive exploitation of inventions." *Id.* at 55,989.

No-No Number 6: The Department believes that mandatory package licensing is an unlawful extension of the patent grant. *Current Position:* "[P]ackage licensing may allow the patentee to maximize the net return on [his] patents, given the constraints on his state of knowledge concerning the value of the patents to different licensees, and on the ease with which he can negotiate separate licenses for his patent. . . . Thus, the practice of package licensing ought not be subject to any general prohibition on antitrust grounds." *Id.*

No-No Number 7: The Department believes that it is unlawful for a patentee to insist, as a *condition* of the license, that his licensee pay royalties in an amount not reasonably related to the licensee's sale of products covered by the patent—for example, royalties on the total sales of products of the general type covered by the licensed patent. *Current Position:* "[W]hat is important is the reasonableness of the patentee's choice of method for metering or approximating the value of the license. Sales may be a reasonable method, but it may not in some circumstances. . . .[A] rule of reason approach must be employed to insure an optimal trade-off between the requirements of the patentee's metering needs, and the risk of unnecessary cartelization. . . .[T]o the extent that the seventh no-no contemplates patentee/licensee relationships that are purely vertical, it sweeps too broadly." *Id.* at 55,989–90.

No-No Number 8: It is pretty clearly unlawful for the owner of a process patent to attempt to place restrictions in his licensee's sale of products made by the use of the patented process. *Current Position:* "[T]o deny the patentee the means to exploit his legitimate monopoly by the most convenient means, simply because those means take the form of restraints on transactions involving the unpatented product, is not only excessively formalistic, but is potentially destructive of consumer welfare."*Id.* at 55,990.

No-No Number 9: The Department of Justice considers it unlawful for a patentee to require a licensee to adhere to any specified or minimum price with respect to the licensee's sale of the licensed products. *Current Position:* "[W]e ... rely ...upon the same analysis employed with respect to distributional practices ... where the relationship between the patentee and licensee is vertical. When that relationship is horizontal, a far more agonizing choice is presented.... There appears to be no clearly superior alternative to a fact-sensitive rule of reason approach where trade-offs of this nature are encountered. It would be constructive to face this inevitable quandary directly, rather than to pretend that it can be resolved by quick reference to a simple rule." *Id.*

Thus, the Antitrust Division seems to have abandoned its adhesion to simple rules to solve quite complex real-world problems. While abandonment of simple rules may appear to make the patent/antitrust interface ambiguous, it is not the abandonment of these rules that creates the ambiguity, but rather the interface itself. The return to a rule of reason approach regarding patent licensing practices is a recognition that "there is little sense in pretending that easy resolutions exist where in fact they do not." *Id.*

Appendix C

100 Factors Involved in Pricing the Technology License

A. Pricing a Technology Is All a Risk Balance
B. Stage of Technology Development; Guarantees
C. Manufacturer's Margin
D. Strength of Protection
E. Distinctiveness of the Market Niche
F. Size of the Market Niche
G. Value of the Technology to the Licensee National Economy
H. Values Brought to the Table by the Licensee
I. Burdens of Enforcement of, and Infringement of, Intellectual Property Rights
J. Favored Nations Clause
K. Ease of Design-around
L. The Number of Patents Involved; Freedom of the Licensee Designers
M. The Facility by which the Licensor Can Reach the Licensee's Markets with the Licensor's Own Manufacture
N. Licensee Competition with the Licensor
O. Tag-along and Derivative Sales
P. The Structure and Time Spread of Payments
Q. Repatriation of Money from the Licensee
R. Risks of Litigation—or Loss of It
S. Risk of Loss of Royalties from Prior Licenses
T. Exposure to Liability for Infringement of Rights of Third Parties
U. What the Market Will Bear
V. Access to Ongoing Technology
W. What Did the Technology Cost the Licensor to Develop?
X. Traditional Division of Anticipated Profits
Y. 100 Factors
    (a) Intrinsic Quality
    (b) Protections and Threats of Protection
    (c) Market Considerations
    (d) Competitive Considerations
    (e) Values Brought to the Table by the Licensee
    (f) Financial Considerations
    (g) Particular Risk Considerations

Licensing

A. Pricing a Technology Is All a Risk Balance

Let me translate "*hope* for profit" into risk of profit to make it grammatically parallel to risk of loss.

There is risk of each profit and loss unavoidably involved in:

—licensing embryo, concept-only, technology by comparison with licensing mature, proven, technology;
—scale-up from prototype product or pilot plant to production model or commercial plant;
—assuming commitments to enforce patent rights;
—future licensee competition with the licensor;
—guarantees of the quantity or cost of production obtainable with the licensed technology;
—the burdens and costs of the license negotiation and the technology transfer itself.

In short, there is risk of profit or loss in everything involved in the license.

France's former President, Georges Pompidou, once said:

There are three ways to ruin yourself: gambling, women and technology.
Gambling is the fastest.
Women are the most pleasurable.
Technology is the most certain.

The total consideration for a license may be payable in whole or in part, in: commitments and guarantees; marketing or other unique talent; equity; debt; front money; postponed sums certain; minimum royalties; running royalties; each tailored partly at least to some risk or hope of profit or loss.

But however structured, the most intelligent price for the license is a balance in the risks of profit and loss—a risk balance.

At the end of this appendix there is a list of about 100 factors in that risk balance. I have selected a very few for discussion here. But each of the 100 factors should be reviewed by both sides of the

296

negotiation in the context of risk of profit and loss in arriving at that risk balance.

If reviewed before and during a negotiation, these considerations will help a party put his own value on the technology and will forewarn him of the thinking of the other side—thinking for which he should be forearmed prior to the negotiation.

B. Stage of Technology Development; Guarantees

The first factor we will discuss is the stage of the technology development, and the related guarantees.

Is the technology at the embryo stage, barely conceived? Or is it a technology fully proven in commercial production, and hence guaranteeable as to annual market, as to cost of manufacture, as to time of getting the plant on stream, as to capacity of the plant, and as to quality of the product?

Many times with some *un*certain amount of time and money the technology can *for certain* be developed independently. But I have represented a licensee willing to pay $50 million for such a technology that could be guaranteed as to

- (a) quality of the product,
- (b) cost of the product,
- (c) capacity of the plant,
- (d) safety of the plant and product,
- (e) the point in time of completion of the plant and entry into the market.

It was primarily the time factor and the guarantee—the elimination of risk—which justified the $50 million price for a technology that conceptually was all publicly available.

The guarantee was not separately priced, but the licensor able to give the guarantee—and convince the licensee that the licensee would never have to collect on the guarantee—could charge extra tens of millions for his technology.

I saw one such deal on low density polyethylene, where such a guarantee was given before the first pilot plant had completed its shakedown.

But usually it is a technology nearly devoid of risk—a technology matured and proven by commercial operation—where such guarantees can be given, and still talked about as part of the price of the technology.

Licensing

A license of tire making technology to a French tire manufacturer is illustrative of the role of the guarantee in licensing even a mature technology.

Some years back a French company purchased a tire manufacturing technology, a complete factory, tools, processes, the works—duly guaranteed as to quantity of production, quality of production, reject rate, etc.

When the training and break-in periods called for in the contract had been completed, the licensor's personnel went home. And the licensee's personnel got only 80 percent of the guaranteed production rate, at twice the guaranteed maximum reject rate.

The licensee complained that the technology was bad. The licensor complained that the licensee was too stupid to use the technology properly. Both were sincere, both were strong, in their beliefs.

Courts, you will understand, are totally incompetent to decide such a case. The kind of evidence that can be brought into the courtroom in such a case simply does not admit to a reliable evaluation and judgment by the court.

So the licensor picked 50 of its best operators out of its own near-duplicate tire factory, sent them to France each with his own interpreter, and in 60 days or so—I of course forget the exact numbers—they had the plant humming along at 110 percent of guaranteed capacity, and half the guaranteed maximum reject rate. You, of course, will understand that guarantees were lower by a good margin of safety than the design specifications the plant called for.

The licensor won the lawsuit without going to court . . . that is, before the suit was filed. But at the cost of the loss of services of 50 of its key people for a couple of months. The licensee paid for their expenses, but not for their lost production.

The guarantee:

—is valuable to the licensee.
—is potentially costly to the licensor.
—is a big factor in pricing the technology whether you are licensing a technology or determining damages in a court infringement suit.

C. Manufacturer's Margin

Some bulk products are sold routinely in hotly competitive markets at a 5 percent margin or less. It is hardly necessary to point

298

out that a royalty in such a market must be less than 5 percent. Much less.

On the other hand, a unique agricultural chemical may be priced in response to value to the customer. For instance, give the farmer three dollars' worth of cost savings or increased crop yield for every dollar of price he pays for the insecticide, herbicide, or fertilizer.

Note that cost of manufacture and selling is not in the pricing formula, a pricing formula that may produce a price that is ten or more times the cost of manufacture and sale. The value of that technology, if it is protected by a solid patent, is tremendous by comparison with a product that must be sold at a 2 percent of 5 percent margin.

I have licensed such an agricultural chemical at 50 percent of the licensee-manufacturers' sales price. And both parties got rich.

Anticipated manufacturer's margin is thus seen to be a very important factor in pricing the technology license.

As with many of the factors, manufacturer's margin is a complex mix of many other factors, such as: strength of the legal protection; uniqueness of the market niche; cost of manufacturer; intrinsic quality of the product in terms of value to the user and absence of close competition; etc.

And some of those constituent factors are highly variable. So let's spend a minute on a few of those factors.

D.   Strength of Protection

Of course the strength of the protection, be it patent, trade secret, or both, is a key factor. For without protection the pricing formula becomes a mark-up over cost—a mark-up that meets competition and is small.

Strength of protection is also important to the next factor, distinctiveness of the market niche.

E.   Distinctiveness of the Market Niche

The distinctiveness of the market niche of the licensed subject matter—the differentiation of the licensed product from its nearest competition—is very important in pricing the technology. For example:

Perhaps ten companies make a soft, stretchable polyethylene film appropriate for garment bags. My client paid extra to Nissan

299

for the technology to produce a relatively nonstretch film strong enough for use as shopping and grocery bags.

Study the distinctiveness of the market niche, and the differentiation of the licensed product from its nearest competition.

That study will influence the price you put on the technology.

F. Size of the Market Niche

The size of the total market and the licensee's share of it are often critical, because small markets often will not support the high cost of the license negotiation and the technology transfer itself, *i.e.,* the employee training cost, etc.

One of our clients had an experience in licensing a sophisticated electronic technology to Hungary. The negotiations went well until the negotiators started studying the amount and cost of the training time required to teach the licensees to maintain and operate the sophisticated equipment.

It was the potential licensee who spoke of the problem first: "Our market is restricted to Hungary and Albania. There is no way that small market will support those training costs."

And so the deal was scrapped because the size of the market niche would not support the cost of the technology transfer.

G. Value of the Technology to the Licensee National Economy

The unique value of the technology to the licensee and his national economy is sometimes critical.

Recall here the Egypt bread factory story. Egypt was in need of bread, and asked for the latest super-duper automated bread factory technology.

But to an experienced licensing man that simple request is a nonsequitur.

Egypt needed jobs even more than it needed bread.

In the U.S. labor is expensive and capital is relatively cheap. And so it is worthwhile to spend cheap capital to automate and avoid expensive labor.

In Egypt labor is cheap and hard currency capital is more dear than a space suit to a man who has landed on the moon.

So ultimately, Egypt purchased an older technology, one adapted to use more cheap labor, and less expensive automatic equipment. It was a win-win deal. The value of the 15-year-old technology was influenced by the economy and labor markets in the licensee country.

H. Values Brought to the Table by the Licensee

Values brought to the table by the licensee can be vital to the pricing of a license.

When Xerox was a small company studying its marketing plan for the European market, it had no market force in Europe; it had no capital with which to build one. Full development of that market before its basic patents ran out was important. This made time an important factor to Xerox.

So Xerox licensed what became Rank Xerox, because Rank brought to the table capital and established marketing muscle, the capacity to penetrate the European market in a hurry.

That value brought to the table by the licensee was an important factor in pricing the technology. And commonly what the licensee brings to the table is very important to the tactics of negotiation as well as to the license price.

I. Burdens of Enforcement of, and Infringement of, Intellectual Property Rights

The provisions of a license dealing with duties and costs of enforcement of patent, trademark, trade secret, and other intellectual property rights are among the most difficult at which to arrive.

The provisions dealing with alleged infringement of rights of others: who will control the defense, who will pay for the defense, who will balance a change in design to avoid infringement against the cost and risk of continuing the litigation? Fairness in these provisions is not easier to arrive at than that in the provisions dealing with offensive enforcement litigation.

Litigation costs alone often run into millions of dollars in the United States. So to indemnify the licensee from infringement of patents to others, or to promise the licensee to enforce the licensed patents, is to assume a responsibility that is very important in pricing the license package. Important to the tune of million dollar orders of magnitude when the U.S. is involved—lesser sums in other countries—that must be accommodated in pricing the technology.

J. Favored Nations Clause

Some form of favored nations clause is often put into licenses almost as a routine throw-away. But should that be so?

If the licensee is paying very much, he cannot afford competition from unlicensed competitors. So he wants an obligation of the licensor to enforce his patents. An obligation to enforce the licensed patents is so plagued with uncertainties and often is so burdensome that the licensor often simply cannot afford to undertake it. If the licensor won't guarantee to enforce his patent rights, the risk to the licensee who is paying substantial royalties is much higher.

So the price he pays must be correspondingly lower, depending upon the presence or absence of a licensor's obligation to enforce his patent rights against infringers who are competitive with the licensee.

K. Ease of Design-around

There are a number of burdens inherently carried by the potential licensee should he elect his alternative choice—development of the same or competitive technology by his own effort, thereby to avoid need for the license. We call that the competitive development alternative to a license.

The most obvious burden of competitive development is cost to the licensee of its own R&D effort. Often of equal importance is time required for that competitive development effort.

Then consider the uncertainty of that effort. Is it certain that a competitive development effort will succeed in producing equal or better technology? Or perhaps might it produce only an inferior technology?

Will the new development give rise to new questions of infringement of patents belonging to others? New questions that will take time as well as money to resolve?

It hardly takes a salesman for the licensor to convince us that: This is baggage, burdensome baggage, that is inherently carried by competitive-development alternative. And that baggage, when properly evaluated and sold in the negotiations, affects the price that the licensor can charge.

L. The Number of Patents Involved; Freedom of the Licensee Designers

In the electronics industry it often occurs that there are a dozen acceptable alternative ways to perform a given function. The component parts for the various alternatives are small and inexpensive, so a royalty must inherently be very very small. Many groups of ten or twenty patents are not worth licensing.

But suppose you have four hundred or a thousand patents on color TV circuits. The burdens of studying all those patents for their scope and validity, and then having your circuit designers plot a track between them all, can be tremendous.

Given the vagaries of the doctrine of equivalents, the scope of patents can be hideously vague and uncertain and expensive to determine.

So often licenses are entered into for all the patents a company has, perhaps with a reservation, for special treatment, of one or two very fundamental patents.

The ideas here are:

(1) to free up the circuit designers to be both quick and uninhibited in their designs, and

(2) to avoid burdening the product with a horrendous patent law study and possible expense and uncertainty of years of litigation.

Royalties in such cases are likely to be a very small percentage of all the licensee's product line without regard to whether a given product infringes any or many patents. This, in order to avoid continuous patent infringement studies and arguments. This, thereby, for the convenience of the accounting by both parties.

If there is no coercion forcing the package license or the royalty on unpatented wares, but rather if those provisions are for the convenience of the parties, they are perfectly legal.

M. The Facility by Which the Licensor Can Reach the Licensee's Markets with the Licensor's Own Manufacture

There is more money to be made in manufacture and sale to a market you can reasonably reach than in licensing to serve that market. There is also more capital commitment, and more risk involved.

The license price is thus going to be affected by the degree of confidence in the feasibility of the licensor serving the licensee's market in lieu of licensing to serve it.

N. Licensee Competition with the Licensor.

Frequently, the licensee's potential for competition with the licensor is a vital factor. That competitive factor may be controlled by geography and related shipping costs, by contractual restraints if effective restraints can be found that are legal. And by pricing the royalty high enough that the licensor retains as much advantage as he really needs to stay profitable in his market.

Of course, if you price it too high and the licensee is put out of the market, you don't really have any licensee at all.

So licensee competition with the licensor is a factor in pricing the technology.

O.   Tag-along and Derivative Sales

If you sell vacuum cleaners, you also can sell vacuum cleaner bags and repair parts. If you sell T.V. antennas, you also get to sell the service of installing them. These are called "tag-along or derivative sales." Very often, these relatively captive sales are at high margins and are highly profitable to a licensee. He may thereby be induced to pay a high royalty on the principal product.

Often the license will enable the licen*see* to pick up some tag-along/derivative sales that may be more profitable than the licensed product itself.

Often the license will cost the licensor some high margin tag-along/derivative sales that he would get by doing the business himself rather than through a licensee. A licensor thereby is induced to charge a high royalty to cover his loss of those sales. Thus, we see an examination of the role of tag-along/derivative sales is important when pricing technology.

P.   The Structure and Time Spread of Payments

The structure and time spread of payments of equity, front money, delayed sums certain, royalty minimums, running royalties, etc., influence the figures to be used in direct proportion to the then value of money.

Depending upon interest rates, $1 million cash up front is perhaps one third more than $100,000 at the end of each of the first ten years, even though the same number of dollars is to be paid in each instance.

The time schedule of payment is a factor in pricing the technology, and this factor is very important in the tactics of negotiation of the license price.

Q. Repatriation of Money from the Licensee

Frequently there are controls on the licensee's capacity to send its local currency out of the country. The cost of repatriation of the money, as by barter exchanges and other deals, becomes a factor in the value of the license.

For example, it once happened that a licensor had royalty money in Peru that it could not get out of the country. A deal was struck with Braniff Airlines, which was then flying routes to Peru.

In rotation each plane was flown to Peru, laid over overnight, outfitted with fine leather seats in the first class section, and flown out with many dollars' worth of Peruvian leather aboard. The licensor paid for the leather seats in his surplus Peruvian money. Braniff paid the licensor in U.S. dollars.

The imagination of the parties in dreaming up and executing such schemes is of course an important factor in the value, and hence the price, of the license.

R. Risks of Litigation—or Loss of It

Patent licenses are commonly entered into not in respect of the patent, but in compromise of a *dis*respect of the patent.

Sometimes the only way the licensor can get a proper respect for his patent is to subject it to reexamination in court in an *inter partes* proceeding.

I have been in the position that the petitioner for license was a prime target for the court-trial reexamination because he was a confessed pirate and his product was a look-alike. In context to this guy's piracy, I did not want to give up my chance for an early judicial reexamination of the patent that hopefully would beget respect of my patent forever thereafter.

That affected my asking price, substantially.

Or the licensee may be buying temporary peace, a settlement of a suit pending in an unfavorable forum, with a plan to litigate later, at a time and in a forum of his choice.

That possibility too may affect the pricing of the technology.

S. Risk of Loss of Royalties from Prior Licenses

It sometimes happens that a valuable patent is licensed for perhaps a million dollars per year worth of annual income.

Then, an importer comes along importing and selling an infringing product, a piracy of the invention.

Licensing

For a variety of reasons patentees lose half of their infringement suits. And under *Blonder-Tongue*[1] if the patent is held invalid against the late-arriving pirate, it is invalid as to the prior and subsequent licensees as well. To litigate against the pirate is to risk not only loss to the pirate, but loss of all that other royalty income.

The late arriving pirate, in our example, may have only the cost of litigation plus $100,000 at risk, whereas the patent owner may have $17 million of royalties at risk.

This is a strong bias for the licensor to avoid litigation by licensing the late arriving pirate cheaply. The likelihood of this problem is also a strong bias to avoid favored nations clauses so that he can deal freely with the pirate and not be contractually bound to carry through a stupid litigation.

Indeed, if in the course of the licensing or litigation effort it should be discovered that there was some gross, deliberate fraud on the Patent Office during the prosecution of the application, and if the patent can be shown to cover a relevant market for antitrust purposes (although commonly it cannot) the licensees may have a possible antitrust claim to recover the prior royalties. Even trebled prior royalties seem possible though no case has yet so held.

This factor influences what the licensor can demand from the pirate importer—or any late infringer of an already licensed patent—and hence influences what the pirate will bargain hard for and how he will go about it.

T. Exposure to Liability for Infringement of Rights of Third Parties

Sometimes the licensee's potential product requires a license not only from Tom, but also from Dick and Harry on their independently owned patents covering different features of the product and the processes of making it.

Regardless of whether there is one patent or ten infringed by a product, a given product in its market context can support only so much in total royalty burden.

So patents owned by others are an important factor in any license price.

---

[1] *Blonder-Tongue Laboratories, Inc. v. University of Ill. Found.*, 402 U.S. 313, 169 U.S.P.Q. 513 (1971).

U. What the Market Will Bear

One of the most common errors in pricing a technology (begot by opinions of courts who do not understand the reality of licensing) is the attachment of a royalty to each of several patents and/or trade secrets in the licensor's package for a single product, as though each licensed item could be separately priced.

There are, of course, situations where such a separate-pricing practice is rational. For example, a patented air conditioning system and a patented stereo sound system each add independent values to a car and such patents are easily assigned individual royalties. But many times, indeed, nearly all of the time, the licensee and the market are looking at a single end product, and what the buyers will pay for that product independently of how many patents may exist on the product and the process and equipment used in making it.

The royalty total becomes, in the greater reality, a single cost figure, supportable nearly in its totality by each of the licensed products. The total, being sometimes dictated more by what the market will bear for the product under the competitive market conditions than by the number of patents, must be divided among the patents on some sort of allocation of the value added by each invention.

If a given product in its market context will support a 7 percent royalty, it likely will nearly support that royalty whether there is only one patent, or five patents and a know-how package all involved in the product and its process of manufacture.

So, at least often, the number of licensable properties involved in the license is only a minor factor in the amount of the total price for the product's technology.

As an aside, I might mention: About four courts[2] have refused to allocate royalty between patents and know-how when the license contract did not so allocate and the patents expired or were invalidated.

Since the courts tend not to so allocate, the parties are thereby encouraged not to indulge a hybrid patent and know-how license

---

[2] *Cf. Meehan v. PPG Indus., Inc.,* 802 F.2d 881, 886, 231 U.S.P.Q. 400 (7th Cir. 1986); *Boggild v. Kenner Prods.,* 776 F.2d 1315, 1319 228 U.S.P.Q. 130 (6th Cir. 1985); *Pitney-Bowes, Inc. v. Mestre,* 517 F. Supp. 52, 61–63, 211 U.S.P.Q. 681, 689 (S.D. Fla. 1981), *aff'd in part and dismissed in part,* 701 F.2d 1365, 218 U.S.P.Q. 987 (11th Cir.), *cert. denied,* 464 U.S. 893 (1983); *Veltman v. Norton Simon, Inc.,* 425 F. Supp. 774, 76, 194 U.S.P.Q. 168 (S.D.N.Y. 1977).

Licensing

for a single royalty, but where feasible (sometimes it is not feasible) to make two separate contracts each for its own royalty.

V.   Access to Ongoing Technology

Many licenses call for grantbacks of licenses under inventions by the licensee. Many licenses license ongoing developments and improvements made by the licensor.

So, look at the other guy's R&D budget and innovation track record. You may find or you may not find that the grantback or grant-forward is an important factor in pricing your license package.

W.   What Did the Technology Cost the Licensor to Develop?

The public's interest in buying a product is essentially unrelated to the cost of developing it. Thus, the value of a technology in the marketplace is essentially unrelated to the cost of developing it.

What the technology cost the licensor to develop often should be disregarded or given little weight—except insofar as it aids estimation of the cost in time and money of the licensee's alternative, competitive development of the same technology.

This is an alternative open to the licensee which limits what the licensor can charge.

X.   Traditional Division of Anticipated Profits

Some authors have published guidelines by precedent.

They suggest a division of projected profits, commonly 20 percent to 50 percent to the licensor and 50 percent to 80 percent or so to the licensee, the larger share commonly going to the licensee because he usually has much more at risk than does the licensor.

Those precedents are based upon some practical experience and hence are not to be totally disregarded. But each license is unique in

—the quality of the technology,
—the solidarity and term of its protection,
—the risk of infringement of rights of others or of having to enforce the licensor's rights by litigation,
—the size of the market niche it will serve,
—the capital required to serve it,
—the exposure of the licensor to subsequent competition from the licensee,

308

—the viability of the licensor electing to set up its own facility rather than to license,

—the actual cost and uncertainty of a litigation alternative,

—etc.

With so many factors, with such important factors, different from case to case, the value of precedents in pricing a license is often greater as a negotiating tactic than as an aid in determining true value.

Y. 100 Factors

We cannot take space and time here to discuss all the 100 factors. So we tabulate them.

Many of the considerations are a mix of anticipated margin, intrinsic quality, strength of protection, market niche, financial and other considerations. So grouping the factors, some of which fit under multiple headings, sometimes begets redundancy.

But it seems that headings and groupings may help the reader some bit in spite of that difficulty.

So, here is the list, including those we have discussed already:

(a) *Intrinsic Quality*

1. The stage of the technology's technical and market development. Barely conceived? Reduced to practice? Commercially proven?
2. The intrinsic quality of the technology as a marketable quality, reliable technology.
3. The *perceived* utility by the buyer or user of the technology or its product.
4. The value to the licensee or its country of educating the licensee employees in the technology. Often developing nations will subsidize a technology-transfer or a licensee-research clause in a license in order to get their citizens technically trained and gainfully employed in a technology.
5. Perceived value of continuing access to technical help and ongoing research and development by the licensor and/or other licensees, including reputation of the seller for innovation and technical development.
6. The possibility of profiting from the good reputation of the licensor.
7. The need for the licensor's technology in the licensee's operations.

8. Pioneering invention or mere slight improvement?
9. Ongoing technical services by the licensor.
10. Whether the technology arose as a by-product of other R&D. (This does not truly change the intrinsic value of the licensable technology, but it seems to have a psychological influence which, when properly advocated, does sometimes affect what a licensor will take.)
11. The type of license (patent, know-how, trademark, copyright, mix, etc.).
12. Whether the product is young with a future market bloom likely in the making, or past maturity and on the downhill side of its life cycle.

(b) *Protections and Threats of Protection*

1. The scope and reliability of the protections of the technology, be it patent, trade secret, trademark, copyright, or chip protection, etc.
2. Whether there is, and the burdens of, a favored nations clause or other contractual duty to sue infringers; or whether the licensee must risk nonprotection of the technology.
3. Precedent, the value in money and other considerations being paid by, or offered as acceptable from, other licensees, particularly if they are likely to be partly competitive.
4. Reputation of the seller for defending its inventions and for technology protection.
5. Whether the higher minimum will convert a nonexclusive to an exclusive license or a lower payment will release an exclusive to a nonexclusive.
6. Can the offered patents or secrets be designed around and at what cost in time, money, legal risks, or technical risks?
7. Enforceability of capacity, volume, location, geographic restriction, or field of use clauses or other restrictions against competition.
8. Is this license a compromise of an uncertain suit for patent infringement or misappropriation of trade secrets, etc.?

(c) *Market Considerations*

1. Size of the total relevant market and licensee's likely share.
2. Distinctiveness of the market niche of the licensed subject matter; differentiation of licensed product. *E.g.,* if 10 companies are making a soft, stretchable quality of polyethylene

as commonly used for garment bags, would a licensee pay more for a license for a nonstretchable film strong enough for use as shopping and grocery bags?

3. Demand for the product of the technology in the licensee's potential market at various potentially available prices and product quality and styles. *E.g.,* the same invention may have a bigger market in a Cadillac than in a Volkswagen, or vice versa.

4. Geographical location of licensee's manufacture or sales base.

5. The importance of and presures for a second source of supply in the market. Many is the market where two quality competitors will sell nearly three times as much as one alone or where the sole customer will buy zero unless he has a second source of supply.

6. Changing market trends in competition.

7. Dynamism of the market.

8. Trade cycles.

9. Political environment and stability in licensee's country.

10. General state of the economy.

11. The possible extent to which the demand for the licensed product may be depressed by unemployment, union attitudes, etc., in the primary marketing area of the licensee.

12. What the market will bear. A given product may support a 7 percent royalty and only a 7 percent royalty—regardless of whether that is for one, four, or ten patents and trade secrets which are necessary to its manufacture.

(d) *Competitive Considerations*

1. Whether the license is exclusive, sole (exclusive except for the licensor), or nonexclusive.

2. The nature and extent of the third party competition with the licensee.

3. The nature and extent of licensee competition with the licensor and/or reaching markets not served by the licensor.
   a. Will the licensee serve markets the licensor can not effectively serve or will the licensee serve competitively the licensor's own markets, etc.?
   b. Whether and to what extent gray-market goods of the licensee will compete with the licensor's products.

4. The scope of the market niche that is protected, and the cross-elasticity of the market within and without the pro-

tected niche. *I.e.,* the degree of exclusivity of the license or the inherent market niche.

5. The nature and degree of differentiation of the projected market niche.

(e) *Values Brought to the Table by the Licensee*

1. Capital, marketing talent, and other values brought to the table by the licensee.
2. Grant-backs of research and development by the licensee.
3. The possibility of acquiring an equity interest in the licensee.
4. Manufacturing and marketing capability of the technology recipient: Whether the licensee has greater talent and capacity effectively to make or to market the invention in the subject market, or to use the technology, than the licensor.
5. The degree of economic and industrial development, the labor and capital availability and cost, etc., in the licensee's country.
6. Whether the licensee has a relevant patent or secret technology position of its own.

(f) *Financial Considerations*

1. Manufacturer's margin. For example, a unique agricultural chemical, medical device or pharmaceutical may often be priced in response to value to the customer, independently of cost of manufacture and sale or competitive prices. Perhaps the farmer can be given a three-dollar return in increased crop yield for one dollar of cost to buy the product, and the manufacturer can still sell such a chemical, if protected, at eight or eighteen times its manufacturing plus sales costs. A much higher royalty (50 percent in one of my cases) is justified in such a case than when the manufacturer's margin is forced to be 1 or 2 percent.[3]
2. Cost of the license negotiation and the technology transfer itself, and profit on that cost. Licenses for small markets often cost more to negotiate than the license is worth.

---

[3] As with many of the considerations, manufacturer's margin is a mix of the considerations of intrinsic quality, strength of legal protection, uniqueness of market niche, competitive, financial and other considerations, so it could be classified many places.

3. Potential for profits at royalties at X percent, Y percent, and Z percent, each to the licensor and the licensee.
4. Availability and cost of capital and labor.
5. Tariffs.
6. Taxes and related considerations—capital gains vs. ordinary income. But "capital gains" as such seems destined to disappear under U.S. Tax Reform Act of 1986.
7. The amount of the licensor's expected cost savings, risk savings, and other burden savings, which follow from licensing a given market in lieu of developing it himself.
8. A comparison of the projected license net income against the potential for profit by the licensor's service of the same market.
9. Can the offered patents be designed around? —Or the secrets be independently duplicated?
10. The burdens on the licensee inherent in its developing the same or competitive technology by its own effort:
    —Cost of licensee R&D.
    —Time for licensee R&D.
    —Quality of licensee R&D result.
    —Unresolved infringement, environmental, and other legal risks involved in likely licensee R&D result.
    —Technological risks in likely licensee R&D result.
11. What did the technology cost the licensor to develop? This should often be disregarded except insofar as it helps evaluate the cost of the licensee's competitive development of the same technology.
12. Cost and risks of enforcing patents or trade secret rights.
13. Cost of warranty service.
14. Cost savings in avoiding litigation to enforce a patent.
15. Costs of obtaining and maintaining local or foreign patent and trademark protection. (Really, not relevant.)
16. Cost of training the licensee's employees; risk that the planned training may prove inadequate.
17. The seller's cost of continually upgrading the project.
18. The nature and type of obligations to be assumed by the licensee under the contract; *e.g.,* books to be audited by the competing licensor, licensor quality control burdens, royalties to be made on sales before goods paid for, force majeure clause.
19. Policing costs: accounting audits, quality control tests/inspections.

20. The *probability* of the license being profitable for the licensee.
21. The *amount* of expected profit or saving incurred by the licensee, including any likely monopoly profit.
22. Different costs in the different countries involved, of capital (either equity or debt capital), of labor, of raw materials.
23. Traditional royalty rates in the industry—a factor relevant more to negotiating tactics and psychology than to what is fair or economically reasonable for the subject technology. Be imaginative in developing reasons for departing from tradition. Precedent-priced technology is often wrongly priced technology.
24. The profit plan; the traditional profit margins in the industry. But again, be imaginative in finding reasons for departure from tradition.
25. Estimated cost of adapting the technology to planned applications like 220-volt power in lieu of 110-, etc.
26. The structure and time spread of payments of equity, sums certain, royalty minimums, running royalties, payments to be of large sum certain in spite of market failure by licensee, etc.
27. Accounting simplicity.
28. The potential for and availability of barter and local manufacture arrangements to cover currency control problems and the like.
29. Follow-on related sales, and profits thereon.
30. The anticipated Return On Investment ("ROI") for each licensor and licensee.
31. The buyer's right to duplicate the seller's technology in subsequent projects.
32. Inflation, in some countries running at 400 percent annually.
33. Varying international exchange rates.
34. The prices (equity, sums certain, royalties) being asked by sellers of competitive or similar technology. Recent industry licensing rates and practices for similar products and processes.
35. Anticipated sales volume of licensed products.
36. Contract administration costs, comfort, and convenience.
37. Division of projected profits, as for example 25 percent to 50 percent, which is common for the licensor, and perhaps

50 percent to 75 percent, which is common for the licensee, who usually has much more at risk.

(g) *Particular Risk Considerations*

1. Exposure to product liability suits.
2. Exposure to and insurance for plant explosions or toxic chemical release, as in Bhopal, India.
3. The licensor's risks and costs of litigation against the licensee, in lieu of license, *e.g.,* risk of loss of royalties from existing licensees if the patent is held invalid.
4. The risk of cost and other burdens upon either party who assumes to police patents and sue infringers.
5. Risk of having to perform uncompensated technical study or training services to verify performance guarantees and specifications.
6. The risk of loss of prior license royalties if the patent is litigated and held invalid. The potential for this risk biases toward an early litigation—which in turn puts at risk all the royalties that might have been collected, usually at lower rates, had the patent never been risked in court.
7. Licensee's credit position.
8. Licensee's willingness to be audited—perchance by a competitor.
9. The risk of a diminished quality of future R&D (a) by the licensor if the licensor does not manufacture, (b) by the licensee if he has no rights in his own innovations.
10. The risks of the licensee's developing the same or competitive technology by its own effort.
11. Uncertainties in cost, time, legal quality and technological quality of licensee R&D result, if independent development is selected in lieu of license.
12. Risk to the licensor and value to the licensee of the licensor's guarantee of performance in
    —time of plant erection,
    —quality of product,
    —production capacity,
    —cost of product,
    —enforcement of patent and know-how protections and exclusivities,
    —indemnity against infringing third party patents,
    —etc.

13. Apart from the guarantee (which often is an incomplete remedy for failure of performance), the licensee's perception of the true reliability of the time of performance quality of product, production capacity, cost of product, enforcement of protections and exclusivities, indemnity against infringements of 3rd party rights, etc.
14. The potential licensee's cost of defending an infringement suit, risk of damages, risk that the license price if any will go sharply up after a litigation, risk of injunction with no license available at all.
15. The term of licensee lock-in (as by a plant design frozen in steel and concrete).
16. The risks of technological obsolescence.
17. Can the offered patents or secrets be designed around (and as aforesaid, at what cost in time, money, legal risks or technical risks)?

(h) Patent portfolios

The number of patents involved, the freedom of the licensee designers, is often an important factor.

Licensees may want to avoid patent lawyers' study of a portfolio of 400 patents on color T.V. circuits, may want to avoid arguments over their validity and scope, may want to turn their circuit designers loose for quick and effective design unencumbered by the need to track a complex course through the maze of outstanding patents of uncertain valid scope.

So the appropriate license may be for all the licensor's patents, with a royalty on all the licensee's items in a given product line irrespective of whether they infringe.

(i) *Legal Considerations*

1. Force majeure clauses.
2. Legal enforceability of restraints on competition.
3. Whether the patent value has been or will be enhanced by a judicial reexamination and decree. Patentees frequently should decline to license or should price a license very high before the first litigation, hoping to precipitate an early litigation with respect to an infringer suffering poor litigation equities, thereby to enhance the subsequent license value of the patent(s).

4. Duration of the license, of payments of sums certain, of the royalty payments, of the obligation of confidence—all of which commonly should be different terms.
5. Favored nations clauses.
6. The risk of, or opportunity for, suit by the licensee to invalidate patents at times and forums of his choice—he may not stay hitched.

(j) *Government Regulatory Considerations*

1. Licensee's government's restrictions and law on royalty rates, royalty terms, etc.
2. Legal restrictions on currency movement.

Bibliography

Arnold, "Basic Considerations in Licensing," 2 *The Law and Business of Licensing: Licensing in the 1980s* 2A-73 (1984).

Bayes, "Pricing the Technology," *1977 Current Trends in Domestic and International Licensing* 369.

Bowler, "Payments for Technology," *1980 Les Nouvelles* 241.

Cruver, D., "The International Marketplace" (Handout at the Society for Marketing Professional Services, Tenth Anniversary Convention, Dallas, Texas, Sept. 16, 1983).

Cruver, D., Interview by author (July 17, 1986) (Donald Cruver is a partner of Blask, Cruver & Evans, Houston, Texas).

Evans, "Packaging and Pricing Technology," *1984 Domestic and Foreign Technology Licensing* 77.

Evans, "Pricing the Technology," *1977 Current Trends in Domestic and International Licensing* 361.

Evans, L., "Turning Patents and Technology into Money" (Handout at the First Annual Licensing Law and Business Institute, Feb. 26–March 2, 1979).

Farley, "Price Fixing and Royalty Provisions in Patent Licenses," 34 J. Pat. Off. Soc'y 46 (1952).

Finnegan & Mintz, "Determination of a Reasonable Royalty in Negotiating a License Agreement: Practical Pricing for Successful Technology Transfer," Vol. 1, No. 2, Licensing Law and Business Report 13 (1978).

Goldscheider, R., "The Art of 'Licensing Out,'" *Les Nouvelles,* Vol. XIX, p. 84, June 1984.

Licensing

Goldscheider, R., *Technology Management Handbook* (1984) (In particular, *see* Chapter 9, "Royalties and Other Sources of Income from Licensing."

Hadji, "Licensing as a Profit Center," *1985 Les Nouvelles* 193.

Janiszewski, "Licensee Evaluation of Payments," *1978 Les Nouvelles* 248.

Leprince, "How Evaluation of Process Technology Affects Licensing," *1974 Les Nouvelles* 182.

Marlow, "Matrix Approach to Pricing," *1978 Les Nouvelles* 11.

Matsunaga, "Determining Reasonable Royalty Rates," *1983 Les Nouvelles* 216.

McKie, "Pricing and Packaging the Technology," *1984 Domestic and Foreign Technology Licensing* 93.

Orleans, "Pricing Licensing of Technology," *1981 Les Nouvelles* 320.

Rahn, "Determining the Royalty—What Is Done and What in Fact Should Be Done," 2 *The Law and Business of Licensing* 657 (1980). (Excellent!—He lists 46 factors ranked by usage by licensing executives.)

Root & Contractor, "Negotiating Compensation in International Licensing Agreements," Vol. 22 No. 2 *Sloan Management Review* 23 (1981).

Scaglione, "Licensor View of Royalty Rates," 1981 *Les Nouvelles* 231.

Table of Authorities

References are to sections

319

Licensing

Cases (cont.)

Ampex Corp. v. Memorex Corp., 205 U.S.P.Q. 794 (N.D. Cal. 1980),
§ 10.01[5]

Ansul Co. v. Uniroyal, Inc., 306 F. Supp. 541, 163 U.S.P.Q. 517
(S.D.N.Y. 1969), *aff'd in part and rev'd and remanded in part,* 448 F.2d
872, 169 U.S.P.Q. 759, 170 U.S.P.Q. 549 (2d Cir. 1971), *cert. denied,*
404 U.S. 1018 (1972), § 10.10, Ch.11

Arbrook v. American Hospital Supply Corp., 645 F.2d 273, 210 U.S.P.Q.
84 (5th Cir. 1981), § 10.01[2][d]

Argus Chem. Corp. v. Fibre Glass-Evercoat, (*Argus II),* 812 F.2d 1381
(Fed. Cir. 1987), § 10.01[2][d]

Argus Chem. Corp. v. Fibre Glass-Evercoat, (*Argus I),* 759 F.2d 10 (Fed.
Cir.), *cert. denied,* 474 U.S. 903 (1985), § 10.01[2][c]; 10.01[2][d]

Armstrong v. Motorola, Inc., 374 F.2d 764, 152 U.S.P.Q. 535 (7th Cir.),
cert. denied, 389 U.S. 830 (1967), § 10.09

Aro Corp. v. Allied Witan Co., 531 F.2d 1368, 190 U.S.P.Q. 392 (6th
Cir.), *cert. denied,* 429 U.S. 862 (1976), § 10.15

Aronson v. Quick Point Pencil Co., 440 U.S. 257, 201 U.S.P.Q. 1 (1979),
§ 10.14, 10.17

Arthur J. Schmitt Found. v. Stockham Valves & Fittings, Inc., 292 F.
Supp. 893 (N.D. Ala. 1966), *aff'd per curiam,* 404 F.2d 13 (5th Cir.
1968), *cert. denied,* 398 U.S. 965 (1970), § 10.13

Atlas Imperial Diesel Engine Co. v. Lanova Corp., 79 F. Supp. 1002, 78
U.S.P.Q. 319 (D. Del. 1948), § 10.09

Atlas Powder Co. v. E. I. DuPont DeNemours, 750 F.2d 1569 (Fed. Cir.
1984), § 10.01[2][b], 10.01[2][c], 10.01[2][d]

Automatic Radio Mfg. Co. v. Hazeltine Research, Inc., 339 U.S. 827, 85
U.S.P.Q. 378 (1950), § 10.02[1], 10.11, 20.03

Baldwin-Lima-Hamilton Corp. v. Tatnall Measuring Sys. Co., 169 F.
Supp. 1 (E.D. Pa. 1958), *aff'd per curiam,* 268 F.2d 395 (3d Cir.), *cert.
denied,* 361 U.S. 894 (1959), § 10.08, 10.09

Barber-Colman Co. v. National Tool Co., 136 F.2d 339, 58 U.S.P.Q. 2
(6th Cir. 1943), § 10.04

Barr Rubber Prods. Co. v. Sun Rubber Co., 277 F. Supp. 484, 156
U.S.P.Q. 374 (S.D.N.Y. 1967), *aff'd in part and rev'd in part,* 425 F.2d
1114, 165 U.S.P.Q. 429 (2d Cir.), *cert. denied,* 400 U.S. 878 (1970),
§ 10.09

B.B. Chem. Co. v. Ellis, 314 U.S. 495, 52 U.S.P.Q. 33 (1942), § 10.04,
10.05, Ch. 11

Beckman Instruments, Inc. v. Technical Dev. Corp., 433 F.2d 55, 167
U.S.P.Q. 10 (7th Cir. 1970), *cert. denied,* 401 U.S. 976 (1971),
§ 10.01[6], 10.11

Licensing

Cases (cont.)

Carpet Seaming Tape Licensing Corp. v. Best Seam Inc., 694 F.2d 570, 216 U.S.P.Q. 873 (9th Cir. 1982), *cert. denied,* 464 U.S. 818 (1983), § 10.02[4]

Carter-Wallace, Inc. v. Davis-Edwards Pharmacal Corp., 443 F.2d 867 (2d Cir. 1971, § 10.01[2][d]

Carter-Wallace, Inc. v. Otte, 1978-1 Trade Cas. (CCH) ¶ 61,976 (E.D.N.Y. 1978), § 10.12

Carter-Wallace, Inc. v. United States, 449 F.2d 1374 (Ct. Cl. 1971), § 10.09, 10.12

CBS v. ASCAP, 620 F.2d 930, 205 U.S.P.Q. 880 (2d Cir. 1980), *cert. denied,* 450 U.S. 970 (1981), § 10.16

Chandler v. Stern Dental Laboratory Co., 335 F. Supp. 580, 171 U.S.P.Q. 100 (S.D. Tex. 1971), § 10.02[3]

Charles Pfizer & Co. v. FTC, 401 F.2d 574, 159 U.S.P.Q 193 (6th Cir. 1968), § 10.01[2][c]

Chemagro Corp. v. Universal Chem. Co., 244 F. Supp. 486, 489, 146 U.S.P.Q. 466 (E.D. Tex. 1965), § 10.09

Chisholm-Ryder Co. v. Mecca Bros., 217 U.S.P.Q. 1322 (W.D.N.Y. 1983), § 10.02[1], 10.02[2]

Christen, Inc. v. BNS Industries, Inc., 517 F. Supp. 521, 216 U.S.P.Q. 928 (S.D.N.Y. 1981), § 10.01[4]

Christianson v. Colt Indus. Operating Corp., 822 F.2d 1544 3 U.S.P.Q. 1241 (Fed. Cir. 1987) § 3.04, § 3.05[6]

Ciba-Geigy Corp. v. Bolar Pharmaceutical Co., 212 U.S.P.Q. 712 (E.D.N.Y. 1981), § 10.09

City of Milwaukee v. Activated Sludge, 69 F.2d 577 (7th Cir.), *cert. denied,* 293 U.S. 576 (1934), § 10.03[1]

Clark, In re, 522 F.2d 623, 187 U.S.P.Q. 209 (C.C.P.A. 1975), § 10.01[7]

Coca-Cola, In re, 91 F.T.C. 517 (1978), *rev'd sub nom.,* Coca-Cola Co. v. FTC, 642 F.2d 1387 (D.C. Cir. 1981), § 10.10

Cohn v. Compax Corp., 87 A.D.2d 364, 451 N.Y.S.2d 171, 1982–2 Trade Cas. (CCH) ¶ 64,800 (N.Y. App. Div. 1982), § 10.11

Columbus Automotive Corp. v. Oldberg Mfg. Co., 264 F. Supp. 779, 153 U.S.P.Q. 97 (D. Colo. 1967), *aff'd per curiam,* 387 F.2d 643, 156 U.S.P.Q. 488 (10th Cir. 1968), Ch. 11

Comparone v. M.J. Caplan Co., 270 Mass. 74, 169 N.E. 667 (1930), § 18.01[1]

Congoleum Indus., Inc. v. Armstrong Cork Co., 366 F. Supp. 220, 180 U.S.P.Q. 40, 180 U.S.P.Q. 264 (E.D. Pa. 1973), *aff'd,* 510 F.2d 334, 184 U.S.P.Q. 769 (3d Cir.), *cert. denied,* 421 U.S. 988 (1975), Ch. 11

Continental Paper Bag Co. v. Eastern Paper Bag Co., 210 U.S. 405 (1908), § 10.03[1]

Licensing

Cases (cont.)

Duplan Corp. v. Deering Milliken, Inc., 444 F. Supp. 648, 197 U.S.P.Q. 342 (D.S.C. 1977), *aff'd in part, rev'd in part on other grounds,* 594 F.2d 979, 201 U.S.P.Q. 641 (4th Cir. 1979), *cert. denied,* 444 U.S. 1015 (1980), § 10.03[2], 10.11, 10.14, 10.15

The Dyer's Case, Y.B.2 Henry V, pl. 26 (1415), Ch. 9

Eastern Scientific Co. v. Wild Heerbrugg Instruments, Inc., 572 F.2d 883 (1st Cir.), *cert. denied,* 439 U.S. 833 (1978), § 10.10

Edward Katzinger Co. v. Chicago Metallic Mfg. Co., 329 U.S. 394, 72 U.S.P.Q. 18 (1947), § 10.07

Eiberger v. Sony Corp. of Am., 622 F.2d 1068 (2d Cir. 1980), § 10.10

Electric Pipe Line, Inc. v. Fluid Sys., Inc., 231 F.2d 370, 109 U.S.P.Q. 24 (2d Cir. 1956), § 10.04

Erie Technological Prods., Inc. v. JFD Elecs. Components Corp., 198 U.S.P.Q. 179 (E.D.N.Y. 1978), § 10.01[3]

Eversharp, Inc. v. Fisher Pen Co., 204 F. Supp. 649, 132 U.S.P.Q. 423 (N.D. Ill. 1961), § 10.09, 10.13

Fashion Originators' Guild v. Federal Trade Comm'n, 312 U.S. 457, 48 U.S.P.Q. 483 (1941), § 9.03

F.C. Russell Co. v. Consumers Insulation Co., 226 F.2d 373, 107 U.S.P.Q. 131 (3d Cir. 1955), § 10.04

F.E.L. Publications, Ltd. v. Catholic Bishop, 214 U.S.P.Q. 409 (7th Cir. 1982), *rev'g,* 506 F. Supp. 1127, 210 U.S.P.Q. 403 (N.D. Ill. 1981), § 10.16

First Beverages, Inc. v. Royal Crown Cola Co., 612 F.2d 1164 (9th Cir.), *cert. denied,* 447 U.S. 924 (1980), § 10.10

Forbro Design Corp. v. Raytheon Co., 532 F.2d 758, 190 U.S.P.Q. 49 (1st Cir. 1976), § 10.01[3], 10.01[4]

Foremost Pro Color, Inc. v. Eastman Kodak Co., 703 F.2d 534 (9th Cir. 1983), *cert. denied,* 465 U.S. 1038 (1984), § 10.02[1]

Fortner Enters. v. United States Steel Corp., 394 U.S. 495 (1969), § 10.04

Foster v. American Mach. & Foundry Co., 492 F.2d 1317, 182 U.S.P.Q. 1 (2d Cir.), *cert. denied,* 419 U.S. 833 (1974), § 10.03[1]

Foster Wheeler Corp. v. Babcock & Wilcox Co., 440 F. Supp. 897, 195 U.S.P.Q. 649 (S.D.N.Y. 1977), § 10.01[3], 10.01[4]

Fowle v. Park, 131 U.S. 88 (1889), § 10.17

Frost, In re, 398 F. Supp. 1353, 185 U.S.P.Q. 729 (D. Del. 1975), *modified,* 540 F.2d 601, 191 U.S.P.Q. 241 (3d Cir. 1976), § 10.01[2][e]

GAF Corp. v. Eastman Kodak Co., 519 F.Supp. 1203, 213 U.S.P.Q. 356 (S.D.N.Y. 1981), § 10.03[1], 10.11

Licensing

Cases (cont.)

Indium Corp. of Am. v. Semi-Alloys, Inc., 566 F. Supp. 1344, 219
U.S.P.Q. 793 (N.D.N.Y. 1983), *motion denied,* 591 F. Supp. 608
(N.D.N.Y. 1984), § 10.01[4]

Industrial Inv. Dev. Corp. v. Mitsui & Co., 671 F.2d 876 (5th Cir. 1982),
cert. denied, 464 U.S. 961 (1983), Ch.7, Ch.13

International Salt Co. v. United States, 332 U.S. 392, 75 U.S.P.Q. 184
(1947), § 9.03, 10.04

International Tel. & Tel. Corp. v. Raychem Corp., 538 F.2d 453, 191
U.S.P.Q. 1 (1st Cir.), *cert. denied,* 429 U.S. 886 (1976), § 10.01[2][d]

International Wood Processors v. Power Dry, Inc., 593 F. Supp. 710, 224
U.S.P.Q. 52 (D.S.C. 1984), § 10.03[1], 10.03[4]

Jack Winter, Inc. v. Koratron Co., 375 F. Supp. 1, 181 U.S.P.Q. 353
(N.D. Cal. 1974), Ch. 11

JBL Enters., Inc. v. Jhirmack Enters., Inc., 509 F. Supp. 357, 210
U.S.P.Q. 438 (N.D. Cal. 1981), *aff'd,* 698 F.2d 1011 (9th Cir.), *cert.
denied,* 464 U.S. 829 (1983), § 10.10

J.C. Ferguson Mfg. Works v. American Lecithin Co., 94 F.2d 729 (1st
Cir.), *cert. denied,* 304 U.S. 573 (1938), Ch. 11

Jefferson Parish Hospital Dist. No. 2 v. Hyde, 466 U.S. 2 (1984), § 10.04

Jenson v. Continental Fin. Corp., 591 F.2d 447 (8th Cir. 1979), § 20.01

Jones Knitting Corp. v. Morgan, 361 F.2d 451, 149 U.S.P.Q. 659 (3d Cir.
1966), § 10.03[3]

J.P. Stevens & Co. v. Lex-Tex, Ltd., 747 F.2d 1553 (Fed. Cir. 1984), *cert.
denied,* 474 U.S. 822, § 10.01[2][b], 10.01[2][c], 10.01[2][d],
10.01[2][e], 10.01[7]

Kansas Jack, Inc. v. Kuhn, 719 F.2d 1144, 219 U.S.P.Q. 857 (Fed. Cir.
1983), § 10.01[2][d]

Kearney & Trecker Corp. v. Cincinnati Milacron, Inc., 562 F.2d 365, 195
U.S.P.Q. 402 (6th Cir. 1977), § 10.01[4]

Kearney & Trecker Corp. v. Cincinnati Milacron, Inc., 403 F. Supp. 1040,
184 U.S.P.Q. 134 (S.D. Ohio 1975), *aff'd,* 562 F.2d 365, 195 U.S.P.Q.
402 (6th Cir. 1977), Ch. 11

Kearney & Trecker Corp. v. Giddings & Lewis Inc., 452 F.2d 579, 171
U.S.P.Q. 650 (7th Cir. 1971), § 10.01[7]

Kewanee Oil Co. v. Bicron Corp., 416 U.S. 470, 181 U.S.P.Q. 673 (1974),
§ 10.14

Kistler Instrumente, A.G. v. PCB Piezotronics, Inc., 220 U.S.P.Q. 631
(W.D.N.Y. 1983), § 10.01[4]

Kobe, Inc. v. Dempsey Pump Co., 97 F. Supp. 342, 89 U.S.P.Q. 54 (N.D.
Okla. 1951), *aff'd on other grounds,* 198 F.2d 416, 94 U.S.P.Q. 43 (10th
Cir.), *cert. denied,* 344 U.S. 837 (1952), § 10.02[2]

Cases (cont.)

Licensing

Cases (cont.)

McCullough v. Kammerer Corp., 166 F.2d 759, 76 U.S.P.Q. 503 (9th Cir.), *cert. denied,* 335 U.S. 813 (1948), § 10.04

McCullough Tool Co. v. Scherbatskoy, 283 F. Supp. 486, 159 U.S.P.Q. 106 (N.D. Okla. 1968), Ch. 11

McCullough Tool Co. v. Well Surveys, Inc., 343 F.2d 381, 145 U.S.P.Q. 6 (10th Cir. 1965), *cert. denied,* 383 U.S. 933 (1966), § 10.11, Ch. 11

McDonald v. Johnson & Johnson, 537 F. Supp. 1282 (D. Minn. 1982), *aff'd in part and vacated and remanded in part,* 722 F.2d 1370 (8th Cir. 1983), § 10.01[2]

Meehan v. PPG Indus. Inc., 802 F.2d 881, 231 U.S.P.Q. 400 (7th Cir. 1986), *cert. denied,* 107 S. Ct. 1301 (1987), § 3.06, 10.14, App. C

Mercoid Corp. v. Mid-Continent Investment Co., 320 U.S. 661, 60 U.S.P.Q. 21 (1944), § 10.04, 10.05

Mercoid Corp. v. Minneapolis-Honeywell Regulator Co., 320 U.S. 680, 60 U.S.P.Q. 30 (1944), § 10.04, 10.05

Michigan Motor Specialities Co., 288 F. 377 (E.D. Mich. 1923), Ch. 16

Mid-America ICEE, Inc. v. John E. Mitchell Co., 1973–2 Trade Cas. (CCH) ¶ 74,681 (D. Or. 1973), § 10.04

Miller Instituform, Inc. v. Instituform of N. Am., Inc., 605 F. Supp. 1125 (M.D. Tenn. 1985), § 10.06

Mitchel v. Reynolds, 1 P.Wms. 181, 24 Eng. Rep. 347 (1711), Ch. 9

Monsanto Co. v. Spray-Rite Serv. Corp., 465 U.S. 752, *reh'g denied,* 466 U.S. 994 (1984), § 10.03[1]

Moraine Prods. v. ICI Am., Inc., 538 F.2d 134, 191 U.S.P.Q. 65 (7th Cir.), *cert. denied,* 429 U.S. 941 (1976), § 10.03[2]

Morton Salt Co. v. G.S. Suppiger Co., 314 U.S. 488, 52 U.S.P.Q. 30 (1942), § 10.04, Ch. 11

Motion Picture Patents Co. v. Universal Film Mfg. Co., 243 U.S. 502 (1917), § 10.04, 10.05

Motorola, Inc. v. Kimball Int'l, Inc., 601 F. Supp. 62 (N.D. Ill. 1984), § 10.11, 10.12

Munters Corp. v. Burgess Indus., Inc., 450 F. Supp. 1195, 194 U.S.P.Q. 146 (S.D.N.Y. 1977), *on reh'g.,* 201 U.S.P.Q. 756 (S.D.N.Y. 1978), § 10.09

National Bancard Corp. (NaBanco) v. VISA U.S.A., 596 F. Supp. 1231 (S.D. Fla. 1984), *aff'd,* 779 F.2d 592, *reh'g denied,* 785 F.2d 1037 (11th Cir. 1986), § 9.02

National Collegiate Athletic Ass'n v. Board of Regents of the University of Oklahoma, 468 U.S. 85 (1984), § 9.03

National Lockwasher Co. v. George K. Garrett Co., 137 F.2d 255, 58 U.S.P.Q. 460 (3d Cir. 1943), § 10.04

Licensing

Cases (cont.)

Power Test Petroleum Distribs., Inc. v. Calcu Gas, Inc., 754 F.2d 91 (2d Cir. 1985), § 10.04

Precision Instrument Mfg. Co. v. Automotive Maintenance Mach. Co., 324 U.S. 806, 65 U.S.P.Q. 133 (1945), § 10.01[1], 10.01[2][d], 10.01[2][e]

Q-Tips, Inc. v. Johnson & Johnson, 109 F. Supp. 657, 95 U.S.P.Q. 258 (D.N.J. 1951), *modified,* 207 F.2d 509, 99 U.S.P.Q. 183 (3d Cir. 1953), *cert. denied,* 347 U.S. 935 (1954), § 10.08

Ralph C. Wilson Indus., Inc. v. American Broadcasting Cos., Inc., 598 F. Supp. 694 (N.D. Cal. 1984), *aff'd,* 794 F.2d 1359 (9th Cir. 1986), § 10.04

Reactive Metals & Alloys Corp. v. ESM, Inc., 769 F.2d 1578, 226 U.S.P.Q. 821 (Fed. Cir. 1985), § 10.01[2][d]

Regents of Univ. of Cal. v. ABC, Inc., 747 F.2d 511 (9th Cir. 1984), § 9.03

Reinke Mfg. Co. v. Sidney Mfg. Corp., 446 F. Supp. 1056, 199 U.S.P.Q. 401 (D. Neb. 1978), *aff'd,* 594 F.2d 644, 201 U.S.P.Q. 344 (8th Cir. 1979), § 10.01[3], 10.01[4], 10.10

Rex Chainbelt Inc. v. Harco Prods., Inc., 512 F.2d 993, 185 U.S.P.Q. 10 (9th Cir.), *cert denied,* 423 U.S. 831 (1975), § 10.04, 10.05

Reynolds Metals Co. v. Aluminum Co. of Am., 457 F. Supp. 482, 198 U.S.P.Q. 529 (N.D. Ind. 1978), *rev'd,* 609 F.2d 1218, 204 U.S.P.Q. 7 (7th Cir. 1979), *cert. denied,* 446 U.S. 989 (1980), § 10.01[3], 10.01[4]

Richmond Metal Finishers, Inc., In re, 38 B.R. 341 (E.D. Va. 1984), *rev'd sub nom.* Lubrizol Enters., Inc. v. Richmond Metal Finishers, Inc., 756 F.2d 1043 (4th Cir. 1985), *cert. denied sub nom.* Lubrizol Enters., Inc. v. Canfield, 475 U.S. 1057 (1986), § 20.02

Riker Laboratories, Inc. v. Gist-Brocades, N.V., 636 F.2d 772, 208 U.S.P.Q. 777 (D.C. Cir. 1980), § 10.14

Robintech, Inc. v. Chemidus Wavin, Ltd., 450 F. Supp. 823, 198 U.S.P.Q. 466 (D.D.C. 1978), *aff'd,* 628 F.2d 142, 205 U.S.P.Q. 873 (D.C. Cir. 1980), § 10.04, 10.10, 10.17

Rocform Corp. v. Acitelli-Standard Concrete Wall, Inc., 367 F.2d 678, 151 U.S.P.Q. 305 (6th Cir. 1966), § 10.11

Rohm & Haas Co. v. Crystal Chem. Co., 722 F.2d 1556, 220 U.S.P.Q. 289 (Fed. Cir. 1983), § 10.01[2][d]

Rohm & Haas Co. v. Dawson Chem. Co., 635 F. Supp. 1211 (S.D. Tex 1986), § 10.01[3]

Rohm & Haas Co. v. Dawson Chem. Co., 557 F. Supp. 739, 217 U.S.P.Q. 515 (S.D. Tex. 1982), *rev'd on other grounds,* 722 F.2d 1556, 220 U.S.P.Q. 289 (Fed. Cir. 1983), Ch. 7, § 10.04, 10.05, Ch. 13

Licensing

Cases (cont.)

SmithKline Corp. v. Eli Lilly & Co., 575 F.2d 1056 (3d Cir.), *cert. denied,* 439 U.S. 838 (1978), § 10.04

Solvex Corp. v. Freeman, 459 F. Supp. 440, 199 U.S.P.Q. 726 (W.D. Va. 1977), § 10.12

Sonobond Corp. v. Uthe Technology, Inc., 314 F. Supp. 878, 165 U.S.P.Q. 731 (N.D. Cal. 1970), § 10.04, Ch. 11

Spartan Grain & Mill Co. v. Ayers, 735 F.2d 1289 (11th Cir. 1984), § 10.04

Special Equip. Co. v. Coe, 324 U.S. 370, 64 U.S.P.Q. 525 (1945), § 10.03[1]

Speed Shore Corp. v. Denda, 197 U.S.P.Q. 526 (C.D. Cal. 1977), *aff'd,* 605 F.2d 469, 203 U.S.P.Q. 807 (9th Cir. 1979), § 10.03[2]

SSIH Equip. S.A. v. United States Int'l Trade Comm'n, 718 F.2d 365, 218 U.S.P.Q. 678 (Fed. Cir. 1983), § 10.01[6]

Standard Oil Co. v. United States, 283 U.S. 163 (1931), § 10.02[4]

Standard Oil Co. v. United States, 221 U.S. 1 (1911), § 9.02

Standard Sanitary Mfg. Co. v. United States, 226 U.S. 20 (1912), § 10.03[1], 10.15

Stanfield v. Osborne Indus. Inc., 7 Kan. App. 2d 416, 643 P.2d 1115 (1982), *modified,* 232 Kan. 197, 654 P.2d 917, 217 U.S.P.Q. 853 (1982), § 10.14

Stewart v. Mo-Trim, Inc., 192 U.S.P.Q. 410 (S.D. Ohio 1975), Ch. 11

Susser v. Carvel Corp., 332 F.2d 505, 141 U.S.P.Q. 609 (2d Cir.), *cert. granted,* 379 U.S. 885 (1964), *cert. dismissed,* 381 U.S. 125 (1965), § 10.04

Tapeswitch Corp. of Am. v. Recora Corp., 196 U.S.P.Q. 348 (N.D. Ill. 1977), § 10.01[3]

Tatum v. Acadian Prod. Corp., 35 F. Supp. 40 (E.D. La. 1940), § 18.01[1]

Technicon Data Sys. Corp. v. Curtis 1000 Inc., 1984–2 Trade Cas. (CCH) § 66,260 (Del. Ch. 1984), § 10.04

Thomson Spot Welder Co. v. Oldberg Mfg. Co., 256 Mich. 447, 240 N.W. 93 (1931), § 20.03

Timely Prods. Corp. v. Arron, 523 F.2d 288, 187 U.S.P.Q. 257 (2d Cir. 1975), § 10.01[2][c], 10.01[2][e]

Timely Prods., Inc. v. Costanzo, 465 F. Supp. 91, 201 U.S.P.Q. 567 (D. Conn. 1979), § 10.17

Tinnerman Prods., Inc. v. George K. Garrett Co., 185 F. Supp. 151 (E.D. Pa. 1960), *aff'd,* 292 F.2d 137, 129 U.S.P.Q. 438 (3d Cir.), *cert. denied,* 368 U.S. 833 (1961), § 10.07

Transitron Elec. Corp. v. Hughes Aircraft Co., 649 F.2d 871, 210 U.S.P.Q. 161 (1st Cir. 1981), § 10.01[5]

Licensing

Cases (cont.)

United States v. Jerrold Elecs. Corp., 187 F. Supp. 545 (E.D. Pa. 1960), *aff'd per curiam,* 365 U.S. 567 (1961), § 10.04

United States v. Krasnov, 143 F. Supp. 184, 110 U.S.P.Q. 411 (E.D. Pa. 1956), *aff'd mem.,* 355 U.S. 5, 115 U.S.P.Q. 70 (1957), § 10.03[2]

United States v. Line Material Co., 333 U.S. 287, 76 U.S.P.Q. 399 (1948), § 10.07

United States v. Loew's, Inc., 371 U.S. 38, 135 U.S.P.Q. 201 (1962), § 10.04

United States v. Masonite Corp., 316 U.S. 265, 53 U.S.P.Q. 396 (1942), § 10.07

United States v. Manufacturers Aircraft Ass'n Inc., 1976–1 Trade Cas. (CCH) ¶ 60,810 (S.D.N.Y. 1975), § 10.02[4]

United States v. Motor Vehicle Manufacturers Ass'n of U.S., Inc., 1979–2 Trade Cas. (CCH) ¶ 62,759 (C.D. Cal. 1979), § 10.02[4]

United States v. National Lead Co., 63 F. Supp. 513, 66 U.S.P.Q. 141 (S.D.N.Y. 1945), *aff'd,* 332 U.S. 319, 73 U.S.P.Q. 498 (1947), § 10.10

United States v. New Wrinkle, Inc., 342 U.S. 371, 92 U.S.P.Q. 158 (1952), § 10.07

United States v. Parker Rust-Proof Co., 61 F. Supp. 805, 65 U.S.P.Q. 563 (E.D. Mich. 1945), § 10.02[2]

United States v. Penn-Olin Chem. Co., 378 U.S. 158 (1964), § 10.02[5]

United States v. Sealy, Inc., 388 U.S. 350, 153 U.S.P.Q. 763 (1967), § 10.10

United States v. Serta Assocs., 296 F. Supp. 1121, 160 U.S.P.Q. 142 (N.D. Ill. 1968), *aff'd,* 393 U.S. 534, 160 U.S.P.Q. 142, *reh'g denied,* 394 U.S. 967 (1969), § 10.10

United States v. Singer Mfg. Co., 374 U.S. 174, 137 U.S.P.Q. 808 (1963), § 10.15

United States v. Socony-Vacuum Oil Co., 310 U.S. 150 (1940), § 9.03

United States v. Studiengesellschaft Kohle m.b.H., 200 U.S.P.Q. 389 (D.D.C. 1978), *rev'd,* 670 F.2d 1122, 212 U.S.P.Q. 889 (D.C. Cir. 1981), § 10.04, 10.08

United States v. Studiengesellschaft Kohle m.b.H., 670 F.2d 1122, 212 U.S.P.Q. 889 (D.C. Cir. 1981), § 10.08

United States v. Topco Assocs., Inc., 405 U.S. 596, 173 U.S.P.Q. 193 (1972), § 10.10

United States v. United Shoe Mach. Corp., 110 F. Supp. 295 (D. Mass. 1953), *aff'd,* 347 U.S. 521 (1954), § 10.02[1]

United States v. United States Gypsum Co., 333 U.S. 364, 76 U.S.P.Q. 430 (1948), § 10.02[2], 10.07

United States v. Vehicular Parking, Ltd., 54 F. Supp. 828, 61 U.S.P.Q. 102 (D. Del. 1944), § 10.02[2], 10.07

Licensing

Cases (cont.)

Western Elec. Co. v. Stewart-Warner Corp., 631 F.2d 333, 208 U.S.P.Q. 183 (4th Cir. 1980), *cert. denied,* 450 U.S. 971 (1981), § 10.06, 10.13, 10.14

Westinghouse Elec. & Mfg. Co. v. Wagner Elec. & Mfg. Co., 225 U.S. 604 (1912), § 10.06

White Cap Co. v. Owens-Illinois Glass Co., 203 F.2d 694, 97 U.S.P.Q. 192 (6th Cir.), *cert. denied,* 346 U.S. 876 (1953), § Ch. 11

Will v. Comprehensive Accounting Corp., 776 F.2d 665 (7th Cir. 1985), *cert. denied,* 106 S. Ct. 1659 (1986), § 10.04

Windsurfing Int'l Inc. v. AMF, Inc., 782 F.2d 995 (Fed. Cir.), *cert. denied,* 106 S. Ct. 3275 (1986), § 10.04

Xerox Corp. v. Dennison Mfg. Co., 322 F. Supp. 963, 168 U.S.P.Q. 700 (S.D.N.Y. 1971), § 10.01[2][d]

Yarn Processing Patent Validity Litigation, In re, 541 F.2d 1127, 192 U.S.P.Q. 241 (5th Cir. 1976), *cert. denied,* 433 U.S. 910 (1977), § 10.13

Yarn Process Patent Validity & Anti-Trust Litigation, In re 398 F. Supp. 31, 182 U.S.P.Q. 323, 185 U.S.P.Q. 334 (S.D. Fla. 1974), *vacated,* 401 F. Supp. 673, 189 U.S.P.Q. 598 (S.D. Fla. 1975), Ch. 11

Zenith Lab, Inc. v. Carter-Wallace, Inc., 530 F.2d 508 (3d Cir.), *cert. denied,* 429 U.S. 828 (1976), § 20.03

Zenith Radio Corp. v. Hazeltine Research, Inc., 395 U.S. 100, 161 U.S.P.Q. 577 (1969), § 10.06, 10.10, 10.11

Secondary Authorities

Andewelt, Roger B., Remarks before the National Institute on Industrial & Intellectual Property, Philadelphia, Pennsylvania, October 11–12, 1984, 53 Antitrust L.J., Issue 3, p. 260 (1985), § 10.02[4], Ch. 12

Collier on Bankruptcy (15th ed. 1979), § 19.01

Countryman, "Contracts in Bankruptcy," 59 Minn. L. Rev. 479 (1974), Ch. 16

Countryman, "Executory Contracts in Bankruptcy: Part II," 58 Minn. L. Rev. 479 (1974), § 20.03

Countryman, "A History of American Bankruptcy Law," 81 Com. L.J. 226 (1976), Ch. 17

Walker on Patents, Deller's edition (2d ed. 1965), § 20.03

Department of Justice Guidelines—Vertical Distribution Restraints, [1985 Transfer Binder] Trade Reg. Rep. (CCH) ¶ 50,473 at 56,200 (April 15, 1985), § 9.02, 10.04

Engel, G. and Radcliffe, M., "Intellectual Property Financing for High Technology Companies," U.C.C.L.J. 19.3 3–33 (1985), Ch. 21, 21.02

References are to sections

Secondary Authorities (cont.)

Ewing, Ky P., Antitrust Enforcement: A Positive Force for Innovation, remarks before the IEEE, September 20, 1978, § 10.02[5]

Ewing, Ky P., Remarks before the San Francisco Patent Law Association, Pebble Beach, California, May 5, 1979, Trade Reg. Rep. (CCH) ¶ 50,398 (1979), Ch. 12

"Justice Department Seeks Termination of Decrees Relating to Patent Licensing," [Jan–June] Patents, Trademarks & Copyright J. (BNA) Vol. 30, No. 735 (June 20, 1985), § 10.02[4]

Klee, "All You Ever Wanted to Know about Cram Down under the New Bankruptcy Code," 53 Am. Bankr. L.J. 133 (1979), § 18.03[3]

Klitzke, "Patents and Section 7 of the Clayton Act: The Significance of Patents in Corporate Acquisitions," 12 Loy. U. Chi. L.J. 401 (1981), § 10.02[1]

Lipsky, Abbott J., Remarks before the American Bar Association Antitrust Section, Washington, D.C., Nov. 5, 1981, Trade Reg. Rep. (CCH) ¶ 50,434 (1981), Ch. 12, App. B

MacDonald, "Know-How Licensing and Antitrust Laws," 62 Mich. L. Rev. 351 (1964), § 10.17

Marsari, "Adequate Protection under the Bankruptcy Reform Act," 1979 Ann. Survey of Bankr. L. 171, § 18.02

Mayers, H., *Drafting Patent License Agreements* (1974), § 20.03

McGrath, J. Paul, Assistant Attorney General, Antitrust Division, Remarks before the Seminar Services International Conference on U.S. Patent Practice, Arlington, Va., April 5, 1984, 27 Pat. Trademark & Copyright J. (BNA) 624 (April 12, 1984), Ch. 12

McLaren, Richard, Assistant Attorney General in Charge of Antitrust, remarks made in London, July 1971, § 9.02

"Principles and Guidelines for the Safe Transfer of Technology," Counseil Europeen de Federations de L'Industrie Chimique, Avenue Louise 250. Btd 71, B-1060, Bruxelles, § 1.02, 3.02, App. A *Restatement of Restitution* (1937), § 20.03

Schenefield, John H., U.S. Department of Justice, Antitrust Division, October 17, 1978 Memorandum, § 10.02[1]

Stern, "A Future Look at Patent Fraud and Antitrust Laws," 52 J. Pat. Off. Soc'y 3 (1970), Ch. 15

Trost, "Business Reorganizations under Chapter 11 of the New Bankruptcy Code," 34 Bus. Law. 1309 (1979), § 18.02, 18.02[3]

Turner, "The Validity of Tying Arrangements Under the Antitrust Laws," 72 Harv. L. Rev. 50 (1958), § 10.04

U.S. Attorney General's Report, Supplement, p. 106 (1968), § 10.04

U.S. Department of Justice, Domestic Policy Review of Industrial Innovation, October 17, 1978, § 10.02[4]

White, R., *Patent Litigation: Procedure and Tactics (1979), § 20.03*

Licensing

Secondary Authorities (cont.)

Wilson, Bruce B., Remarks before the Michigan State Bar Antitrust Law Section, Detroit, Mich. September 21, 1972, Trade Reg. Rep. (CCH) ¶ 50,146 (1972), Ch. 12

Statutes and Model Codes

11 U.S.C. § 101, Ch. 17, § 18.01[1], 18.01[3]

11 U.S.C. § 301, Ch. 17

11 U.S.C. § 302, Ch. 17

11 U.S.C. § 303, Ch. 16, Ch. 17

11 U.S.C. § 323, Ch. 16

11 U.S.C. § 361, § 18.02

11 U.S.C. § 362, Ch. 16, Ch. 17, § 18.01, 18.01[2], 18.02

11 U.S.C. § 363, Ch. 16, Ch. 17, § 18.01[2], 18.01[3], 18.02, 18.02[2], 18.02[3]

11 U.S.C. § 365, Ch. 16, Ch. 17, § 19.01, 19.02, 19.03, 19.04

11 U.S.C. § 501, Ch. 17

11 U.S.C. § 502, Ch. 16, Ch. 17

11 U.S.C. § 506, Ch. 17

11 U.S.C. § 507, § 19.04

11 U.S.C. § 541, Ch. 16, Ch. 17, § 18.01

11 U.S.C. § 544, Ch. 17

11 U.S.C. § 545, Ch. 17

11 U.S.C. § 547, Ch. 17, § 18.01[1], 21.01[1], 21.01[3][a]

11 U.S.C. § 548, § 21.01[1]

11 U.S.C. § 701, Ch. 17

11 U.S.C. § 702, Ch. 17

11 U.S.C. § 704, Ch. 16, Ch. 17, § 18.01[1]

11 U.S.C. § 727, Ch. 16, 18.01

11 U.S.C. § 1101, Ch. 16, Ch. 17, § 19.01

11 U.S.C. § 1104, Ch. 16

11 U.S.C. § 1106, § 18.01[1]

11 U.S.C. § 1107, Ch. 16, § 18.01[1], 19.01

11 U.S.C. § 1108, Ch. 16

11 U.S.C. § 1122, § 18.02[3]

11 U.S.C. § 1123, Ch. 17

11 U.S.C. § 1129, Ch. 17, § 18.02[3]

11 U.S.C. § 1141, Ch. 16, § 18.01

11 U.S.C. § 5601, Ch. 16

Sherman Act, 15 U.S.C. § 1, Ch. 9, § 10.02[4], 10.02[5], 10.03[2], 10.04

Sherman Act, 15 U.S.C. § 2, Ch. 9, § 9.02, 10.01[1], 10.01[3], 10.02[1], 10.02[2], 10.02[4], 10.03[4], 10.04

Sherman Act, Section 7, Ch. 13

Robinson-Patman Act, 15 U.S.C. § 13(a), § 10.12

Licensing

Miscellaneous (cont.)

"Commonwealth Nations Adopt Resolution Criticizing U.S. Treble
  Damage Judgments," 963 Antitrust & Trade Reg. Rep. (BNA), p. A-10
  (May 8, 1980), Ch. 7, Ch. 13

Index

341

Licensing

Antitrust-misuse law: specific areas considered—*Cont.*
Settlement of patent interferences and patent infringement litigation, 10.15
Tied restraints, control of unpatented goods, 10.04
Territorial restrictions, 10.10
Trade secret, know-how, and show-how licenses, 10.17
Assignees, *see* **Bankruptcy**
Assignment
And bankruptcy, *see* **Bankruptcy**
Current Antitrust Division position on, App. B
Assignors, *see* **Bankruptcy**

B

Balancing act
Court, between materiality and intent, 10.01[2][e]
Bankruptcy
Clauses, Ch. 16
Licensee use of technology after licensor's rejection, 20.04
Liquidation and reorganization proceedings, synopsis of, Ch. 17
Lubrizol case under code, 20.02
Avoiding *Lubrizol* problem, 20.06
Nonexclusive licensor advantage
Code protects licensor, 19.02

Bankruptcy—*Cont.*
Nonexclusive licensor advantage—*Cont.*
Nonexclusive license assignable, 19.03
Practice cannot continue if license rejected, 19.04
Trustee cannot assume nor assign personal contract unassignable by licensee, 19.01
Pending legislation, 20.05
Pre-code law, 20.01
Rejection of "naked" immunity from suit, 20.03
Security interest and control at bankruptcy: assignee-debtor's interest in patent will belong to estate, 18.01
Assignor with no security interest at mercy of trustee and secured creditors, 18.01[2]
Debtor's royalty obligation discharged and patent rights sold free of royalties, 18.01[3]
Recovery of property transferred before bankruptcy filed, 18.01[1]
Security interest and control at bankruptcy: assignor with enforceable security interest and well-drafted default clause, 18.02

343

Licensing

NOTES

NOTES

NOTES

NOTES